Green, Inc.

Green, Inc.

An Environmental Insider Reveals
How a Good Cause Has Gone Bad

Christine MacDonald

THE LYONS PRESS
Guilford, Connecticut

An imprint of The Globe Pequot Press

To buy books in quantity for corporate use
or incentives, call **(800) 962–0973**
or e-mail **premiums@GlobePequot.com.**

The Lyons Press is an imprint of The Globe Pequot Press.

Text designed by Sheryl P. Kober

Library of Congress Cataloging-in-Publication Data is available on file.

ISBN 978-1-59921-436-8

Printed in the United States of America

10 9 8 7 6 5 4 3 2 1

Table of Contents

Abbreviations

Center for Environmental Leadership in Business	**CELB** (a division of CI)
The Conservation Fund	**CF**
Conservation International	**CI**
Environmental Defense Fund	**ED**
Environmental Investigation Agency	**EIA**
Forest Stewardship Council	**FSC**
Global Aquaculture Alliance	**GAA**
International Union for the Conservation of Nature and Natural Resources	**IUCN,** also known as World Conservation Union
Leadership in Energy and Environmental Design	**LEED**
Marine Stewardship Council	**MSC**
National Audubon Society	**NAS**
National Park Foundation	**NPF**
Natural Resources Defense Council	**NRDC**
The Nature Conservancy	**TNC**
Rainforest Action Network	**RAN**
Sustainable Forestry Initiative	**SFI**
United States Climate Action Partnership	**USCAP**
U.S. Agency for International Development	**US AID**
Wildlife Conservation Society	**WCS**
Wilderness Society	**WS**
World Wildlife Fund–US	**WWF**

Acknowledgments

I would like to thank everyone who shared their thoughts and recollections of conservation movement, without which I would not have been able to write this book. Not everyone who spoke with me is quoted here by name. Many people did not want to be identified for fear that their comments could hurt their ongoing business in the conservation world. But even those whose names are not mentioned provided valuable insights. I would like to thank them for trusting me to respect their confidentiality.

I would also like to thank my agent Nancy Love for believing in this book and finding it a home. It was a pleasure working with The Lyons Press Associate Publisher Eugene F. Brissie, his colleagues Jennifer Taber and Linda Cowen, and everyone else at The Lyons Press whose hard work went into the book.

Many friends and family members were generous with support and guidance. I'd like to thank accomplished wordsmith Tom Sheehan for his encouragement, comments, and the headline-writing acumen that led to the title of the book. The astute Mark Abel and the savvy Sarah Cardozo Duncan also read early portions of the book and kindly shared their views. My sisters Nancy Saux and Maria Byford, and my sister-in-law Sophia Davila provided help and encouragement at different stages along the way. Another person I would like to thank is my former boss at Conservation International, Haroldo Castro, an intrepid Brazilian conservationist, who took a chance that a veteran reporter could become a conservationist. Working for Haroldo offered a crash course in international nature conservation concerns. While things turned out differently than either of us had envisioned, I'm grateful to him and my colleagues in Haroldo's international communications team for their friendship and professionalism and for sharing many positive aspects of the conservation world.

This book is for my mother Constance MacDonald for introducing me to the joys of good books and good conversation and for my husband Alberto Roblest, who shares my love of both.

Introduction

As I sat down to write this book in early 2007, a new consensus was forming around climate change and the threat that it poses to people and the planet. When a United Nations commission of the world's leading scientists concluded in February that global warming is "unequivocal," resistance to the notion was melting away nearly as fast as the Arctic ice shelves.

By mid-month, ExxonMobil had abandoned its long-held denial of global warming. In a full-page advertisement published in the *Washington Post*, the company declared, "let's talk about climate change." The top executives of ten large U.S. corporations had issued a call for mandatory carbon emissions limits. Before the month was out, another energy company, TXU, announced a $45 billion buyout that included an unprecedented twist: The buyers promised to cancel plans for several coal-burning power plants that had riled environmentalists. These newly "greened" companies were joining hundreds of other enterprises already working to brand themselves as environmentally friendly.

Big business was finally stepping up to the environmental challenge. What could be better? Well, if the actions of today's "green corporations" are anything to go on, this is no time to celebrate.

By the time Exxon had come around to the negotiating table, I had already learned a few nasty details about so-called green corporations and the conservation groups that line up eagerly to vouch for them. The previous spring, I had left journalism to take a job at Conservation International, one of the world's largest environmental organizations. I was tired of writing news stories about what other people were doing; working to save endangered species sounded like a dream job. Not long after I reported to CI's headquarters in Washington, D.C., however, it became all too apparent to me that something is deeply wrong in today's clubby, well-upholstered world of conservationists.

I have written thousands of news stories over the years; among them are hundreds of profiles of people and places. But actually spending all day, every day, at the same organization—getting to know people, observing how things work, and traveling abroad to see operations in field countries—offered insights it would take a reporter years to gather. What I learned was far from what I had expected—it was quite disillusioning, really. So when my job was eliminated in a division-wide reorganization, I was relieved. Well, of course, there was the initial panic about being jobless, despite the comfort of knowing I wasn't being let go for poor job performance.

After I had adjusted to the shock, the relief started to wash over me, and that's when I decided to write this book. Once I began, it didn't take long to learn that the objectionable behavior I observed at CI was by no means restricted to that organization. It permeates the entire conservation world.

Groups that once dedicated themselves solely to saving pandas and parklands today compete for the favors of mining operations that remove entire mountaintops, logging and paper companies that clear-cut old-growth forests, and homebuilders who contribute to urban sprawl. They rely on funds from cruise ship companies, despite the industry's record for polluting the oceans. Among the most generous donors are the biggest environmental scofflaws of all: energy companies.

As a practical matter, I have winnowed the list of organizations playing leading roles in this story to three of the largest U.S.-

based conservation groups: Conservation International, The Nature Conservancy, and World Wildlife Fund–US. Several others are supporting players in this tale. Each group is different. Some work only in the United States. Others only work abroad. Some shun corporate donations altogether. But they all have corporate executives on their governing boards and work to advance corporate interests in a variety of ways. It is not an exhaustive list of business-friendly nonprofit groups, nor are all environmental groups too closely aligned with the corporate world. There are many organizations that resist the lure of corporate money or take donations under strict guidelines designed to minimize the companies' influence on their behavior.

The groups mentioned here represent only a tiny fraction of the thousands of environmental organizations across the country. But they warrant a closer look because, together, they spend billions of dollars on international conservation and loom large on the national political scene and in conservation fights underway across the globe. But even within this small sampling, there is a lot of variety.

The Nature Conservancy: TNC, with more than $1 billion a year in revenues, is the world's largest conservation group, boasting chapters in all fifty states. It has more than $4 billion in assets, mostly tied up in U.S. conservation land managed though its state chapters. But TNC also runs international programs in more than thirty countries. The organization has partnered with oil and gas, power, mining, homebuilding, high-tech, financial services, carmakers, and aircraft builders, among others. Its ties to big logging companies and paper- and pulp-industry conglomerates have been controversial, along with TNC's policy to log and ranch many of its "conservation lands."

Conservation International: CI is headquartered in a suburb of Washington, D.C., but does all of its conservation work abroad in about forty countries on four continents. It began in 1987 as a scrappy group of TNC rebels, who set out on their own to forge a new, more humane way to work in developing countries. It hasn't done too well in that regard: The organization has been the center of controversy with local communities in many places where it works. CI has had more success developing fundraising operations tied to big oil and gas, power, mining, construction, financial services, consumer goods industries, carmakers, and the cruise ship industry.

World Wildlife Fund–US: WWF is part of WWF-International's network of groups with operations in one hundred countries. The country groups often act as one multinational institution but carry out fundraising and conservation work independently of the international headquarters. The U.S. outfit, WWF-US, is the entity most closely examined here. Its partners include mining, logging, consumer goods, financial services, high-tech, and large retailers.

All of these groups accept corporate money but report a relatively modest level of contributions, usually no more than 10 percent of total revenues. Whether they give too much away for such small change is a discussion for the coming chapters. For now, it's worth noting that the figures appear deliberately vague. Since donations from corporate foundations tally as "foundation" grants, and endowments from corporate philanthropists go into the "individual" piggy bank, it is difficult to accurately assess corporate financial influence.

The lawyerly organizations that will also make appearances in the story—Environmental Defense Fund and Natural Resources Defense Council—are more cautious about accepting corporate donations that could lead to awkward questions about conflicts of interest. In fact, ED has a detailed policy against taking money from a long list of industries. If this policy was applied to WWF, CI, and TNC it would disqualify the vast majority of their corporate partners. But both ED and NRDC are considerably business friendly and accept funding from the family foundations built on corporate fortunes. For example, ED receives money from the Walton Family Foundation operated by the Wal-Mart heirs, while the Turner Foundation, Inc., started by CNN founder Ted Turner, has funded NRDC work.

Natural Resources Defense Council: NRDC is sometimes called the "brain trust" of the U.S. environmental movement. Staffed by scientists and lawyers, NRDC is at the forefront of defending, among other things, federal environmental laws such as the Clean Air and Water Acts that have been under rollback pressure almost ever since they were passed into law in the 1970s. Although the organization frowns on corporate sponsorship, NRDC was an influential force behind the U.S. environmental movement's acquiescence to the North American Free Trade Agreement and subsequent trade agreements.

Environmental Defense Fund: ED likes to call itself nature's lawyer, but ED's longtime president Fred Krupp is seen more as corporate America's most effective mediator on environmental questions. ED won't take money from oil, gas, mining, agricultural, forestry, fishing, heavy construction, and an array of retail, transportation, and telecommunications sectors. But it has conducted "projects" aimed at greening such companies as Federal Express, S. C. Johnson, and DuPont that critics say have allowed those companies to greenwash their images.

How do these environmentalists justify their dealings with the world's biggest polluters? The most common refrain: They can influence corporate leaders to change their polluting ways. The argument sounded good to me at first. There is plenty of evidence, however, that the companies are getting more out of the current setup than the endangered species. Although there is change afoot in the corporate world, it appears propelled by concern about consumer views and pressure from activist groups and shareholders. If anything, the big conservation organizations seem more like "enablers" that are slowing down the corporate awakening to environmental and social responsibilities by providing the companies with easy ways to appear green without making significant changes.

It's important to distinguish between the organizations' leaders and their staff members. Not everyone in the conservation world has sold out to corporate interests. Many of the scientists and hardworking conservation educators I met inside these organizations share my concerns about the growing corporate influence, though few are willing to say so publicly for fear of losing well-paid careers in a competitive industry. These groups make important contributions to global knowledge of endangered species by bankrolling rigorous scientific research by some of the most respected biologists in the world. Their field workers do the difficult and sometimes dangerous job of trying to convert local people to a conservation mindset. These scientists and local environmentalists have my respect. Their organizations' leadership, fundraising, and public relations staffs, however, have led the groups astray in the endless quest to keep the corporate dollars flowing into their coffers.

For decades, the conservationists running these groups have escaped harsh criticism by coasting on an altruistic image that has thrown a green sheen over even the most undeserving corporate sponsors. With the stakes higher than ever, it's time to examine these questionable practices and unsavory corporate ties. In this book, I will share with you what I've learned about the leading conservation groups. It will chronicle the exploits of heavy-polluting corporations and conservation groups apparently unable to turn down any donation, regardless of the taint of greenwashing. The expression, a twist on the term "whitewashing," was coined to describe corporate efforts to appear "green" without actually delivering on their environmental promises. Cultivating ties to big conservation groups has proved a cost-effective greenwashing strategy for many companies. The corporate interest has had an unseemly influence on the conservation groups: Having succumbed to the competitive rush to raise cash, conservation organizations are deforming themselves in ways that would probably make them unrecognizable to the committed nature lovers who started the movement decades ago. But fundraising success has not brought the groups closer to completing their missions.

Despite unparalleled conservation efforts in the last three decades, the planet is hurtling toward the largest mass extinction since the age of the dinosaurs. As we learn more about global warming, the outlook only grows dimmer for the Earth's most vulnerable species. A quarter of all mammals and coniferous trees, a third of the world's frogs and amphibians, and one in eight birds are under threat of extinction. The last gazelles are vanishing from the Sahara Desert. Hippopotamuses may soon be gone from the Congo River. Overfishing is emptying the oceans. Illegal logging is threatening the last towering mahogany trees. Deforestation and pollution from encroaching human outposts are devastating once remote rainforests in Asia and Latin America, while real estate development in the Mediterranean has nearly obliterated the Iberian lynx.

While the lynxes grow ever scarcer, conservation groups are thriving. They have become fat cats of the nonprofit realm. And yet the national parks and protected areas that conservationists tout among their chief accomplishments are faltering. There are tens of thousands of protected areas around the world today. They take up a tenth of the Earth's landmass, an area equal to the combined territories of China and India. Too many of these so-called protected lands, however, are little more than "paper parks." Despite legal protections on paper, a shortage of park managers and rangers leaves them vulnerable to illegal logging, wildlife poaching, drug trafficking, and other illicit activities. The "paper parks" scenario is only part of the problem. There's also the "shell game": New protections declared on marginal tracts or remote lands, under no immediate threat of development, deflect attention from lucrative real estate deals. The result: biologically important land bulldozed to make way for tourist resorts or vacation homes.

Conservation groups become accomplices to the subterfuge, unwilling to jeopardize ties to regimes and corporations that provide money, access to powerful decision-makers, and public relations opportunities they can boast about to wealthy donors and tout in their annual reports. But such power politics has led to friction with the residents of the very rainforests conservationists are trying to save. They have squandered opportunities for natural grassroots alliances by siding consistently with corrupt regimes and powerful but environmentally hostile corporations. But the conservationists would rather hide this unpleasant fact from the public. In fundraising brochures and reports, the big groups repeatedly describe how they work in harmony with indigenous people. The truth is they are often seen as the bad guys in the developing world, where much of the Earth's remaining biodiversity exists.

In the first part of this book, you will learn about the professionalization of conservation and the "double lives" of today's top brass, while part two focuses on how the groups and their corporate partners have acted in the name of conservation around the world. You will hear from people inside and outside the conservation movement, from chief executives to tribal chiefs, field biologists to community activists. After visiting Texas oil fields, Brazilian rainforests, and Pacific island fishing villages, the book returns its focus to the United States with the truth about biofuels, "green" homebuilding, off-setting your carbon footprint, and other consumer fads that enjoy slick but misleading sales pitches.

With more companies than ever rushing to reinvent themselves as environmentally friendly, now is the time to take a hard look at what it means to be green. Will the emerging corporate environmental ethos ring in serious changes or merely provide PR cover for industries that continue to ravage the planet? "The devil is in the details," said Exxon's spokesman when the company first signaled its willingness to negotiate curbs on greenhouse gas emissions. What could be more obvious? Whether those details serve the interests of environmentally hostile corporations or a broader global public will have an enormous impact on the planet's future health.

In the rainforest, the towering trees of jungle canopy and the delicate orchids that attach themselves to their trunks and grow like vines up their branches rely on the Amazonian rains to nourish their symbiotic relationship. We, the consumers, the voters, and the donation-givers, are the raindrops that nurture the corporate-conservationist symbiosis. The companies and the nonprofit groups want and need our respect, our brand loyalty, and—most importantly—our hard-earned cash.

It's time to use our influence to grow a greener economy.

Green, Inc.

Part One

Chapter One

From Gentleman's Hobby to Multibillion-Dollar Industry

At eighty-six, Russell Train is still an imposing figure. The longtime leader of World Wildlife Fund comes to work in a three-piece suit and tie, starched white shirt, and breast-pocket handkerchief. His hair is short and parted on the side, just like his official photo as Environmental Protection Agency administrator in the mid-1970s. Once dark, it is now entirely white. But his voice is deep and steady and only, perhaps, a bit more gravelly today than during decades as a Republican Party stalwart and one of the country's most influential environmentalists.

He's been retired for more than a dozen years. But Train and Catherine Williams, his longtime secretary, still go to work a few times a week. His is a corner office on the fourth floor of World Wildlife Fund's environmentally friendly "green building" in Washington, D.C. The distinctive structure is one of the only office buildings in the capital designed to recycle just about every bit of trash and reduce energy consumption by harnessing sunlight that filters through the extra-large windows. Recycled materials were used in everything from the ceiling tiles to the carpets. The office furniture is made of timber hewn from a sustainable forest in Pennsylvania. The distinctive white-brick facade, set off by colorful flags bearing the institution's panda mascot, stands out on a block of drab and ordinary buildings as if to remind the neighbors of the Fund's place in the vanguard of international nature conservation. It's a neighborhood teeming with environmental groups. Train protégés Thomas Lovejoy and Russell Mittermeier, who went on to lead other groups, worked within a few blocks of the Fund for several years. Hundreds of other organizations—among the more than twelve thousand environmental groups that now exist in the United States—have offices in Washington or the surrounding suburbs.

In many ways, Train personifies the modern conservationist. From the mid-1950s, when he first became an activist, until he resigned as World Wildlife's U.S. chairman in 1994, he presided over the movement's transformation from essentially a hobby for "gentlemen of wealth" to a professional and lavishly funded industry. The popular idea of an environmental activist may be a scruffy "tree hugger" or shadowy "ecoterrorist," but conservationists like Train are a more conservative lot, members of a traditionally right-leaning branch of a vast movement. Left-wing environmental militants trace their roots to late 1960s and 1970s fights over toxic-waste dumps and urban air quality. Conservationist history goes back at least to 19th-century naturalists Henry David Thoreau and Sierra Club founder John Muir.

A Conservationist Awakening

Far from anti-establishment, environmentalists of the conservationist ilk tend to trace their nature-loving roots to privileged childhoods spent hunting, fishing, and camping on tracts of wilderness owned by their own families. As a boy, Train went duck hunting with his father, a rear admiral, on the banks of the Potomac River outside Washington, D.C.

"There was an interest in my family in sort of traditional conservation. My father was a naval officer and he liked to shoot ducks. So he was concerned with the conservation of ducks and waterfowl," he recalls.

Train and his wife, Aileen, had their "awakening" while on safari in Africa in the mid-1950s. A few years earlier, Ernest Hemingway's celebrated story "Snows of Kilimanjaro," about an American writer injured while hunting in Africa, was made into a Hollywood movie staring Gregory Peck and Ava Gardner. The Trains were a young, recently married couple. And safaris were exotically fashionable in the way that visits to Tibet or Tierra del Fuego might be today.

As Train remembers it, he and his wife were the only tourists in their party. Led by a big-game hunter, they traveled with a crew of nearly a dozen people "ranging from everything from a gun bearer to an automobile mechanic or a cook." Aileen never really enjoyed the hunting. By the couple's second and last expedition in 1958, she would simply walk along the trails, taking in Africa's natural beauty, her husband recalls. Train, however, loved everything about tracking elephants, tigers, and other big and dangerous game. Hiking through lush jungle, fragrant with unknown smells and alive with the rustle of animals, nearby but hidden from view, was "an impressive experience on the self," Train recalls. Though in his many later trips to Africa Train was more likely to shoot the endangered species with a camera than a rifle, the hunting safaris marked a turning point in his life.

U.S. Conservationists Abroad—
The Beginnings of International Efforts

Moved by the beauty they found in East Africa's game parks and nature preserves, the Trains launched a nonprofit in 1959 and named it the African Wildlife Leadership Foundation. The group arranged for African schoolchildren to visit nature preserves in their countries and offered wildlife management scholarships to Africans, poised for independence from their European colonists.

Africa's national parks and other protected areas were run almost exclusively by white colonizers, who had arrived on the continent a century before when European empires had scrambled to carve up Africa amongst themselves. By the early 1960s, the long and bloody struggle for independence had come to a climax in British East Africa, where the Trains had focused their interest. Uganda gained independence in 1962; Kenya followed the next year. Tanganyika united with Zanzibar to form the United Republic of Tanzania in 1964.

"All these colonies were becoming independent," Train recalls. "With independence, what was going to happen to the wildlife and the wild places that drew so many of us to Africa?"

"You couldn't really assume that the African people taking charge were going to have the same motivation that the European colonizers had had. Native African people and communities tended to view wildlife as a source of food, primarily, and otherwise damn nuisances as far as their crops are concerned and other things of importance at the time, all of which is very understandable. But it made you wonder what the future held."

The only native Africans he had ever encountered in national parks were game scouts on antique bicycles, toting old Winfield rifles. More often than not, the scouts had no bullets for the guns and probably didn't even know how to shoot, recalls Train, who had, by that time, joined a small but committed group of foreign conservationists who considered Africa's unique wildlife and breathtaking natural places the heritage of the world.

Train set out to educate African nationals in wildlife management on the theory that they would form a new cadre of conservationists personally invested in preserving the continent's natural wonders. The foundation's first graduate became the first African head of the Wildlife Service of Kenya. Others finished degree programs at Colorado State College, Humboldt State University in Arcata, California, and other U.S. universities with the money the Trains' foundation raised from American philanthropists, and went on to work at nature preserves in other East African countries.

At the time, Train supported his family as a judge in federal tax court. But soon he would join the ranks of a new profession: the paid conservationist. His African conservation work brought him to the attention of Fairfield Osborn, head of the New York Zoological Society, today called the Wildlife Conservation Society (WCS), that runs the Bronx Zoo. Osborn initially looked on Train as an interloper on the Society's international turf and tried to convince him to shut down or merge his foundation with the Society. At the time, it was one of the only established U.S. groups working to promote land conservation in foreign countries. Train didn't think the group was doing nearly enough. But his concern for Africa wasn't the only reason he refused Osborn's offer: "I enjoyed doing my own thing. I wasn't going to become a subordinate—a typical, personal motivation."

When he couldn't convince the judge to work for him, Osborn, whose nickname was "Fair," suggested Train replace Samuel Ordway Jr., a philanthropist who hailed from a Minnesota industrial empire, as the president of the Conservation Foundation, an obscure nature group founded by Osborn. But he was shocked to learn Train wasn't independently wealthy and insisted on a salary of $50,000 a year, the equivalent of his pay as a judge. "Fair was somewhat taken aback," Train recalled in his 2003 memoir *Politics, Pollution and Pandas*. "The CF tradition was to have gentleman of wealth at the top, who would serve without compensation."

While he wasn't as wealthy as many of his fellow conservationists, what he lacked in fortune he made up for in connections. The great-grandson of New England Puritans, Train grew up a third-generation Washington insider. His wife Aileen came from a prominent family and was a bridesmaid at the wedding of Jacqueline Bouvier and John F. Kennedy. The couple attended Kennedy's 1961 presidential inauguration. But his deeper connections were Republican. As a high-ranking member of the Nixon administration's Department of the Interior, years after he became involved in conservation work, he helped establish the Environmental Protection Agency and craft landmark laws such as the Endangered Species Act. He went on to serve as the country's second EPA administrator from 1973 to the end of the Ford administration in 1977 and later campaigned for President George H. W. Bush. Like his parents had before him, Train and his wife hobnobbed with a succession of American presidents, wealthy philanthropists, and captains of industry. They were guests at the White House and summered on Cape Cod. They spent weekends at their Maryland farm and owned a winter home on Jupiter Island in Florida, where the Bush family spent part of the year.

World Wildlife Fund Establishes a U.S. Beachhead

Train helped create the U.S. branch of WWF in 1961, the same year the organization was established in Europe with Prince Bernhard of the Netherlands as its international president and the Duke of Edinburgh heading up the U.K. branch. At the behest of the British gentleman explorer Sir Julian Huxley, Train agreed to serve as a founding director and vice president—volunteer posts at the time.

Nearly two decades later, Train would become the first paid president of World Wildlife Fund's U.S. operations, another sign of the movement's drift away from gentlemanly pursuit and toward a more corporate-style business model. Today most large conservation nonprofits devote about half of their annual budgets to paying their employees and consultants. Presidents and top managers earn hundreds of thousands of dollars a year plus benefits and expense accounts. The situation was much different, however, when Train first became involved. Back then, few environmental groups existed. The only one he had heard of was the Sierra Club, the country's oldest conservation organization, founded in 1892. The Nature Conservancy was established only a decade before Train started his African philanthropy, while another well-known group, Greenpeace, didn't set up shop until 1971.

By the time he took over as president of WWF's U.S. office in 1978, the operation had a small staff but was seen as something of an underachiever by the home office in Switzerland. Train was determined to change that. One of his first moves was to stop giving grants to other U.S. environmental groups and start his own international program.

Like other WWF branches, the U.S. office had operated essentially as a fundraising outfit that sent appeals through the mail to a variety of types of donors—from schoolchildren, who collected pennies to save pandas, to charitable foundations and wealthy philanthropists. Part of the money went to the Swiss headquarters, the rest to U.S. envrionmental groups.

Thomas Lovejoy, a recently graduated biologist, fresh from two years' field study in the Brazilian Amazon, had joined the Fund in 1974 and oversaw grants that launched international programs at three groups: the NRDC, ED, and TNC. It was the only U.S. grantmaker funding international environmental projects in the mid-1970s, Lovejoy recalls. The funds provided the seed money for what is today's global environmental industry.

Once Train took over, however, those groups found their benefactor had turned into a fierce new competitor. Train hired away their staff members and put them to work building WWF's international programs. Among those who joined him were Michael Wright, who had used the Fund's money to start TNC's international program; and Russell Mittermeier, a respected primatologist from the New York Zoological Society.

TNC and the other groups soon rebuilt their international operations. Within a few years U.S. efforts for nature conservation worldwide started attracting much larger sums of money and employing an increasing number of biologists and support staff.

After Wright's departure, TNC gave the international post to Spencer Beebe, a Peace Corps veteran, who learned fluent Spanish working with Honduran fishermen. A third-generation Oregonian, Beebe grew up camping and hiking his family's conservation land. He had a graduate forestry degree from Yale and spent two years sailing around the world before returning home to the Pacific Northwest, where he rose quickly through the ranks of TNC's West Coast hierarchy.

The Nature Conservancy
Opens an International Department

Beebe left the West Coast for the Conservancy's Washington, D.C., headquarters in 1980. At the time, U.S. groups had largely focused their efforts in Latin America, but those initiatives were far from robust. "It was pretty scattered," says Beebe, who recalls that WWF-US's two-year-old program was the most prominent on the international scene at the time. A short list of other conservation efforts abroad was fronted by the federal government's U.S. Agency for International Development, the World Bank, a few fledgling nonprofit groups, and Peace Corps veterans like himself.

Train was unhappy about Beebe's arrival in Washington. Just as Osborn had seen him as an interloper two decades earlier, Train felt TNC was horning in on the Fund's international turf. Competitive and territorial, Train didn't want other contenders for the attentions of donors.

"I make no bones about that," Train says of the episode. "But I found that we did have competitive problems often in fundraising and in publicity. Everybody wants to blow their own horn and not give anybody else credit. And all that is very irritating."

If his stance was ironic considering he had wooed away the Conservancy's international program manager only two years earlier, Train didn't see it that way. A decade later, however, the tables were turned when Beebe and a group of dissidents from The Nature Conservancy hired Russell Mittermeier to become president of a new group they had christened Conservation International. Mittermeier, then a senior member of World Wildlife Fund's U.S. staff, had been passed over for Train's job leading WWF. "So he took the [Fund's] science department and he bolted and went to CI," remembers Wright, who witnessed the coup from afar. A longtime member of the U.S. conservation community, Wright has also worked for the John D. and Catherine T. MacArthur Foundation, which provides grants to conservation groups like the Conservancy and Conservation International. He is currently the managing director of the Natural Capital Project, a partnership created by TNC, WWF, and the Woods Institute for the Environment at Stanford University.

Since its upstart beginnings, CI has joined the Fund and the Conservancy on the list of the largest U.S. conservation organizations, but it's never lost its "pirate quality," Wright says. The jockeying for talent and funding among conservation groups would only increase as the financial stakes multiplied.

When Beebe started the Conservancy's international department, the organization was about thirty years old and in the middle of a growth spurt that would continue after Beebe left in 1987. By that time, the Conservancy operated chapters in all fifty states plus the international department, which had a staff of about fifty people and operated as a sort of super-chapter. But its leaders were struggling with how to integrate the foreign projects with its work in the United States, where it was one of the best-regarded land conservation organizations in the country. This struggle precipitated the mutiny that gave birth to CI. While it was a major blow to the organization, the walkout didn't have lasting effects on the Conservancy's evolution into a multinational institution.

TNC traces its roots to an obscure scientific group called the Ecological Society of America, established in 1915. But it wasn't until 1951 that it was incorporated in Washington, D.C., under its present name by a group of scientists determined to protect the country's wilderness from sprawling suburbs and industrial operations that had begun to spiral out from urban centers.

TNC's founders completed the first of what would become the organization's signature land acquisition and management strategy a few years later. The first deal involved a sixty-acre parcel along the Mianus River Gorge on the New York–Connecticut border. By 1958, the year Train went on his last African safari, the Conservancy had saved more than 2,500 acres.

In the beginning volunteers held bake sales and raffles to pay for saving a few acres at a time. Since then, TNC has gone on to manage more than 117 million acres of land and thousands of miles of river. It is the largest among the many thousands of conservation groups in the world. It raised nearly $1.3 billion in fiscal 2007 and spent $806.7 million on conservation programs internationally. The group, which hired its first full-time, paid president in 1965, now has net assets of $4.7 billion and employs more than three thousand people in the United States and more than two dozen foreign countries.

U.S. Environmental Groups Experience Explosive Growth

The environmental movement worldwide has followed a similar growth trajectory. Public awareness surged after publication of Rachel Carson's landmark book *Silent Spring*, credited for bringing concerns about the impact of pollution and pesticides to a world stage for the first time in 1962. The first Earth Day followed in 1970, consolidating a new movement that would wax and wane over the next several decades. But the net effect has been one of enormous growth.

When Train took World Wildlife's U.S. helm in 1978, the operation had an annual budget of less than $2 million and a staff of about a dozen. Today, its employees fill its D.C. headquarters and field offices scattered around the world. The Swiss-based WWF-International operates in more than one hundred countries with four million members worldwide. It has traded in the unwieldy full name for the acronym WWF, and its cute panda logo has become one of the conservation world's most recognized and trusted symbols. Groups such as WCS, ED, NRDC, CI, The Conservation Fund (CF), Sierra Club, National Audubon Society (NAS), and Greenpeace have also experienced dramatic growth, and thousands of new organizations have sprung up.

At last count, there were nearly twelve thousand environmental groups in the United States alone. They reported more than $9.6 billion in annual revenues and assets amounting to more than $27 billion in 2004, according to the Urban Institute, a nonpartisan think tank in Washington.[1]

Even as the movement has gone "mainstream," however, it has struggled to reflect the diversity of the country. While conservationists prefer to focus on the movement's crusades to protect imperiled landscapes and animals, its history isn't without dark chapters. Many early conservation clubs were whites-only establishments.[2] Even some of the early national parks had "whites-only" postings designed to keep out African Americans. As the movement's grown, it's become more middle class, but few people of color have joined. According to one University of Michigan study, a third of mainstream green groups and 20 percent of government agencies dealing with environmental protection don't have a single person of color on staff.[3] Today's leadership is also decidedly white and stacked with millionaires. Of the top ten national groups, only one has a female chief executive.

Still, Kierán Suckling, executive director of the Center for Biological Diversity in Tucson, Arizona, sees a shift in the national agenda as a direct link to the changes wrought to the movement over the last few decades. As recently as the early 1990s, the conservation movement's wealthy "old guard" were focused on protecting "extremely scenic" landscapes, valued for their beauty, not on today's more scientific basis of where the animals live and how much old-growth forest and wildlife corridors are needed to support them.

"To me it goes back to a kind of a blueblood thing," says Suckling. "The sublime landscape that looks like a [Edward] Hopper painting—that's kind of an old blueblood agenda. Whereas talking to a bunch of scientists, and drawing the lines mapping where the species live, is a much more techie middle-class approach. That's now the much more common approach to wilderness designation. So there's been a big shift."

The Dramatic Climb in Charitable Giving Funds a New Nonprofit Sector

The exponential growth of international conservation efforts was made possible by an equally dramatic transformation in the world of philanthropy. Environmental groups and other non-profits traditionally depend on endowments from the wealthy, usually bequeathed to favored institutions at the time of the donor's death. While this money continues to flow, new streams in recent decades have bubbled to the surface, propelled by growing worldwide concern about global warming, endangered creatures, and their vanishing habitat. Newly minted foundations launched by self-made billionaires have led the way, followed by corporations and government agencies and multilateral lenders. These new funding flows are propelled by different interests but together have financed and sustained a multibillion-dollar global environmental movement.

Social commentators have for decades criticized the growing gap between rich and poor worldwide. In what seems like irony, this disturbing trend has been a boon to nonprofit groups. While more and more people are slipping into poverty worldwide, there has also been an unprecedented proliferation of self-made billionaires. Internet gurus, finance barons, and media moguls, who made their fortunes in the stock market booms of the 1980s and 1990s, are the new patrons of today's thriving nonprofit realm, according to Katherine Fulton and Andrew Blau, experts on trends in charitable giving.[4]

In 1987, when Sam Walton was the richest man in America, he was one of only 49 billionaires on *Forbes* magazine's list of America's four hundred richest people. In 2007, everyone on the list was worth at least a billion, according to the magazine. High-profile billionaire-philanthropists who made the cut included Bill Gates, ranked number one with $59 billion; his philanthropic partner Warren Buffet, who ranked number two with $52 billion; Pierre M. Omidyar, number thirty-two with $8.9 billion; George Soros, ranked thirty-three with $8.8 billion; Gordon Moore, number sixty-eight with $4.5 billion; and Ted Turner, number 195 with $2.3 billion.

Billionaires Among the Four Hundred Richest People in America

Year	Percentage
1987	12 percent
2007	100 percent

Source: *Forbes* magazine

These self-made billionaire-philanthropists and their family foundations have been the single most important new source of funding to conservation groups, offering them previously unimaginable sums of money. Unlike philanthropists of bygone eras, who bequeathed their fortunes and didn't bother with the details of how it was spent, "living donors" such as Turner, the Waltons, and Moore are deeply involved in deciding how best to use their money. The Walton Family Foundation gave $21 million to Conservation International in fiscal 2005, nearly a quarter of CI's total revenues that year. In 2002, CI was also the beneficiary of a $261 million ten-year grant from the Gordon and Betty Moore Foundation. It was the largest conservation donation in history. eBay founder and philanthropist Omidyar donated a conservation easement to The Trust for Public Land to save 1,500 acres on his ranch in Colorado's Wet Mountain Valley. The Turner Foundation, meanwhile, has made hundreds of grants to conservation groups since it was founded in 1991.

Environmental causes have not been the only beneficiaries of these new financial wellsprings. In the last three decades or so, these new cash flows have nurtured a wide variety of nonprofit institutions that have formed what economists would call an entirely new economic sector. Today there are more than a million nonprofits nationwide. Together they bring in more than a trillion dollars in revenue each year and have even more assets.[5]

Nonprofit Revenues and Spending				
U.S. Nonprofits	1994	1999	2004	percentage change*
Revenues	$678	$950	$1.36	62 percent
Expenses	$621	$851	$1.26	63 percent
Assets	$1.25	$2.1	$2.97	91 percent

In billions of dollars. Source: *Nonprofit Sector in Brief: Facts and Figures from the Nonprofit Almanac 2007*, Urban Institute. *Adjusted for inflation.

A Global Phenomenon

It is not just a U.S. phenomenon either. Nonprofits around the world are seeing growth in revenues, spending, assets, and job expansion that outpace growth of their local economies. They have experienced such explosive growth by picking up the slack left by shrinking government authorities around the world. Just as the private sector has taken on jobs—such as trash collection in Allentown, Pennsylvania, or military base security in Iraq—once carried out by local, state, or national governments, nonprofits have stepped up with cultural and educational offerings, social work, and environmental protection. In Brazil, for instance, environmental groups are a significant employer. Meanwhile, foreign investment in nature conservation projects is an important source of hard currency in Madagascar, an impoverished island off the east coast of Africa, home to a large variety of endangered lemurs, the world's smallest monkeys, found nowhere else on Earth.

There are no good estimates of the total number of people conservation employs worldwide. The World Conservation Union, also know by its formal name the International Union for the Conservation of Nature and Natural Resources, or IUCN, estimates that more than 83,000 work in parks and protected areas. At least as many more work for independent conservation groups and nonprofits around the world.

Since most of the world's remaining biodiversity hotspots exist outside U.S. borders, U.S. groups have close relationships with nonprofits abroad that carry out field work in impoverished developing countries. Alone, the five largest U.S. conservation groups—TNC, CI, WCS, WWF-US, and CF—spend more than $1 billion a year on saving endangered species and landscapes around the globe.

Billions more are spent running the protected areas that cover nearly ten million square miles of the Earth, though it's hard to say exactly how much money is spent annually, since there is no clearinghouse for reporting conservation work done by many different agencies and organizations. The World Conservation Union has made several unsuccessful estimates to tally the total spent by governments, nonprofit groups, foundations, individual donors, multi-lateral institutions, and corporations, according to Jeff McNeely, the Union's chief scientist. It is more than $6 billion a year, he says. Whatever the amount, it's not nearly enough to stop the habitat destruction fueling global warming and mass extinction of plant and animal species, according to McNeely and other experts.

How much money is spent and how much more it would take to save the planet's biodiversity are matters of debate. There is little doubt, however, that today's conservation efforts have grown to a magnitude unimaginable when Russell Train joined the cause half a century ago. And the groups doing the work have also changed. There are more skilled "conservation workers" in the field today. The amount of money has increased exponentially as has the number of newly created protected areas.

"These organizations no longer talk about working themselves out of a job," notes Train protégé Michael Wright. "I think they see themselves now as permanent transnational organizations."

While the international conservation industry's survival is a sure thing, much less certain is the fate of the giant panda, symbol of human efforts to save endangered species. Despite half a century of conservation efforts, only about a thousand may remain in their dwindling forest habitat in central China. One day the panda may exist only as an image on a logo.

Chapter Two

The Double Lives of Conservation Leaders

Leading the nation's fight to save endangered critters and pre-serve the world's rainforests may seem like the kind of job that would make up in personal satisfaction what it lacked in remu-neration. But the leaders at the country's top environmental groups do surprisingly well, earning annual compensation that puts them in the top 1 percent of Americans.[1]

The National Park Foundation's James Maddy's $833,290 in earnings won him the dubious distinction of highest-paid environmentalist on the American Institute of Philanthropy's 2006 list of U.S. nonprofit executives with the priciest com-pensation packages. Maddy's pay only slightly outdid that of Steven E. Sanderson, the chief executive of the Wildlife Con-servation Society, who earned $825,170. Natural Resources Defense Council's John Adams took away $757,914 in total compensation when he retired after more than two decades at the organization's helm.

The men are among the executives at prominent national groups who made $350,501 a year or more—more than 99 percent of U.S. taxpayers. The worst-paid among the nation's best-known national groups is the Sierra Club's Carl Pope. But Pope doesn't do too badly: He made nearly a quarter of a million dollars in 2005. That's still way above the country's median household earnings of $48,201 a year.

While these merely rich nonprofit executives don't make nearly as much as their "mega-rich" colleagues in corporate America, they are in one of the fastest-growing job brackets, according to the Chronicle of Philanthropy's annual compensation survey. Salaries across the nonprofit sector have risen faster than inflation for a decade.

WWF-US founder Russell Train set a respectable bar when he demanded a salary for his conservation work equal to his pay as a federal tax court judge, nearly half a century ago. In the intervening decades, a judge's salary has increased a little more than threefold to about $160,000 a year. That's nothing compared to the way conservation pay has soared. WWF-US president Carter Roberts makes about seven times as much as Train made in his first paid conservation job. Meanwhile Maddy at NPF and Sanderson at WCS each earned about sixteen times as much as Train once did and more than five times as much as a federal tax judge earns today.

Some conservation fat cats, in fact, are doing so well that their compensation packages have begun to raise eyebrows. Sanderson qualified for a place on the Chronicle of Philanthropy's list of nonprofit chief executives with the plushest fringe benefits. His pay package includes a $115,200 housing allowance. Steve McCormick, who led The Nature Conservancy until 2007, had a similar deal, with a $75,000 signing bonus, $75,000-a-year housing allowance, and a $1.6 million low-interest mortgage loan from TNC when he took the CEO post in 2001.

Some of the Highest-Paid U.S. Conservation Executives

Organization	Individual	Title	Total Compensation
NPF	James Maddy	past president	$833,290
WCS	Steven E. Sanderson	president, CEO	$825,170
NRDC	John Adams	past president	$757,914
ED	Fred Krupp	president	$468,615
CF	Richard L. Erdmann	exec. vice president	$461,576
CI	Peter Seligmann	chairman	$391,398**
NAS (National Audubon Society)			
	John Flicker	president	$390,716**
CI	Russell Mittermeier	president	$381,759**
CF	Lawrence A. Selzer	president, CEO	$347,588
WWF-USA	Carter Roberts	president	$347,190
DoW (Defenders of Wildlife)			
	Rodger Schickeisen	president, CEO	$295,602
WS (Wilderness Society)			
	William H. Meadows	president	$294,063
NRDC	Frances Beinecke	president	$279,837
Sierra Club	Deborah Sorondo	CEO	$264,310
Sierra Club	Carl Pope	exec. director	$239,508

All compensation is for 2006 excepted *2004 and **2005. Sources: Organizations' tax returns.

Not only do these raconteurs of mass extinction earn some of the highest salaries of the nonprofit world, the presidents and CEOs of today's most prominent conservation groups speak the gospel of environmental sustainability but live like carbon junkies, burning many more times the greenhouse gases responsible for global warming than the average American. They have grown accustomed to celebrity lifestyles and lavish working vacations to places most people won't see in a lifetime. They explore the

Galápagos Islands, safari in Botswana, and dive the Great Barrier Reef off Indonesia, often with a rock star, famous actor, or corporate scion in tow. But their fondness for gas-guzzling private jets and electricity-hogging multiple homes leaves these so-called conservationists vulnerable to the same accusations of hypocrisy that have dogged former Vice President Al Gore and Hollywood's "green glitterati."

The highest-paid environmental leaders in the country are comfortable with top corporate executives because it's a world they know well. Current NPF president Vin Cipolla is a former Internet entrepreneur and serial CEO—he served as the CEO of six companies before taking the NPF helm. NRDC president Frances Beinecke is the daughter of the former CEO of Sperry & Hutchinson, the company that pioneered discount coupons more than a century ago with S&H Green Stamps. While TNC prides itself on its science, its top leaders in the last two decades have been an economist, a lawyer, and an investment banker. ED's longtime president Fred Krupp is a Yale-educated lawyer, who appears more often in a business suit than hiking boots. Perhaps the most jet-setting of them all is Peter Seligmann, CI cofounder and chairman of the board. He is a millionaire from a family of investment bankers. Even the left-leaning Sierra Club, with its pugnacious stance against Wal-Mart and an elected board of directors, has been derided as a martini-sipping "club Sierra" by its own dissidents, who say the organization has become too quick to make compromises and cut deals.[2]

Public Perceptions

The nonprofit leaders are well aware that their members and the public in general frown on their corporate ties. Holding focus groups and carrying out market research has become routine at many nonprofits. A 2001 report prepared for TNC, and subsequently made public, offers insights into what the "consumers" of conservation think of corporate alliances.[3]

The consulting firm Wirthlin Worldwide conducted two focus groups at TNC's Virginia headquarters. One group was comprised of TNC members, while the other had only a passing knowledge of the Conservancy and other environmental groups. Most participants agreed that corporations could provide the organization with needed funding and had no objections to corporate donations with no strings attached beyond some good public relations for the company.

But when it came to sponsorships, partnerships, and other arrangements that imply that TNC is vouching for the good corporate citizenship of the company, both focus groups agreed it was unacceptable to partner with a whole range of polluting industries. Participants said it would be "an inherent conflict of interest" for TNC to partner with petroleum refining, mining, forestry and paper products, energy utilities, and chemical industries. For some, even accepting a donation from those industries would be tantamount to a payoff.

Asked specifically about partnership with BP, most said the idea was inappropriate. Wal-Mart? Absurd! They suggested dealings with a beer company would be wrong given the amount of cans and bottles that litter public places. For several other companies mentioned, the groups struggled to find relevance between the corporations and TNC, prompting researchers to conclude that the public views with suspicion most corporate alliances with the organization.

These findings are far from shocking and seem like simple common-sense guidelines. In fact, ED's corporate donation policy closely mirrors the conclusions TNC's focus groups reached. And several subsequent opinion polls have confirmed the public skepticism of corporate efforts to green their images.[4] TNC, however, has relationships with just about every company its own focus groups admonished against. And TNC is not alone.

The Corporate Ties

Corporate executives run the boards of many of these organizations. NRDC's board includes Robert J. Fisher, Chairman of Gap Inc.; Alan Horn, president of Warner Brothers; and Daniel R. Tishman, CEO of Tishman Construction Corp. of New York. TNC has high-tech representatives, such as John P. Morgridge, former chairman of Cisco Systems, Inc.; finance and banking-industry types including Roberto Hernandez Ramirez, chairman of Banco Nacional de Mexico; and Roger Milliken Jr., president of the logging company Baskahegan. On WWF-US's board of directors is Pamela Ebsworth, the wife of retired cruise ship baron Barney Ebsworth; GE executive Pamela Daley; and S. Curtis Johnson, the Johnson & Johnson heir. CI's board members include Fisher from Gap Inc.; Moore, the former Intel chief; Nicholas J. Pritzker, vice chairman of the hotel chain Global Hyatt Corp.; and Henry H. Arnhold, chairman Seligmann's uncle and co-chairman of Arnhold & S. Bleichroeder, the New York investment-banking firm that gave George Soros his start.

Besides being run by moguls, these groups have set up an array of joint marketing partnerships, sponsorship programs, and advisory groups catering to corporations such as Exxon-Mobil of the infamous *Valdez* oil spill; PG&E Corporation, the gas and electric company that settled a $28 million water contamination suit made infamous by the movie *Erin Brockovich*;

and the British energy conglomerate BP, owner of the Texas refinery dubbed the most polluting plant in the United States by the Environmental Protection Agency in 2006.[5]

Many of the worst corporate scofflaws spread their attentions around to multiple groups. BP and Shell have given to CF, CI, and TNC and have relationships with ED and NRDC. Also well represented are power companies that rely on coal-fired power plants—a principal driver of global warming. American Electric Power, which gets three-quarters of its generating capacity from dirty coal-fired plants, gives to CF and has partnered with TNC. CF, in fact, has ties to five power companies, including Entergy Corporation, which has a seat on CF's board of directors.

Other corporate sponsors of the conservation industry include Centex and International Paper Co. Both companies are linked to forest destruction and nevertheless have ties to CF and TNC. Bunge and Cargill, agribusiness companies contributing to the disappearance of the Amazon rainforest, have ties to CI, WWF, and TNC. The auto industry has also been a generous corporate partner.

Several of the biggest corporate sponsors of conservation groups are also part of a not-so-flattering club: "The Toxic 100," an annual list of the worst corporate air polluters by the Political Economy Research Institute at the University of Massachusetts. Six of the companies that made the 2008 list's "top ten" are E. I. du Pont de Nemours & Co., General Electric, Eastman Kodak, ExxonMobil, Nissan, and Dow Chemical. Each one of those companies and twenty-three others among the top 100 polluters are major contributors to big conservation groups.

Financial institutions like Citigroup, JPMorgan Chase & Co., and Bank of America also appear to take cover behind their conservation contributions. These institutions have been the subjects of campaigns in recent years by the Rainforest Action Network (RAN) and other groups for providing the financing for illegal logging, sprawling residential and vacation developments, coal-fired power plants, and other environmentally challenged projects. Nevertheless, big conservation groups have not turned them away. Bank of America has partnered with CI and TNC. Citigroup is a WWF partner. JPMorgan Chase's former chief executive William B. Harrison Jr. is on CI's board and the company has a partnership with WWF.

But donations are only one way corporations influence the environmental movement. Environmental Defense played a key role in arranging the $45 billion sale of TXU, one of the most notorious coal-powered energy companies in the country. Its acquisition by Kohlberg Kravis Roberts & Co. was celebrated in the press as a victory for environmentalists and people everywhere who value cleaner air. Krupp was praised in *The New York Times* for taking "a page from Wall Street's deal-making playbook."[6]

But, not everyone was pleased. Before the Kohlberg deal, the mayors of Dallas and Houston were leading a coalition of nineteen Texas mayors against the company's plans to build eleven coal-fired plants in the state, where the air quality is already among the worst in the nation. Lawsuits, petition drives, and anti-TXU Web sites were already working to block all new coal plants, when ED announced it had mediated a deal that would eliminate eight of the planned plants but would allow three of the largest to be built by the new owners.[7]

Some observers saw it as a classic bait and switch. They doubted whether TXU ever really planned to build all eleven power plants, which would have cost an investment outlay of $1 billion apiece. By threatening to build that many, the company left the new buyers in good position to push through approvals for three large, dirty coal-burning plants and avoid looking like global-warming villains. In any event, ED's maneuvering appeared to undercut local environmental efforts. Laura Miller, Dallas mayor at the time of the deal, told the *New Republic* that Krupp's agreement was "feckless and unenforceable."[8]

There was another noteworthy element to the ED–TXU deal: In an indication of the kind of cross-pollination that goes on between conservation and the corporate worlds, William Reilly, a former EPA administrator and a past president and chairman of WWF-US, led the negotiations for the buyers. According to the *New Republic* story, Reilly convinced them to meet with Krupp by saying, "Look, this is a guy who can keep secrets" . . . "and he'll do deals."

Corporations and Their Ties to Conservation Groups

Company	CF	CI	ED	TNC	NRDC	WWF-US
Alcoa		•			•	•
AEP	•		•			
Anheuser-Busch	•	•				
BP	•	•	•	•	•	
Bechtel	•					
Centex	•		•			
Chevron Corporation	•	•	•			
Chrysler			•	•		
ConocoPhillips	•	•	•	•		
Entergy	•					
Exelon				•	•	
ExxonMobil	•		•			
First GEN Corp.		•				
Ford Motor Co.		•		•	•	

27

Company	CF	CI	ED	TNC	NRDC	WWF-US
General Motors				•	•	
Home Depot	•			•		•
International Paper Co.	•			•		
Johnson & Johnson	•			•	•	•
PG&E				•	•	•
Rio Tinto		•	•	•	•	
Royal Caribbean Cruises	•	•				•
S. C. Johnson & Son		•	•	•		
Shell Oil	•	•	•	•	•	
Starbucks		•	•			•
USX	•					

Relationships include donations, partnerships, programs, projects, joint councils, and advisory boards. Sources: Web sites and tax returns of the organizations and corporations.

The History of Triple-Digit Pay

While it's business as usual for today's top conservation leaders to earn huge salaries and act like corporate moguls, the environmental movement's original corporate sweetheart might have been the late Jay D. Hair, who served as the National Wildlife Federation's (NWF) president from 1981 to 1995, followed by one term at the helm of the prestigious IUCN. Hair was pulling down an annual $300,000 in those days, twice as much as any of his peers. During Washington's sweltering summers, he reportedly kept his limo idling outside his elegant Washington office, the air-conditioning cranked, apparently unconcerned about global warming! This, though the first major international furor over climate change took place in 1988, smack in the middle of his NWF reign.[9]

Hair pioneered the kind of corporate ties that have become all too common today. He set up NWF's Corporate Conservation

Council and raised more than $1 billion during his time at the organization's helm. But that was apparently a more innocent era: Hair's corporate overtures were met with outrage by the rest of the environmental community at the time. Today every large conservation group has followed his lead by establishing their own public-private sector boards. TNC has an International Leadership Council. ED has a National Council. CF has a Corporate Council; CI has the Center for Environmental Leadership in Business, known as CELB. The groups also spearhead several industry-specific committees and task forces.

After Hair retired from conservation work, he became the secretary general of the newly formed International Council on Mining and Metals (ICMM), an appointment meant to signal that the mining industry "wants to do things differently" according to the ICMM's chair, Douglas Yearley, then the CEO of Phelps Dodge Corp. The ICMM was formed in 2001 by the leading international mining corporations with the stated purpose of promoting their commitments to environmental, economic, and social responsibility. But several of their members have since been involved in controversies in which their actions on environmental and human rights fronts have been called into question. The scandals have undermined the ICMM's credibility.

Industry Crossover

As Reilly's role in the TXU sale attests, that sort of crossover is commonplace now. Not only are conservation groups vying for the favors of Wal-Mart, Adam Werbach, the youngest-ever president of the Sierra Club and protégé of the late environmental iconoclast David Brower, went to work as a consultant for the company in 2006. It was a major reversal for the Club's former wunderkind, who once referred to the retailer as a "virus, infecting and destroying American culture."

There was a brief furor over Werbach's defection. But, for the most part, even the watchdogs have turned blasé. The growing corporate influence in conservation boardrooms and donation rosters fails to fluster environmental journalists such as Kelpie Wilson.

"It's the way the world works. And it's just not my focus," says Wilson, the environmental editor of an online journal called *Truth Out*. Wilson says she works with conservation groups and prefers not to harp on their corporate ties. It's the same stand taken by the growing horde of environmental e-journals and publications, which seem loath to air the movement's dirty laundry. They prefer to give the benefit of the doubt to just about any corporate environmental initiative, apparently taking the attitude that anything is better than nothing at all. The most scathing exposés have appeared occasionally in the pages of mainstream newspapers such as the *Washington Post, Sacramento Bee,* and *Los Angeles Times.*

Though conservation groups do not often come under the harsh glare of scrutiny, their corporate makeovers have not been without a certain number of public relations glitches, scandals, and eyebrow-raising conflicts of interest that beg the question: Would this be tolerated at a publicly traded corporation?

Allegations and Ethics

Allegations of financial impropriety and unethical behavior have flourished as the groups have grown. The largest, most respected conservation groups in the world have been investigated for shady real estate deals, padding their books, and accepting quid pro quo payments—equivalent to payoffs—from petroleum companies and other corporations.

Nepotism is widespread. At Conservation International, where I worked, the children, spouses, and close personal friends of executives, donors, and board members held posts ranging from interns to senior staff. My boss and his wife worked in the same division. But at least they had been at the organization for years, nearly since its inception, a time when CI was a fledgling start-up and in danger of extinction itself. In those days, the organization was far from the professional operation it is today and friends and family were often called on to help out. The few staffers would bring their kids to the office on weekends to help stuff envelopes or whatever else was needed. Entire families pitched in, often on a volunteer basis.

Once an organization has grown into one of the largest of its kind in the world, it seems inappropriate to continue in the same vein. But in 2007, CI named Cristina Mittermeier, the wife of its president, Russell Mittermeier, to the post of senior director in my old division, communications. It was CI's twentieth anniversary year. A marine biologist by training, Mrs. Mittermeier hadn't worked in her field in years. Before being hired by CI, she had devoted much of her time to traveling around the world as a sort of informal first lady. She took wildlife photographs and collaborated with her husband on CI coffee table books.[10] And nepotism is by no means unique to CI. Instances at the Conservancy and other conservation organizations are common knowledge in the close-knit conservation world, where business and pleasure seem too easily mixed.

Conflict of interest involving their corporate board members, supporters, and sponsors is another murky and confusing landscape; it's difficult to discern where altruism ends and inappropriateness begins at many groups. TNC was prompted to make sweeping reforms in the mid-2000s after a newspaper scandal led to a congressional investigation and an Internal Revenue Service audit. But other groups have relationships with the companies of their board members that raise questions. For instance, Tishman Construction Corp. received hundreds of thousands of dollars in project management fees for the remodeling of NRDC's Los Angeles offices. Was Tishman giving the nonprofit a good deal? Or was the company making some easy money because its chairman sits on NRDC's board? Is it appropriate that Banco Nacional de Mexico handles all of the banking for TNC's Mexico operation, when the bank's chairman, Roberto Hernandez, sits on TNC's board of directors? Is the fact that ED is working closely with Wal-Mart and even opened an office in the company's Bentonville, Arkansas, hometown related to Wal-Mart scion Sam R. Walton's seat on ED's board? Who gets the most out of these relationships? When is the public's interest served? When is the public's trust abused?

A conservation land deal made by Henry Paulson, Goldman Sachs' chief executive, before he left the post to become treasury secretary during the George W. Bush administration, was the focus of protest in 2007 by shareholders who objected to a Goldman Sachs land donation to the Wildlife Conservation Society, a group with a relationship to Paulson's son, Merritt.[11] The company had acquired 680 acres of forestland in Tierra del Fuego, an archipelago off the southernmost tip of South America, at auction as part of a debt portfolio. Instead of treating it as a company asset with valuable timber stocks, the company donated the land to WCS and paid TNC nearly $145,000 in consultancy fees in the arrangement. Shareholders were incensed about the deal, because of the apparent personal gain and conflict of interest for Paulson and his son. Merritt Paulson is a member of WCS's advisory board. His father was a member of TNC's board of directors at the time. One month after the land donation took place, Paulson became the chairman of TNC's board. According to press reports, Paulson and his wife had become fond of the archipelago during previous camping and bird-watching trips. One of the groups that filed shareholder proposals regarding the Tierra del Fuego transaction, Action Fund Management LLC, demanded that Paulson reimburse the company for "any shareholder assets spent to advance his personal interests." The group also alleged that Goldman Sachs lied to shareholders at the 2006 annual meeting by asserting that TNC had been deliberately excluded from the transaction. In fact, TNC's 2004 tax return states that Goldman Sachs paid the environmental group $144,895 between August 2003 and June 2004 for consulting services on the Chilean land deal.[12]

Both TNC and WCS pride themselves on basing their operations on models straight out of business schools. The Tierra del Fuego episode is illustrative of the lack of professional standards all too often exhibited at organizations that claim to function like corporations. Conservation board members, who hail from top international businesses, have engaged time and again in behaviors that would not go unnoticed in the corporate world. These corporate moguls join conservation groups for the wrong reasons and often never learn enough about the group's scientific objectives to play their roles effectively, says Huey Johnson, former California Secretary of Resources and stalwart of the environmental movement, who helped build TNC and founded the Trust for Public Lands and several other influential groups. "Many of the corporate board members come on because they want social rewards," Johnson says, such as "their kids' respect and something to talk about at cocktail parties."

If the board members of conservation groups tend to look on the groups as their own exclusive social clubs, the same seems true for the leaders of the nonprofit institutions. In an industry where international travel and adventure is part of the job, fuzzy boundaries between the personal and professional spheres also prove a problem on the spending front. When the Pacific island government of Papua New Guinea tried to kick CI out the country in mid-2006, part of the uproar was caused by CI executives who used money earmarked for a community center for unauthorized expenses. For instance, $30,000 in project funds was used on "visa runs," frequent international travel to renew visas because CI had failed to obtain work permits for the international staff and their families. Another $200,000 was spent reimbursing the foreign staff members for income taxes they paid because the organization did not take advantage of the tax exempt status that was available to project staff as employees of a UNDP-funded operation.[13] A few years earlier, during the messy 2003 divorce of CI chief Peter Seligmann, his wife, Susan, accused him of charging personal meals and other expenses to his corporate credit card and using CI funds to pay for a trip to Africa for himself, his mistress, and her children.[14]

The Nature Conservancy was in the habit of issuing low-interest and no-interest loans to key executives, including its president Steve McCormick. McCormick also controlled a $23 million no-strings-attached discretionary fund used to finance pet projects, which had raised questions of propriety.[15]

Despite the scandal, McCormick remained at the helm of the organization for another four years, when he quit abruptly after a proposal to merge TNC and CI was scuttled. He later surfaced as the new head of the Gordon and Betty Moore

Foundation, CI's most important funder. Mark Tercek, an investment banker from Goldman Sachs, was picked to replace McCormick as TNC's president and CEO.

A Lavish Culture

But the conservation world is not alone in its excesses. Similar scandals have plagued many other public organizations, including the Smithsonian Institution and the World Bank. Smithsonian chief Lawrence M. Small was forced from his job in 2007 after a public airing of his annual salary of nearly $916,000 and questionable expense account charges including chartered jets, catered meals, a luxury car service, and expensive gifts. He used Smithsonian funds to pay for his wife's trip to Cambodia, according to the Smithsonian inspector general. The investigation also revealed that Small had received an allowance of more than a million dollars from the institution for holding official functions at his Washington, D.C., mansion, but that he hardly ever held events at his home. Small, it turned out, wasn't the only Smithsonian official living what one congressman called "the Dom Pérignon Lifestyle" on the public's dime.[16] Several other Smithsonian senior staff members were found to have similar failings. At the World Bank, meanwhile, Paul D. Wolfowitz resigned after a months-long crisis over revelations that he used his position to engineer a promotion and raise for his girlfriend.

After years of excesses, the Internal Revenue Service finally stepped up in 2004, announcing plans to increase policing of nonprofit groups. As part of the crackdown, the IRS reviewed pay practices and levied its first fines in March 2007. Twenty-five nonprofits were charged with owing $21 million in back excise taxes for, among other things, paying their top executives excessive salaries and picking up the tabs for vacation homes, personal automobiles, and legal fees.[17] The nonprofits were also found to have let executives pay for personal meals and gifts that should not have qualified as business expenses.

The IRS never discloses who it investigates. So, while the scandal at TNC is widely believed to have prompted the IRS inquiry, there is no way to know if conservation groups were among those fined. In any event, the questions raised by the exorbitant salaries and luxury lifestyles of today's nonprofit leaders have more to do with ethics than legality.

Although earning more money than 99 percent of Americans while working for a charity raises ethical questions, it doesn't break any laws. In fact, conservation groups aren't even at the very top of the nonprofit pay pyramid. While nonprofit pay, in general, has galloped along faster than inflation, the windfalls are not felt across the board: Hospital administrators and university chiefs make the most, often pulling down a million or more dollars a year. The top executives of conservation groups are in the upper-middle class of their industry's pay scale. Sadly, it is those nonprofit professionals who run after-school programs and work with the elderly, the poor, and the homeless, who make the least money. They earn modest salaries on par with public school teachers. Who decides? The same private consulting firms that help corporate boards determine executive compensation often decide nonprofit pay, basing their recommendations on norms in the particular nonprofit industry. It's a self-perpetuating process that critics say can only push top compensation ever higher, at the expense of each organization's mission.

A Growing Controversy

Besides the increased government oversight, the brouhaha over CEO pay has led to plenty of private sector studies, reports, and consternation.[18] Responding to a survey by the charity watchdog GuideStar about whether nonprofit execs are overpaid, Judy Powell of the Parent Guidance Center in Montgomery County, Texas had this to say: "Just like the for-profit world, some executives are compensated outrageously TOO HIGH while others are not compensated nearly enough. It only proves that the nonprofit world is subject to the same competitive principles of capitalism as the profit world." Nonprofit consultant Elizabeth Gibbs had similar concerns about top-paid nonprofit leaders: "One of the problems society faces today is a race by corporate executives to see who can get the highest salary. Corporate salaries are over the top and way out of line with performance. It seems as though nonprofit salaries are taking the same path."

Kierán Suckling, executive director of the Center for Biological Diversity, a midsized conservation group based in Tucson, agrees the salaries of many top conservationists are outrageous. Suckling, who makes $76,535 a year including benefits, is among the environmentalists who have shunned corporate-style compensation packages and corporate sponsors. Besides the salaries, Suckling and others are even more concerned with the cozy relationships their colleagues have established with dirty industry barons.

"To me, it's not a matter of whether you should work with them," said Suckling of corporate executives with whom he often collaborates on government-mandated advisory boards and other public ventures. "The issue is whether you allow them on your board of directors. Should you be endorsing their products?

"There are folks who say, 'if you're going to work with these people, you can't beat them up at the same time. Either work with them or beat them up.' Our position is, of course we can do both because we come from a position of strength," says Suckling, whose group has a reputation as a hard-lined defender of nature.

Timothy G. Hermach, who has been called the conscience of the U.S. environmental movement, has a similar view—that many large groups have been co-opted by their donors.

"Today, you have 'gang green,' part of the D.C. political process with a seat at the table, negotiating terms and conditions for more of the liquidation of nature," says Hermach, the founder and president of the Native Forest Council in Eugene, Oregon.

Bill Turnage, former president of the Wilderness Society, also dislikes the deal-making culture that has taken over as the U.S. environmental movement has grown large, rich, and too polite.

"To me it is war and we need some more warriors in the environmental movement. People who aren't afraid to take off the gloves and really get in there," Turnage says. "We need a few leaders who aren't careerists. People who aren't worried about where they are going to get their next job, who just say, 'I'm going to give this my all and when I'm done, I'm done.'"

Chapter Three

The Conservation Corporation

Environmentalist Judson Barros is in the thick of battle over the future of Brazil's vast biodiversity. He lives in Piauí state in northwestern Brazil, a region traditionally dominated by dirt-poor family farms and tropical woodland savannahs, a region known as El Cerrado. It's Brazil's second-largest ecosystem after the Amazon and crosses a broad swath of the country's mid-section. Scientists say it is one of the most biologically diverse savannahs on the planet.

In 2001, Barros and his wife established the nonprofit Fundação Águas do Piauí, or the Waters of Piauí Foundation, known as Funaguas. Two years later, New York–based agribusiness company Bunge Ltd. opened a soybean-crushing factory in the city of Uruçuí, in the south of the state. A number of commercial soybean farmers had already moved into Piauí from southern Brazil soy-growing strongholds in search of cheap land. Once the Bunge plant arrived, the conversion of Piauí's Cerrado into industrial farmland began in earnest. The state's soybean cultivation nearly tripled over the next three years. Such was the rush to expand the agricultural frontiers that new fields were often cleared without the proper land titles and required environmental permits.[1] By 2006, soybeans became the state's number-one cash crop.

But such remarkable changes weren't without an environmental toll. To clear the land, a common method involves stretching a long chain between two bulldozers and ripping out the vegetation along their path. Then the roots and top layer of soil are swept together and set on fire.[2] Besides the destruction of the Cerrado with its attendant consequences to the air and water quality, soil erosion, and climate regulation, the native wood was carted off to be burned as fuel at the Bunge plant. The state government helped the company fast-track government permits required to open the plant plus a waiver giving it a fifteen-year holiday from paying taxes. Bunge also obtained permission to clear-cut the land within a seventeen-mile radius of the factory and use what was cut down as firewood. It plans to keep using wood as fuel even after the local vegetation is exhausted by switching to fast-growing plantation timber, grown just for this purpose.[3]

When Bunge arrived in Piauí, Funaguas teamed with the attorney general's offices of both the state and federal governments and sued the company for failing to comply with Brazilian environmental law by burning native wood as fuel. Bunge was slapped with a sort of Brazilian version of a consent decree called a "TAC," or Term of Adjustment of Conduct, mandating that the company find a more environmentally friendly alternative. After the company threatened to close the factory and leave the state, however, a deal was cut that allowed Bunge to continue using wood to power the plant. Piauí's governor Wellington Dias proudly took the credit and issued a press release calling attention to a visit from Bunge's plant managers, who had stopped by the Piauí government palace to personally thank him for his persistence in the matter.[4]

But the members of Funaguas were outraged and filed a formal objection to the ruling in 2004.

Bunge countered with a flurry of criminal and civil lawsuits against Funguas and against Barros personally. The criminal charges were quickly settled. But the company continues to pursue four civil suits demanding the equivalent of about US$1 million for alleged "moral damages" to its reputation. Bunge officials disagree with the assessment, however. "From the start, our request has simply been that Funaguas cease publishing factually incorrect information about our operations," Bunge said in a statement. The company also defends its use of wood, which it refers to as "biomass," saying many other Brazilian manufacturers use biomass instead of more conventional fuels and that the practice is environmentally sound. Human rights advocates funded by the Ford Foundation, however, concluded that Bunge's legal pursuit of Barros is a case of harassment through the courts system, a common tactic used by corporations in Brazil to intimidate journalists and grassroots activists.[5]

CI also works in Piauí state. Like Funaguas, CI wants to save what's left of the Brazilian Cerrado. But, CI and Funaguas are on opposite sides of what Barros describes as an all-out war. Rather than ally itself with the Brazilian grassroots group, CI has partnered with Bunge and joined in the company's demands that Barros drop his legal case and retract his public statements.[6]

"This is war, a very unequal war," says Barros, who supports his family as a civil servant and receives no pay for his environmental work. He and his collaborators are volunteers. He admits he's sometimes short on time and on the bus fare to get to meetings he must attend on the business of the foundation, which operates on a budget of less than US$10,000 a year raised primarily from sympathetic fellow Brazilians.

"We are fighting against a multinational corporation that makes billions of dollars each year in Brazil, one of the world's most important companies. We are fighting against the governor of the state. And, we are just a small NGO consisting of one room and one environmentalist," says Barros, who also considers CI among the enemies he must vanquish to save what remains of El Cerrado. "In Piauí, CI is good for nothing," he says. "It just gives a seal of approval to Bunge's brutality."

The Corporate NGO

Not only has CI sided with Bunge in the fight in Piauí, the organization and others like it more closely resemble multinational corporations than the shoestring nonprofit groups they once were. As they have increased financial ties to corporations in recent decades, they have remade themselves in the image of their benefactors. Posh offices, large expense accounts, and public relations budgets mirror the practices of the corporate world. Groups like CI use business operating practices and jargon. Their leaders go by titles such as president, CEO, and chairman of the board. Fluent in corporate speak and philosophy, they "contract" with local NGOs to work in large conservation "markets" like Indonesia or Brazil and call their donors "customers."

Field offices are usually located in the most fashionable business districts in the countries where they work. Just as an employee at the IBM offices in São Paulo makes a much lower salary than her or his counterpart in the United States, the conservation field staff makes much less money than their U.S.

colleagues. But the jobs are far better than those at the local organizations that act just like "suppliers." While Ford purchases auto parts for its China plants from local suppliers in China, for instance, organizations like CI rely on local partners to work in remote areas thousands of miles away from the decision centers of their organizations. As outsourcing has grown popular in the corporate world, the world's largest conservation groups have embraced the business model, as well, reaping impressive cost savings but inflaming existing friction over the salary differentials in the global environmental movement.

"CI talks so much about poverty alleviation and treating people fairly, but we are paid less than the poverty line. They do not care about us," remarked one of CI's contract workers in Papua New Guinea.[7]

Indeed, the two top executives at CI make hundreds of times more each year than that Papua environmentalist.

The Man at the Helm

For most of its life span, CI has been run by two men—Peter Seligmann, its chairman and cofounder, and Russell Mittermeier, its president. Mittermeier is more famous and charismatic, having been named one of *Time* magazine's "Heroes for the Planet." A Harvard-trained primatologist, Mittermeier is most at home canoeing down the Amazon River or hiking an African wilderness with a cuddly lemur clinging to his shoulders. The talents of Seligmann, a Yale man, lie in another realm of nature conservation—the rarefied world of the wealthy donor.

The chairman of Conservation International is perhaps the most audaciously successful of a new breed of corporate courtiers. His comfort level with the fabulously rich probably started in childhood. He comes from a long line of German Jewish investment bankers, known for handling the business transactions of "high asset" individuals.

World War II set events in motion that led both men's families to the United States. Mittermeier arrived in New York by steamship from Germany as a toddler a few years after the war and settled in the city with his mother, Bertha. Seligmann's mother Esther Arnhold and her family escaped the Nazi regime just before the war's outbreak. The family business started in Berlin in 1803. In 1937 Esther's brother Henry Arnhold reestablished Arnhold and S. Bleichroeder Advisors in New York City, where it continued to thrive. Today, it manages nearly $30 billion in assets.

Peter's mother, Esther, married Otto Seligmann. The couple settled into life in Princeton, New Jersey, where Peter was born in 1950, one of four Seligmann children. Esther also taught dance. Otto, until he retired at age eighty, was the treasurer of Arnhold Ceramics, one of the many companies in the portfolio of his wife's family. The Seligmanns summered in Grand Teton National Park. In fact, when he is not traveling with mega-rich philanthropists, Seligmann divides his time between a home in Seattle, a Virginia horse farm, and the family's compound, an "inholding" located within the boundaries of Grand Teton National Park, near Jackson Hole, the exclusive hunting and skiing resort area in Wyoming where Vice President Dick Cheney and actors including Harrison Ford, a longtime CI board member, own homes. Seligmann would later say, "This place shaped all of our lives, and for me, it was the foundation for my involvement with conservation."

Peter Seligmann's uncle Henry Arnhold, the investment banker and eventual CI board member, must have cut a romantic figure for Seligmann as a boy. Arnhold gave George Soros, investment banker turned philanthropist, his start as a portfolio manager. In 1962, the Budapest-born Soros had his first successes there. The Double Eagle Fund, a hedge fund Soros started in 1969, is still a centerpiece of the Arnhold and S. Bleichroeder offerings. By 1973, when Soros jumped ship to start his own operation, he left with a sizable amount of its assets and went on to greater glory.

As an adult, Seligmann has been constantly in the company of such highfliers, which may make his pay as a nonprofit executive seem meager. His former wife says he had a habit of cashing in assets from the family fortune to subsidize his proclivity for living large and traveling by private jet.[8] It's a lifestyle common among his friends and benefactors, who include the biggest corporate raiders of our times.

Seligmann is often hailed as the most successful fundraiser in the history of the conservation movement. His strategy of snaring donors of great wealth transformed CI from an "endangered" start-up to an organization at the top of the conservation world's food chain. Seligmann created a team of conservationists specialized in cutting deals with leading corporations, from BP to Wal-Mart. CI helped the cruise ship industry develop environmental practices. And, years later, when other environmentalists complained that the industry had failed to fulfill its promises to stop polluting the oceans with waste from its floating cities, Seligmann has been available with a quote or a sound bite in the industry's defense. He has spoken glowingly of oil companies, regardless of their records for being among the world's foremost polluters.

He has defended longtime CI benefactor William Clay Ford, Jr. from complaints about Ford Motor Company's efforts to sabotage tougher fuel efficiency standards. The Ford scion and executive chairman of the company's board once sat on CI's board. But, he traded that seat for another on the executive board of CI's Center for Environmental Leadership in Business (CELB), established with $25 million from the Ford Motor Company. CELB's mission is "to engage the private sector worldwide in creating solutions to critical global environmental problems in which industry plays a defining role." Critics call it CI's greenwashing center.

CI, of course, is not the only big conservation group guilty of making deals with the devils of deforestation, habitat destruction, and global warming. What really sets CI apart from the pack is Seligmann's talent for cultivating moguls. While many groups rely on mass mailings and constant membership drives, Seligmann's method has centered on fewer and richer marks. He first met Gordon Moore in 1987, the same year CI was formed and the cofounder of the computer-chip maker Intel Corporation stepped down from Intel's day-to-day operations as chief executive.

According to the well-worn lore, Moore mailed CI a check for $100. Seligmann noticed the name and sent him a note. After that, he called. Moore was incredulous at first, asking if Seligmann called everyone who donated a hundred bucks, to which Seligmann replied: "No, but they're not all Gordon Moore, either."[9] Soon Moore joined CI's circle of super-rich backers onboard with Seligmann's big-picture vision for saving the world's natural riches. It's a now-familiar marketing pitch that CI and its rivals revamp every few years, promising to revolutionize nature conservation by "thinking big," "scaling up," and tapping into "the multiplier effect."

In 1998, Moore gave CI $35 million to start the Center for Applied Biodiversity Science, the organization's research arm.

Three years later, he announced a $261 million contribution to be spent over ten years. The money would finance CI's Centers for Biodiversity Conservation, new regional centers that promised biodiversity conservation at previously unimaginable scales. It wasn't only the largest grant ever made to an environmental group; it was four times larger than any other at the time.

Other big donors include Starbucks founder Orin Smith. After the company faced a barrage of criticism for purchasing beans from sources fueling rainforest conversion in Southeast Asia to expand coffee crops, Starbucks launched a multiyear "Conservation Coffee" effort with CI. And, in 2004 the Walton Family Foundation put up $21 million for marine science and ocean protection programs over several years.

Smith, Moore, and Walton sit on the CI board. Other board members include Kristen Moore, the Intel founder's daughter, and Moore Foundation trustee Lewis W. Coleman, an investment banker with few conservation credentials before Gordon Moore hired him to head up his foundation in 2000. The presence of so many Moore Foundation bigwigs on the CI Board has raised murmured complaints about conflict of interest. But few CI competitors are willing to talk too loudly, for fear of losing a shot at the Moore funds. Still, behind the scenes the foundation, its pro-business stance, thin conservation knowledge, and unusual grant-making, which some see as smacking of favoritism, has fueled lots of gossip. Some critics go so far as to call the foundation a glorified fishing club.[10]

The guy arranging the trips is Peter Seligmann. These aren't your average fishing expeditions either. They usually involve the world's best big-fish destinations and exotic locales off the coast of South America or the breathtaking Pacific island atolls. To give them a little more serious air, Seligmann likes to refer to them as "creative councils."

CI even operates its own high-end travel service called Sojourner that caters to the exotic vacation whims of "high-asset" individuals, who might donate to the cause. Tour guides? It depends on the size of your fortune. The mega-moguls and other high-profile prospects such as Pearl Jam guitarist Stone Gossard and celebrity journalist Thomas Friedman, whose wife sits on CI's board, travel with the top brass. Less deep-pocketed donors must make do with biologists or field staff doubling as unusually knowledgeable tour guides.

Seligmann's prowess at reeling in the philanthropic world's biggest fish has landed him many accolades. Some hail him as a conservation hero. But he is viewed with skepticism by many in the movement and even within his own organization, which, true to its corporate structure, has a top-down hierarchy that tends to stamp out open dialogue but breeds rampant gossip and behind-the-scenes political machinations. Top managers spend most of their time globetrotting. While I worked there, Seligmann and Mittermeier were rarely seen in the organization's offices. They tended to turn up only for quarterly meetings and organization-wide pep talks broadcast live to CI's field offices around the globe. In these "all-staff meetings" they would update the rank and file about their travels to far-flung places. Mittermeier, particularly, is master of a folksy storytelling style that seemed to hearken back to more earnest and egalitarian origins. Still, the atmosphere inside CI's two floors in a fluorescent-lit office building in suburban Washington would probably be unrecognizable to the small band of dissidents who started CI two decades ago.

CI History

The night CI was founded was an unseasonably cold Tuesday, even for late January. The week before, a rare blizzard had slammed Washington, D.C., the first of two major snowstorms that dumped two feet of snow on the capital over five days. The storms had buried the entire East Coast, leaving at least forty-five people dead from Alabama to New England. In D.C., hardware stores sold out of shovels and road salt, and business boomed at neighborhood restaurants, bars, and corner stores catering to snowbound residents.

On the evening of January 27, 1987, two days after the last snowflakes had fallen, ill-prepared city officials were still struggling to clear the streets. Temperatures hovered around twenty degrees. Thoughts had turned to warmer climates at the Tabard Inn on N Street, however, where a few dozen young ecologists were crammed inside a guestroom, wedged onto the bedroom furniture and seated on the floor with knees drawn up under their chins, deep in conversation.

That afternoon they had walked off their jobs at TNC, even at that time one of the country's largest environmental groups, and were now hammering out the precepts that would guide a new organization dedicated to saving tropical rainforests and other endangered landscapes around the world. The meeting stretched through the night and well into the next day.

"We didn't know what was going to happen. We might be left without jobs. But they could assure us that there were a few people [financial donors] who were there to support us for a few months," according to Raquel Gomez, who was among the defecting staff members who trekked a few blocks through the snowy streets from the Conservancy's Massachusetts Avenue offices to the Tabard that bitter-cold and blustery afternoon. "It was very emotional. People would cry and laugh and hug and kiss."

"It was a coup d'état. There were articles [in newspapers] all over the world, all over Latin America. I think TNC called us a group of bandits," smiles Gomez, an administrative assistant, who joined the walkout along with Martin Goebel.

"We were a pretty tight-knit group," recalls Goebel, "and we felt like we belonged together and that we were doing historic work."

They christened the new organization Conservation International. And, in many ways, it would become symbolic of the new "multinational" character that the U.S. conservation movement had begun to embrace at a time when scientists were sounding a drumbeat of alarm about global warming, habitat destruction, and mass extinctions.

Depending who you talk to, the split was either about money, control, or how to do the work of preserving nature in some of the poorest countries on the planet. Several observers say all three factors had something to do with it. TNC, which had focused on buying and protecting conservation land in the United States for most of its existence, was struggling to find the best way to work internationally, mainly in Latin America's impoverished but biologically rich rainforests. Goebel, who became CI's assistant science director, remembers battles over strategy. As he recalls it, TNC's science department wanted the international team to buy up as much ecologically sensitive land as possible and put it under conservation management.

He and his colleagues, however, were determined not to embark on conservation work in the U.S. style, believing such an approach was not only doomed to fail in Latin America, but could blow up on them. Like Goebel, who grew up in Mexico, many members of the international department were Latin American natives with a strong grasp of the politics of the region. While TNC's strategy had been successful in the United States, they believed it could open the group up to attacks of neo-imperialism in nationalistic Latin American countries, where social critics would not look kindly on a U.S. organization buying up the region's most spectacular real estate.

"We used to have heated debates with the [TNC] science department. They were particularly perplexed that we weren't buying land [in Latin America] because it was so cheap," he says. "We decided there was no way that we were going to go out and raise billions upon billions of dollars to go buy somebody else's territory on behalf of a U.S. entity. . . . It was a politically unwise thing to do."

Despite the acrimony, the international team was caught by surprise when the word came down a few weeks after Frank Boren, the new TNC president, took office. Boren's daughter worked for the international department at the time, a fact that had lulled many into thinking he could never break up the department. But there were powerful undercurrents at play. The international program had grown rapidly by January 1987, stepping on toes among TNC's state chapter members in the process.

The Conservancy's state chapters had long abided by strict rules governing fundraising. If one chapter had developed a relationship with a certain philanthropist or foundation, the other chapters were barred from approaching the donor. The international program, however, had no state territory to claim as its own, and its foreign mandate gave it a unique appeal with some donors all over the country. As Seligmann and his boss

Spencer Beebe increased their fundraising, they were seen as poachers, Sumner Pingree and others recall.

"Very quickly, it engendered a lot of suspicion and competitive response," says Pingree, one of the TNC defectors who would become CI's first vice president for development and communications. "I remember going to national board meetings and playing this public relations game with not only national staff and board but also with state chapter people, who were kind of very concerned about their base."

Humble Beginnings

The early days, once they had defected, were lean and uncertain times. For the first few months of 1987, headquarters were three rooms in the Tabard, a labyrinthine hotel carved out of several adjacent townhouses near Dupont Circle. The hotel bill and payroll were picked up by an anonymous donor—one of a small number of early supporters who kept the organization going during those early days, Pingree recalls.

The hotel rooms became frequent gathering spots "to maintain confidence and a sense of the group," he said. "But basically people moved into their home offices. People were house-bound and snowbound and otherwise kind of making do."

Before Washington's cherry trees were in bloom, the group had secured an office in a D.C. building owned by the father of one of its founders. But furniture was not in the budget.

"We were all working on the floor, lying on the floor. These biologists were working on maps on the floor. The telephones were in a closet," Gomez recalled. "And everybody was so happy," she said. "It was so lovely."

In those early days, she recalled, everyone chipped in what they could, worked long hours. At night, the "office" often shifted to people's homes, including her apartment in the nearby Adams Morgan neighborhood. Late-night work sessions would end in sing-a-longs with her husband playing the guitar and everybody following along to the words of "Nuevo Cancion" South American songs about love and revolution. Her husband designed the first newsletter. And trips to the field meant seat-of-the-pants budget travel to remote South American rainforests in World War II–era airplanes, trips packed with real risks and adventure.

Within the first six months, CI pulled off a coup that put the organization on the map: It became the first environmental group in the world to do a debt-for-nature swap, stealing the thunder of larger, more established groups. It was the height of the debt crisis in which impoverished countries were defaulting under staggering debts to banks in the United States and other developed countries. Today, these swaps are just one instrument in the toolkit international conservation groups use to expand protections in developing countries.

In those days, CI's small but passionate staff was determined to work with local groups to find new and culturally appropriate ways to conserve nature. In terms of finding more people-friendly ways to work, the results have been middling to poor, as we will discuss later in greater detail. If fundraising prowess were the only measure, however, CI would be one of the most remarkable nonprofits operating today.

But not everyone sees the rise of corporate values as a good thing. There has been significant pushing back by veterans in the conservation movement, particularly scientists, who feel the credibility of their organizations is being undermined in the emphasis on marketing, fundraising, and corporate relationships. Among CI's forty-odd founders, Seligmann and one other executive are the only ones who remain working for the organization. Many who were forced out are still livid over the direction in which Seligmann has taken the group. He is known as one of most polarizing figures in the conservation movement today and one of the chief architects of the entire movement's corporate makeover.

"It's the 'Wal-Martization' of conservation," quips one CI cofounder, who—like many people interviewed for this book—declined to speak on the record because of ongoing business in the conservation world, where CI is a major player controlling who gets funding.

Others see what has happened at CI as symptomatic of the entire movement, which has grown large, fat, and complacent. It's a moment, critics say, that is run today by environmantalist who are more like bureaucrats or corporate executives than the passionate crusaders who took a chance and started CI two decades ago.

Sustainable Development

While it may just be the inevitable conclusion of age and growth, one important factor propelling the transformation of the environmental movement into something like an industry has been an uncritical acceptance of "sustainable development." The concept has been kicking around for decades, supplying the philosophical underpinnings for today's corporate-conservationist embrace. It emerged from the confrontational politics of the 1960s and 1970s environmental movement that generally left business communities and environmentalists with no common ground. The idea that development could be environmentally sustainable opened the door to dialogue and innovation aimed at merging two of society's biggest concerns.

In recent years, corporate America has embraced the idea as its own, propelled by consumers who are increasingly informed about the consequences of environmental degradation and climate change. According to a global survey by the business consulting firm McKinsey & Company, corporate executives are more concerned than ever about how environmental problems will affect their companies' bottom-line performance. The report concluded that corporate leaders are now more worried about climate change than the public at large. Nine in ten executives fret over global warming, while only 3 percent said they don't believe it is happening. The vast majority said they understand the public expects them to improve their handling of sociopolitical issues. They expect the environment, including climate change, to influence shareholder value "far more than any other societal issue during the next five years."[11]

As a result of shifting mind-sets, companies have rushed to come up with green marketing campaigns and lavish cash on environmental groups. Lengthy sustainability reports have become commonplace among the world's leading corporations today. These reports chronicle good works that include reducing waste and pollution, developing environmentally friendly products, combating poverty, and other social ills.

This is undoubtedly a positive development. However, several social corporate-responsibility studies note a wide gap between the rhetoric and the reality. One study published by the Boston College Center for Corporate Citizenship found that three-quarters of high-level executives polled agreed corporate citizenship needs to be a priority but far fewer had incorporated concrete action into their operations.[12] Their concern hadn't prompted them to start making environmentally sustainable products or rethinking their relationships with employees and suppliers.

While the emerging socially responsible discourse among business leaders is encouraging, it is important to remember executives are not motivated by purely altruistic goals. Corporate social responsibility holds attraction with many business leaders for its utility as a defensive posture in the face of possible new government regulations on carbon emissions and increasingly savvy and interconnected watchdog groups around the globe. Corporate leaders, who run businesses with interests in many far-flung places, have found a proactive sustainability stance can help avoid costly environmental accidents, avert PR messes when they occur, and mute protests, particularly in developing countries, where the bulk of the world's raw materials and finished goods come from these days.

But some ask whether sustainability makes any sense in nature conservation, where ancient forests, oceans, fresh water, and other natural resources have been taken to the brink of collapse after human exploitation dating back millennia. How to harvest these resources sustainably is a concept that has eluded humankind for centuries.

Two projects that illustrate the dilemma of how to strike a truly "sustainable" balance are the Forest Stewardship Council, or FSC, and the Marine Stewardship Council, or MSC. The product certification programs were launched separately by consortiums made up of corporations and environmental groups. As such, they are the product of compromise, deal-making, and behind-the-scenes wheeling and dealing that critics say have done a disservice to the very nature they set out to protect. While both labels have prominent environmentalist supporters, their detractors say the FSC and the MSC are half-measures that mislead the public but won't head off extinctions.

The FSC came under heavy fire in 2007 on the news that Asian Pulp & Paper Co. Ltd. would start using the FSC label. The Singapore-based conglomerate is one of the world's largest logging companies, with a record of laying waste to forestland in the developing world. After the uproar, FSC severed its relationship with Asian Pulp and discussion ensued about tightening its standards. It was not the first time FSC had come under fire for the actions of companies that wear its label.

One of the biggest arguments between FSC's supporters and detractors concerns old-growth forests. While the FSC standards require its members to protect "high conservation value" areas, it does not prohibit them from logging in the few remaining ancient stands. The detractors say the FSC rules only confuse people and undermine years of public education about the importance of preserving ancient forests.

In New Jersey, for instance, activists who had first campaigned in the 1980s against using a Brazilian rainforest timber called *ipê* to refurbish the state's many seaside boardwalks had a bad feeling of déjà vu in 2007: In Ocean City, New Jersey, local officials approved a contract to buy FSC-certified *ipê* to replace a block of the boardwalk, going against the recommendation of its own environmental commission. The decision angered FSC critics who say there is no way to sustainably log an ancient rainforest.

"If the *ipê* trees were 30 years old when you logged them, then you could argue that this is sustainable. But these trees are 250 to 1,000 years old. That is not sustainable at all," Tim Keating, executive director of the New York City-based Rainforest Relief, told *The New York Times*.[13]

The MSC, meanwhile, has certified hundreds of wild-caught seafood products from more than a dozen fisheries since the label was established in 1996 by Unilever and WWF. But critics say MSC's current standards are too lenient to actually support a recovery of the most threatened species. And, there are not enough well-managed fisheries in the world to meet demand from Wal-Mart, Whole Foods Market, and other retailers looking to sustainable labels to ally consumer concerns about overfishing that experts predict could lead to the collapse of fish stocks.

Other examples abound of corporate sustainability projects that received seals of approval from green groups despite their absurdly unsustainable practices. They reach back at least as far as the early 1990s when Waste Management Inc.'s ties to the NWF and WWF prompted grassroots activists in Wheeler, Indiana, to raise a ruckus.[14] At the same time it touted its ties to the nature conservation groups, Waste Management was accused of polluting local drinking water there.

Since the late 1990s, ED has bragged about its successes greening the operations of United Parcel Service and Federal Express. Yet a 2007 industry study by the nonprofit group Climate Counts placed the two companies' sustainability practices at the very bottom of the list of top shippers.[15] The nonprofit graded companies on a scale of one to one hundred based on criteria such as their positions on climate policy initiatives and whether they've taken meaningful steps to reduce their climate impact. FedEx ranked last with a score of twenty-eight, while UPS did slightly better with a ranking of thirty-nine: failing grades in both cases.

Fundraising Treadmill

Political scientist Christopher J. Bosso and others suggest the nonprofits have gotten so good at fundraising in recent decades that their success has left them on a sort of treadmill, where they must forever try to keep up with their fundraising goals at the detriment of their missions.[16]

Corporate funds are only part of the mix, but the relationships are the most troubling of all. David Morine, who launched TNC's corporate outreach nearly two decades ago, told the *Washington Post* that the corporate embrace was a big mistake. "These corporate executives are carnivorous," he said. "You bring them in, and they just take over."[17]

I have heard similar comments from other conservationists. One senior executive at a large group once told me he preferred not to reach out to corporations, because the cash always came with strings attached. "They tend to buy you up first and want to talk about conservation later," he said.

And, then, the corporate leaders too often end up believing the very spin they orchestrate. When I was at CI, Cemex, the Mexican cement maker, was known as an insatiable publicity hound. At a time when it needed some "reputational rehabilitation," the company began sponsoring coffee table books CI published with gorgeous photo layouts and texts by Mittermeier. Cemex executives were constantly pushing for CI to get it more press coverage for its conservation work, apparently oblivious to concerns that a higher profile could lead to unflattering scrutiny that could hardly conceal Cemex's true environmental record. Besides the negative impact of its cement-making mainline, its forestry subsidiary lost several management concessions in Brazil after federal investigators there charged the company with illegal logging.[18]

Julian Teixeira, a former public relations manager for CI's CELB unit that dealt directly with corporate partners, puts the blame on the nonprofit leaders. As he sees it, the conservation groups are greedier than the companies, seeking to partner with as many corporations as possible but failing to follow through with the companies and push them toward sustainable business practices. Instead, conservation groups flit from one "sexy" cause to the next; one day it's sustainable farming, the next it's global warming.

"The sexiest is being able to partner with one of the worst corporations and being able to change them," says Teixeira, who says that although he loved working for an environmental group and hoped the work he did had a net positive impact on the planet, the appetite for corporate dollars led to more than one bad decision at CI. "There were companies we should not have partnered with. There were times I was very uncomfortable."

He still cannot reconcile CI's willingness to partner with some industries, such as mining, a sector where CI has at least half a dozen corporate ties but that is also one of the most environmentally evasive industries on the planet. Teixeira says he was particularly discomforted working with Newmont Mining Corporation, a CELB partner that has been embroiled in human rights and environmental scandals on several continents.

Instead, he muses, perhaps it would be more ethical for CI to publicize mining's negative impacts and conduct a public campaign to raise awareness of the costs associated with making our computers, cell phones, iPods, and a vast universe of other products. Then again, he wonders how successful such an approach would be since people are unlikely to give up the comforts of modern life.

Seeing the Big Picture

Just as some corporate executives end up believing their own spin, CI executives seem to lose sight of reality after awhile, as the organization's partnership with Bunge attests. The company and the nonprofit have made their partnership into a high-profile PR vehicle. Bunge brags about it on its Web site and in its sustainability report. CI recounts it again and again as a "success story." The relationship spawned Aliança BioCerrado, the BioCerrado Alliance, a coalition made up of Bunge, CI, and CI's local partner Oréades, to evangelize the model among other companies and NGOs in Brazil.

The alliance has had a hard time gaining traction, however, given Bunge's public relations travails in Brazil and with international environmental and human rights groups. The company has not only run afoul of rights organizations with its lawsuits against Barros and its contributions to deforestation and global warming; Bunge outsourced the job of cutting down of all those trees it uses as firewood to a Brazilian company called Graúna, which human rights activists allege engages in modern-day slavery. Several of the state's large soybean plantations have also faced government prosecution for forced labor. Bunge implicitly acknowledged that slavery was an issue in its industry in April 2006, when the company signed Brazil's National Slavery Eradication Pact, pledging to sever ties with any company or plantation owner convicted of labor crimes.

A Brazilian appeals court finally weighed in on Funagua's appeal in March 2008. The court ruled that the company's use of firewood as fuel violates Brazilian environmental laws. Citing satellite images that show rapid deforestation and desertification underway in El Cerrado, the Brazilian tribunal ruled that Bunge should stop using native wood as fuel and consider liquid natural gas, petroleum, and other options that would be less environmentally damaging.[19]

Bunge is appealing the decision and points out that its permit from Brazilian environmental authorities has not been revoked, despite the court ruling.

"We have studied the efficacy of biomass as a fuel source, and third party research has stated that it is the most efficient method of generating heat at our facilities. There are no natural gas lines to many of our facilities and trucking fuel oil hundred of kilometers is inherently inefficient from an energy perspective," according to the statement provided by Bunge officials.

CI executives, incidentally, use Bunge's own arguments to defend the company's use of firewood, arguing that transporting conventional fuels to the factory would burn up a lot of greenhouse gases. It's also a much cheaper alternative than relying on petroleum products, given today's high prices. But wouldn't a company truly interested in environmental sustainability look into alternatives such as solar energy? Solar panels could provide a renewable source of energy in this part of Brazil, where it is hot and sunny most of the year.

But CI did not set out to make such a compromising partnership. The project had a more positive beginning. Under Brazilian law, the owners of large agricultural holdings are required to set aside a portion of their properties in private nature preserves and maintain the natural vegetation around lakes, streams, and other waterways to keep them from being contaminated by runoff containing chemical pesticides and fertilizers. But few farmers comply with the law. And they aren't the easiest people to approach, as the average plantation owner is known to greet strangers with a shotgun more often than a welcoming smile. After much debate and internal dialogue about how to approach the farmers, CI staff members finally decided the best intermediaries would be seed and fertilizer suppliers such as Bunge. Their salespeople usually have biology training and an understanding of how good land management practices could benefit the environment and the long-term productivity of the farms their customers own.

For its part, Bunge was facing public outcry over its role in fueling the deforestation in another ecologically critical part of Brazil, the Amazon rainforest, and was in need of reputation rehabilitation. The company is a diversified agribusiness conglomerate that sells everything farms need to plant oilseed crops, and later buys up the harvest and processes it into a wide variety of products sold under dozens of brand names. Bunge has operated in Brazil for more than a century and sells oils and soy drinks under brand-name labels such as Delícia, Primor, Salada, and Soya. In the United States, India, and several European countries, Bunge is a wholesaler of products from eatable oils and shortenings to animal feed and biofuel.

It took CI two years of visiting with Bunge managers in Brazil and at their White Plains, New York, headquarters before the company dropped its guard and agreed to make the introductions with farmers around the Emas National Park in central Brazil, a region where at least 80 percent of the land is privately owned. Once the contacts were made, CI and its local partner provided high-tech mapping services to help the farmers establish the boundaries of their reserves and file the paperwork with the Brazilian government. The collaboration led to private conservation reserves on nearly one hundred farms, achieving an important objective of preserving and restoring natural areas around the Emas park, where the original vegetation had already been nearly unrecognizably transformed into farmland.[20]

Things got murky when CI agreed to help Bunge replicate the project in Piauí, where the woodland savannah was still largely intact when they arrived. By holding Bunge up as a shining example of environmental sustainability, CI provided the company with cover to deflect valid concerns by Funaguas and other critics about the impact of Bunge's operations there.

I think there is no doubt that there are people at CI who want to save El Cerrado. John Buchanan, senior director of business practices at CI's CELB unit, who runs the Bunge program from the group's Crystal City, Virginia, headquarters, expressed his concern in an interview with Grist.com: "Deforestation in the Cerrado is actually happening at a higher rate than it has in the Amazon. If the actual deforestation rates continue, all the remaining vegetation in the Cerrado could be lost by the year 2030. That would be a huge loss of biodiversity."[21]

But it seems like CI lost its way in the relationship. One longtime observer of the conservation movement notes that CI, because of its rebel origins, always had a sort of an underdog sensibility about it, a sense of barnstorming for biodiversity that it retained even as it grew to be one of the biggest and most powerful groups in its niche. "But when they are barnstorming with a 747, it can be a little intimidating," he notes.

In dealings with Funaguas, CI can no longer be seen as the underdog. That role belongs to Barros, who has faced intimidating phone calls and anonymous death threats. He equates his fight with Bunge to a battle of biblical proportions. "This is a battle like the one in the story of David and Goliath. But, here in Piauí, we survive on hope. We trust that, just like in the story, David will win," says Barros, who was ecstatic that his group's appeal persevered. But his fight with Bunge is far from over. Besides appealing the court ruling, Bunge says it will continue to pursue its civil suits against him.

Chapter Four
"The Marketing Enterprise"

When IKEA came under fire for selling dining room sets made from trees stolen from endangered forests, the Swedish home furnishing giant turned to what seemed an unlikely quarter for a public relations boost: WWF.

WWF is one of the chief campaigners against illegal logging, which is razing the planet's last old-growth forests at an alarming rate, endangering species, and speeding global warming. Without naming names, WWF says U.S. and European retailers sell the vast majority of the world's illegally forested timber products. Purchasing items made from illegally acquired wood is "frighteningly easy—as easy as stepping into a wood product retail store and purchasing a chair or a table whose origins are unknown," WWF says on its Web site. Such crusading on behalf of nature has earned WWF public credibility.

But WWF also takes millions of dollars from corporations. IKEA, for instance, is a "marketing partner." So WWF dispatched Duncan Pollard, director of its Forests for Life Program, to vouch for the company at an April 2007 press briefing in which IKEA acknowledged its products very well might have come from stolen timber.

"Unfortunately, IKEA can never guarantee that IKEA products are not made from illegally logged wood," said Thomas Bergmark, the company's head of social and environmental affairs.[1]

The question is, can't or won't?

It is certainly true that it's difficult to tell where timber comes from today given the number of middlemen and "spot markets" where raw wood—legally and illegally harvested—is mixed, sorted, and sold to the highest bidder. According to the company, it would take too many resources to trace back every wood shipment.

But all it really has to do is insist that its suppliers work with WWF's own Global Forest and Trade Network or any of the other independent auditing services created in recent years to ensure stolen wood does not end up in international supply chains. On paper, IKEA has a strong policy: According to the company, it "demands that the wood in our solid wood products does not originate from intact natural forests, unless they are certified." In practice, however, IKEA could do better.

"With the consolidation of the retail sector and the rise of the 'big-box' store, individual retailers now have the leverage in the market to set the rules of commerce," said David Groves, a campaigner with the nonprofit Environmental Investigation Agency, which has gone undercover to expose the illegal timber trade. "For example, if Wal-Mart, Home Depot, IKEA, etc. were to strictly enforce such a purchasing policy, then they would only need a handful of staff making unannounced inspections that would inevitably turn up unscrupulous suppliers. If these huge retailers were to terminate their relationships with these suppliers, it would send shockwaves through the Chinese manufacturing sector. Relatively quickly, you would see supply chains shortened, middlemen eliminated, no purchasing from 'spot markets,' and a rush for independent certification."

But the WWF emissary did not mention his group's Global Forest and Trade Network or that IKEA was woefully behind schedule on a pledge to sell more wood products certified as "sustainably" harvested. Instead Pollard praised IKEA for sponsoring WWF's efforts to educate people in Russia about the downsides of deforestation, efforts that had resulted in several glossy full-color brochures extolling the company's good works. Ironically, a *Washington Post* exposé published the same day linked the illegal timber trade to a factory in China that produces 100,000 pine dining room sets a year for IKEA. The lumber had come from the Russian Far East, where illegal logging is rampant.

But as Groves pointed out, IKEA is not alone in abetting the transformation of the world's forests into cheap plywood, coffee, vegetable oils, and other consumer goods that end up in our homes and on our dinner tables—sometimes even *as* our dinner tables. Home Depot, Lowe's, and other large retailers have been implicated by journalists, activists, and investigators in the illegal logging trade. Unilever, Cargill, Nestlé, Procter & Gamble, and Kraft have been named in fueling today's environmentally evasive palm oil industry, while Starbucks and dozens of other coffee companies have been linked to beans harvested on illegally cleared rainforest land. All those companies have relationships with big conservation groups.

From Rainforest to Dinner Table

How do rainforests end up in our dining rooms? It usually begins with a dirt road built into an untapped wilderness. Sometimes the builders are looking for oil, diamonds, or deposits of coal, minerals, or precious metals. Often the object is hardwood that brings top dollar from homebuilders in richer countries. Once the roads go in and the raw materials come out, landless peasants follow, clearing patches by the roadsides for subsistence farming. Eventually the dirt roads get paved. The small plots are bought up and consolidated into large tracts of land. The transformation is complete when these former rainforests become vast pasture lands for cattle grazing or soy, palm oil, or coffee plantations supplying markets in the United States, Europe, Japan, and elsewhere. Sometimes the subsistence farmers are cut out of the equation by large conglomerates that clear-cut the land and immediately turn it into cash-crop plantations.

This process plays out again and again all over the world—sometimes even inside protected areas, as WWF-UK documented in the Bukit Barisan Selatan National Park, on the southern coast of the Indonesian island of Sumatra. The 800,000-acre park is a World Heritage Site containing some of the island's last lowland forests and a quarter of the country's wild rhino and elephant populations, plus tigers and other unique and threatened plant and animal species. So much of the surrounding forest has already been destroyed by illegal logging, animal poaching, and farming that invaders have started to colonize the park itself, despite its ill-enforced legal protection as a World Heritage Site. Coffee farmers are the biggest threat. Almost a third of Bukit Barisan Selatan's original forest cover has been lost, according to WWF-UK, which tracked the coffee grown in the park to regional markets where it comingled with other beans and was sold to importers from at least fifty-two countries. The United States, Germany, Japan, Italy, and the United Kingdom were among the largest importing countries. The coffee was sold under many well-known brand names including Nestlé, Folgers, and Italy's Lavazza.[2]

Marketing Conservation

Not only do the largest conservation groups take money from companies deeply implicated in environmental crimes, they have become something like satellite PR offices for the corporations that support them. It's part of the large role marketing plays in the nonprofit world today. Besides operating multi-million-dollar efforts to attract and retain their own members, these groups have developed a variety of revenue-generating products and services that cater to the needs of their corporate benefactors.

Even a straightforward donation with no strings attached can give a company a public relations boost. But these days there is an array of other possibilities. Membership in the various corporate councils or advisory boards usually entails a hefty donation. Scaling up from there are building endowments and naming rights. For a donation of land and $150,000 in construction costs, the country's most profitable company, for example, snagged naming rights for The Nature Conservancy's ExxonMobil Education and Volunteer Center at Galveston Bay Prairie Preserve in Texas. Depending on the level of support, corporations can even get their names associated with entire centers such as CI's CELB, started with $25 million from Ford Motor Co. There are exclusive deals like International Paper Co.'s pledge to kick back a penny to its partner the National Park Foundation for each biodegradable commemorative cup it sells to concession operators inside the country's national parks. There are credit cards, carbon credits, and "cause-related marketing."

"Marketing" is a relatively new term. It entered the language only about a century ago, according to the American Marketing Association. The concept encompasses all aspects of selling a product—from its packaging and advertisement and promotion to sales and distribution and the management of customer relations.

Since first thought up, marketing has been the subject of countless innovations and offshoots. One of those is nonprofit marketing; another is green marketing. Still another is "cause-related marketing," generally described as marketing alliances between the for-profit and nonprofit groups or government agencies designed to meet the objectives of each party. In plainer English—those objectives are usually to sell the company's product, while improving the world in some way. WWF's partnership with New Line Cinema to advertise the plight of today's polar bears with the young audience of the film *The Golden Compass* is one example. But not all of these deals make for good bedtime stories.

Greenwashing is another relatively new expression. As green marketing took off, greenwashing claims have skyrocketed. In fact, green marketing—and its abuses—has so swiftly entered the corporate mainstream that the Federal Trade Commission launched a review of environmental marketing guidelines in 2008, a year ahead of its previously announced schedule. But so far, fear of consumer backlash has done more to rein in corporate greenwashing than enforcement action by the government.

Study after study shows that consumers are skeptical of corporate green marketing. General Motors found this out firsthand in January 2008 when it opened an interactive Web site aimed at stimulating discussion on future automotive technologies.[3] It was immediately bombarded by postings from the carmaker's critics, who didn't take kindly to GM's efforts to derail tougher fuel economy standards or the fact that the company killed the EV1, the rechargeable electric coupes it built in the late 1990s. Saying it was losing control of the site, GM quickly eliminated the interactive functions. GM, incidentally, has ties to TNC and NRDC.

Despite their deep skepticism about green advertising, consumers have made it clear they want companies to become more socially responsible. And, increasingly, consumers say they want environmentally friendly products and are willing to pay a premium for them. The combination of these trends has made green marketing an increasingly important—if often misused—part of both the corporate and conservation worlds. It's sometimes referred to as "reputation insurance," a sort of "get out of jail free" card for companies with environmental rap sheets.

While wealthy philanthropists and the average $20-a-year WWF member may be swayed solely by the idea of saving endangered species, corporate leaders are frank about their very different expectations for the relationships: Every transaction with a nonprofit—donation, partnership, or marketing arrangement—is calculated to help the company's image and boost its bottom line.[4] It is not necessarily bad that the corporate leaders expect "a return" on their charitable investments. But it is an important distinction between corporate and individual giving.

It's not hard to understand why companies want to piggyback on environmental groups. The Edelman Trust Barometer, an annual report ranking the most trusted institutions around the world, consistently ranks nonprofits above governments, corporations, and the media.[5] Several environmental "brand names" are as widely recognized as those of major corporations such as Sony or Microsoft. World Wildlife Fund's panda logo is the eighth most-trusted brand in the United States and the second most-trusted in Europe, according to the company's market research. TNC was named the most-trusted organization among thirteen well-known national nonprofits, think tanks, and associations, according to a poll conducted by market research firm Harris Interactive.[6] Nearly eight in ten people familiar with the Conservancy said they trusted the organization, the highest trust score of any organization tested.

Harder to understand is why conservation groups risk their reputations to partner with companies that take a harsh toll on the environment.

One example among many is the bottled water industry. An estimated sixty million plastic bottles a day end up in landfills, where they will linger for up to a thousand years before they biodegrade. And that's only the trash problem. The bottles took millions of barrels of crude oil to produce, not to mention the impact on the springs that supply the water and the environmental costs involved in shipping it from source to market. Nevertheless, WWF and CI have partnered with bottled water companies. WWF is helping Coca-Cola, which makes Dasani purified water, improve its image by teaming up on conservation projects involving seven freshwater river basins.

Fiji Water, meanwhile, hired CI to advise the company on ways to obliterate its carbon footprint. The company has launched a plan to reduce to negative 20 percent the amount of greenhouse gases it generates by implementing energy efficiency measures and offsetting the rest by paying CI to preserve a rainforest in Fiji, among other things. The plan, according Fiji and CI, sets out to make the company the first ever to venture into "carbon negative" territory, meaning its actions remove more carbon from the atmosphere than its manufacturing and shipping operations put in. Whether actions to mitigate carbon emissions actually justify the emissions to begin with is a topic of lengthy debate taken up in a later chapter. Suffice it to say, the announcement received splashy publicity in news outlets around the globe in late 2007. The coverage was overwhelmingly positive except for bitter complaints from Michael J. Brune, executive director of the Rainforest Action Network.

"Bottled water is a business that is fundamentally, inherently, and inalterably unconscionable," Brune told *The New York Times*.[7] "No side deals to protect forests or combat global warming can offset that reality."

Kierán Suckling, executive director at the Center for Biological Diversity, worries such questionable corporate partnerships could hurt the reputation of the entire movement.

"There is just no excuse beyond revenue generation," he says. "And at that point, haven't you made the devil's bargain?"

Not All Corporate Deals Are Good Ones

While their brand names are often as recognizable as those of major corporate products, nonprofit leaders apparently don't have the business savvy to match. Too often they commit their organizations to cozy partnerships with corporations. The deals are sold to the public as boons for the charities, but actually yield more benefits for the companies involved.

Credit card arrangements are a good example. These so-called "affinity" cards, which bear the logo of the charity and the card issuer, have proliferated rapidly in the last decade. The TNC Visa card comes in a choice of picturesque views of Idaho's central mountains, the Colorado River, or a cute shot of an endangered orangutan from Indonesia.[8] Banks like these cards because consumers who choose them tend to be more affluent and loyal. And they are more likely to pay their bills than the average customer. At 15.99 percent annual interest, however, the card is hardly the best deal on the market. And, it's not much of a deal for the charity either. TNC gets a one-time activation fee, followed by 25 cents on every $100 you spent. If you spent $100 a month on the card, it would net TNC $3.00 in a year. Because it's coming from a credit card, the contribution is not even tax deductible.

Cause-Related Marketing

Credit card relationships are just bad business for the charity. Cause-related marketing deals, like the one IKEA has with WWF, are even more questionable. According to regulators and charity officials, these arrangements come with a myriad of legal and ethical pitfalls.

A task force of attorneys general from sixteen states and the District of Columbia's Corporate Council concluded that cause-related advertisements often communicated false and misleading messages.[9] The arrangements usually entail the rental of a nonprofit group's name and logo to help promote a company's product. Consumers are often left to believe that the nonprofit is endorsing the product as being superior to its competitors, when that is seldom the case. The ads are deceptive, the state law enforcers concluded, because they usually do not disclose that the transactions are of a purely financial nature.

These marketing relationships have stirred controversy inside groups as well, as the Sierra Club's national leadership found out in early 2008, after the makers of Clorox bleach approached them with a cause-related-marketing proposal.

The bleach maker wanted the club to endorse its new Green Works line of "environmentally friendly" household cleaners in exchange for an undisclosed percentage of sales.

The Sierra Club's Corporate Accountability Committee advised the group's national executive committee to turn down Clorox's offer. Or, if club leaders wanted to endorse the products, they should at least refuse to take money from the company, the committee advised, voicing concerns similar to those raised by the report of the Attorneys General. They warned that taking money from a company with a product the club endorsed would amount to a conflict of interest, or at least the appearance of a conflict, that could hurt the club's standing with members and the general public. An endorsement could confuse consumers into thinking the club had compared Green Works to other products in the "green" cleaning niche and found it to be the best.

"We were concerned that we weren't really set up for consumer analysis like *Consumer Reports*," said Stuart Auchincloss, the committee's chair, referring the independent consumer product comparisons published by the nonprofit Consumers Union.

Despite those objections, the group's national executive committee voted to take the money in exchange for lending its logo and name to Clorox's advertising efforts. When the deal went public in early 2008, controversy erupted. Leaders in the club's Florida chapter passed a measure condemning the Clorox deal. The Massachusetts chapter sent a letter urging the national leadership to return the company's money, and individual members around the country engaged in a heated debate about the ethics of accepting money for endorsing a product line, particularly one created by a company best known for making an environmentally harmful product like bleach. [10]

Carl Pope, the Sierra Club's executive director, defended the decision in a lengthy e-mail to members, saying the association with Clorox would put "green" products in the hands of a wider public and bring the club to the attention of Americans, who didn't already know about the group. Besides encouraging a major manufacturer to "green" its products, the Clorox brands were cheaper than other environmentally friendly cleaners on the marketplace, which would make them attractive to more consumers. And, Pope asserted in several press interviews and again in his e-mail to club members that Green Works was better than the other products. "We think our name and credibility can help Americans separate truly superior products from the many fake 'natural' labels out there," Pope said in the internal e-mail titled "Why we chose Green Works." To the *New York Times*, Pope said: "We made sure these chemicals were all something we could be comfortable with."[11]

The only problem is the club's Toxics Committee never did carry out an analysis to determine if the Green Works line was environmentally friendly, let alone "superior" to other products. Despite Pope's repeated assurances that the Toxics Committee had vetted them, committee co-chair Jessica Frohman said the committee was never asked to do a comprehensive review. Frohman and a club colleague, who co-chairs the Toxics Committee with her, took a quick look at Clorox product information and asked a few questions at the behest of the national leadership, she said. That was the extent of the committee's role in the transaction until early 2008, when Pope announced the deal and that the Toxics Committee approved the move.

"Our committee members were dismayed, as were our committee advisers," Frohman says. "We clearly corrected the record. We never approved the product line."

W. William Weeks, a former senior executive at TNC who served as acting president in the early 2000s, agrees cause-related marketing agreements are especially dangerous for nonprofits.

"It's very easy for a charity to forget that rather than soliciting a donation with no strings attached, it is in the midst of a negotiation. It's making a commercial transaction and linking its name commercially to the other organization," said Weeks, now the director of the Conservation Law Center in Indianapolis.

"It's advertisement. There are lots of things that can go wrong," he says.

In fact, during Weeks's tenure at the organization, TNC was criticized by congressional investigators for entering into several cause-related marketing agreements with the companies of its board members. The more questionable arrangements included the rental of its mailing list to General Motors and a $100,000 contract with S. C. Johnson & Son to promote its toilet bowl cleaner. [12]

TNC responded to the public outcry by banning the companies of board members from doing business with the organization. But there is no indication other groups have followed suit. CI's deal with Fiji Water had a similar taint. Fiji is owned by Roll International Corporation, whose chairman, Stewart A. Resnick, sits on CI's board of directors.

Science Questioned

Publicly, all the major conservation organizations pride themselves for using the best science to guide their conservation work. Inside these organizations, however, long-running debates are raging about whether the science mission hasn't been eroded by the quest for quick results easily translated into glossy annual reports and full-color fundraising appeals.

"It is difficult because TNC says we are science based, but internally the pressure is not to do science, but to produce results. It's very hard to do one without the other and remain a credible organization," said one scientist in a 2001 internal report assessing the state of TNC's science program.[13]

The report, based on opinions shared by scientists working at TNC chapters across the country, depicted a demoralized science staff that felt increasingly pushed aside as fundraising and public relations operations gained influence. Several questioned whether the Conservancy could still be considered an organization that based its actions on sound science. They noted high turnover rates and time constraints that undermined the science mission. One person lamented that the organization infrequently chose scientists for top leadership posts, leaving few career development options open to them. Others complained that scientists didn't earn as much as other TNC executives.

Similar concerns were later expressed by a group of leading scientists from around the world, who disparaged the approaches used by large international conservation groups as mere "branding" with dubious grounding in science.[14]

While conservation scientists may increasingly question the quality of the science these groups conduct, "science," as a concept, has become a centerpiece of marketing efforts and an integral part of their brand identities today. CI touts itself as "science driven," while TNC says it's "science based"; WWF claims it has "a foundation in science." It is a selling point with donors and an effective club to bat away critics, who can be dismissed as failing to grasp the "pure science" behind their work.

Membership Services

Catering to corporate sponsors is only one facet of a conservation group's marketing machine. Most large conservation groups spend many millions of dollars on building and managing their own brands. TNC is unique in that it earns a portion of its income from business activities such as logging and ranching. Until 2003, TNC also derived large revenues from oil drilling on its conservation lands. For many groups, individual donations and membership fees are still the number-one source of income. Organizations have developed large marketing and membership retention departments charged with packaging nature into a commodity and selling it "retail," so to speak, to millions of individual donors.

Membership provides clout and moral authority. Over time it becomes a bellwether of the organization's health. For groups with large membership rolls, those numbers are almost like a corporation's stock price. Slipping figures can make "investors" jittery and the organization appear to be losing public confidence. So much effort goes into keeping members and replacing ones that leave that groups established to protect nature have also become purveyors of an array of merchandise designed to sell the organizations to conservation "consumers."

Memberships usually come with subscription to the organization's magazine, discounts on calendars, books, and special ecotravel offers, and e-mail updates on the organization's work to protect nature in exotic places. The Sierra Club also has limited-time enticements like the official Sierra Club "Expedition Pack," a backpack bearing its logo that comes free with a $25 membership. NRDC, meanwhile, has enlisted the rock band Green Day. For a $10 donation, you can get dog tags specially designed out of recycled metal by lead singer Billie Joe Armstrong and his wife, Adrienne Nesser. WWF sells panda coffee mugs, T-shirts, and safari hats.[15]

What about the "carbon footprints" involved in making these products? The raw materials, manufacturing, and shipping come with greenhouse gas bills attached. These consumer offerings seem almost absurdly out of step with the movement's core mission to improve the environment. The contradiction has led some to remark wryly that WWF, TNC, the Sierra Club, and others would have us believe we can save the environment by shopping.

Timothy W. Luke, a political scientist at Virginia Polytechnic Institute and State University, argues that green groups have been obliged to repackage "dead nature" into "environment" and sell it to the public in order to remain relevant in today's consumer-driven world. The "green goods and services" come in many forms. TNC has repackaged nature as real estate, while other groups have remodeled it into visions of "the good life," "paradise," and a variety of "bioresources."

"To save the habitat, one must reshape the habitus," says Luke, who also points out that cute endangered species have become "biocelebrities."[16]

Then there are the Hollywood celebrities that help the groups sell themselves to the public. Besides Green Day, NRDC has Robert Redford and Leonardo DiCaprio. CI has Harrison Ford, Pearl Jam, and the Dixie Chicks. TNC has used Paul Newman to narrate advertisements, to name a few of the bulging ranks of green glitterati.

Conservation organizations spend millions of dollars on focus groups, marketing consultants, and advertisements in an effort to distinguish themselves from the competition. TNC started a major push after a study it commissioned noted the group was better esteemed but less well-known than Greenpeace. Its consultants concluded TNC could easily position itself as "the most respected and well-known conservation organization." But it would have to move quickly since WWF was also preparing a major advertising campaign.[17]

The organization where I used to work was one of the few latecomers to such marketing efforts. CI had sworn off expensive mass marketing after its attempts to attract a membership base failed shortly after the group was established in the late 1980s. The organization still managed to grow into one of the world's largest conservation groups by cultivating corporations, wealthy donors, foundations, and government grants. In the mid-2000s, however, its leadership changed tacks and decided to raise its profile as part of plans to dramatically ramp up its fundraising.

I was among about a dozen global communications staffers assembled in a sixth-floor conference room in September 2006 when Laura Bowling, CI's new vice president of global communications, unveiled plans to whip our division into "a marketing enterprise" capable of catapulting the organization and its chairman Peter Seligmann into the limelight.

"Peter wants to be a household name," Bowling confided.

That same month, Seligmann had announced in an "all-staff meeting" that CI was working with the producers of Live Earth, a 24-hour concert for nature that would have a worldwide television broadcast in July 2007, bringing CI quite literally to a world stage.

As it turns out, CI wasn't included when the Live Earth concert aired. Seligmann was left backtracking, praising the event as a boon for the group's work even if it didn't give the organization the PR luster he had hoped for. The episode illustrates how competitive the world of environmentalism is today, perhaps providing some insight into why top conservationists are so willing to make deals with corporate polluters.

Chapter Five
Excess and Oversight

When John Sawhill took over The Nature Conservancy in 1990, it was already far and away the country's largest conservation group. It had the highest revenues and impressive numbers of members and acres of land saved from development. During the ten years he was at the helm of the organization, however, Sawhill took it to new heights. He brought in previously unheard-of revenues, extended TNCs reach into dozens of countries across the globe, and turned it into one of the biggest landholders on Earth.[1]

He had come from McKinsey & Co., one of the foremost management consulting groups in the world with a client list of Fortune 500 companies. Before that he served in the Energy Department under the Nixon and Ford administrations and ran New York University, where he had proven himself a prodigious fundraiser. When Sawhill was the school's president from 1975 to 1979, the university and the City of New York were near bankruptcy. Sawhill was widely credited with the financial turnaround of the country's largest private university, a recovery that coincided with the city's own comeback.[2]

When he came to TNC, he convinced his former colleagues at McKinsey to conduct a complete review of its operations.

Then in its fortieth year, the organization appeared to be extraordinarily healthy. But the consultants reported back that TNC was in need of an overhaul.

In the course of the next few years, Sawhill rewrote the mission, revamped the conservation approach, and established the kind of concrete organization-wide goals common to many corporations. The idea was to harness the efforts of fifty different state chapters and an international division and get them working like a multinational corporation to accomplish conservation at a much more ambitious scale than ever before. For that purpose he hired so many McKinsey alumni for key jobs and regional board positions that one critic told *Range* magazine "it began to look like a rite of passage for them."[3]

Sawhill also presided over TNC's foray into a series of "for-profit" businesses, areas the venerated conservation organization had never before explored. He took special pride in the Virginia Eastern Shore Sustainable Development Corporation, launched under his guidance. The plan, which Sawhill often cited as an example of the Conservancy's cutting-edge approach, was to create fifty small businesses that would each generate 250 jobs in ecotourism, organic farming, and other environmentally friendly trades. The goal was "low-impact" development that would be less likely than, say, a large tourism resort to threaten the ecosystems surrounding the Virginia Coast Reserve, a chain of barrier islands on the state's Eastern Shore that the Conservancy had purchased years before as a sanctuary for migratory birds and shorebirds.

"Our mission leads us to this kind of activity because once you say you're going to work on the scale of an entire landscape to protect biological resources, you've touched the tar baby whether you like it or not. You're in the community-development business and the conservation business; the two are inextricably linked," he told the *Harvard Business Review,* going on to exclaim, "We think of ourselves as Adam Smith with a green thumb," referring to the eighteenth-century Scottish moral philosopher whose writings are the most famous rationale for capitalism.[4]

A tall, lanky man with the jowls of a bulldog, Sawhill had a reputation as a blunt-talking workaholic. When he wasn't power-lunching with corporate moguls or high-ranking government officials, the Princeton-educated economist was a devotee of eating lunch at his desk, where he had posted a little sign that read, "If you're not the lead dog, the view never changes."[5]

Well connected to politics and business through his former jobs, he strengthened TNC's ties to those worlds as well. At the same time, Sawhill protected millions of acres of land during his tenure while dramatically increasing TNC's corporate donors.

After his unexpected death from diabetes in May 2000, the *High Country News* ran an obituary that described him as "one of those rare men who could contemplate the significance of ecosystems in the morning and then pop off to lunch with a corporate CEO or bank president at a Wall Street restaurant."[6]

Like many of his colleagues in big conservation, Sawhill studiously avoided taking a position on oil drilling in the Arctic National Wildlife Refuge, which was to become a huge public debate toward the end of his tenure.[7]

To some in the environmental movement, his silence made him a traitor to the cause. But Sawhill protégé W. William Weeks says his former boss was simply acting in the tradition of the organization. While he took things to a higher level, Sawhill didn't really change the Conservancy's pro-business stance, says Weeks, who spent more than two decades at TNC and was named the acting president while a search committee selected a successor after Sawhill's death.

"The Conservancy always had a philosophy that it would work with corporations to the extent that it could find common ground with the Conservancy's mission rather than confront corporations on all environmental issues," says Weeks, who defends this approach as sound, since each group must "choose every day the battles that they are going to fight and the times they're going to keep their powder dry.

"When you have limited resources, you don't get to the tenth thing down on the priority list, which might have been fuel economy," Weeks says. "So are you vulnerable to being charged with couching your words in order not to get into conflict with General Motors? [GM was a TNC donor with board representation at the time of Weeks's employment with the nonprofit.] Or is it the case, that with the resources and time that you have, that you pursue the first four things on your biological conservation list and you never get to fuel economy?"

During his decade at TNC's helm, Sawhill raised $300 million and had begun a new fundraising push with a goal of $1 billion.[8] His unapologetic attempts to meld conservation and capitalism echoed through the environmental movement, spurring other groups to look for ways they could make money while doing good work. He presided at TNC at a time when the largest groups in the movement made a decided turn toward corporations and TNC lost much of its earlier earnestness. Sawhill was one of the influencing forces, noted Fred Krupp, the executive director of the Environmental Defense Fund. After his death, Krupp praised Sawhill for sharing his management philosophy with his colleagues in other groups:

"Environmental Defense was but one of many organizations that benefited from his wisdom."[9]

The organization's critics, however, questioned the apparent quid pro quo nature of TNC's alliances with big business. The year before Sawhill's death, TNC gave a "conservation leadership award" to Shell Oil Company, at a time when Shell needed a PR boost to temper the international condemnation of the company after Nigeria's brutal military dictatorship executed Nigerian writer Ken Saro-Wiwa for opposing oil drilling by Shell that had devastated the Niger Delta. Shell, it turned out, had donated hundreds of thousands of dollars to TNC and went on to give the Conservancy more than $1 million in the years that followed.[10]

Inside the organization, trouble was also brewing. Sawhill led the Conservancy but never really embodied it. Some employees had been stunned, in the first place, when the TNC board tapped a member of corporate America to run one of the country's preeminent environmental organizations. Sawhill seemed a particularly strange choice since he had spent the previous ten years working as a consultant to the world's biggest polluters: energy companies. He hadn't exactly proven himself as environmentally sensitive during his tenure in the Ford administration's Energy Department in the mid-1970s during the energy crisis. In fact, he horrified many by suggesting it might be acceptable to pursue strip mining coal despite the heavy environmental costs. Recommending that policymakers consider offshore oil drilling in New England did not endear him to environmentalists either. In those days, he also frequently ran afoul of Ralph Nader, then at the height of his consumer protection powers, for hiring petroleum industry executives for key posts in his government department.

When he ran the Conservancy, years later, veteran conservation scientists never really got used to Sawhill and interpreted his overhaul as shifting the emphasis from conservation work to fundraising. Sawhill alluded to this ongoing internal struggle in his 1995 interview with the *Harvard Business Review* when he said, "Some people at the Conservancy think our customers are the plants and animals we're trying to save. But our real customers are the donors who buy our product, and that product is protected landscapes."[11]

But the corporate drift created problems of its own. In "tightening up" the operation, Sawhill had fundamentally altered the way the Conservancy worked. Like most nonprofit groups, it had long been a consensus-driven outfit, slow moving in decision-making because many people in the organization had a voice. Sawhill, seeking to reduce the time spent on management hassles, consolidated decision-making power with the senior staff.

Tensions only grew after Steven J. McCormick was selected to replace him. McCormick, who Sawhill had picked to oversee the redesign of TNC's mission statement six years earlier, had risen to the top post at TNC's California chapter. At the time of his selection he had left the organization to practice law in Northern California. To entice him to the East Coast, the Conservancy offered perks not often seen in the nonprofit world. But the generous signing bonus, housing allowance, and low-interest home loan McCormick received would later come back to haunt him and his employer. He did not hit it off with the national staff. Eventually, TNC employees blew the whistle on the organization, going to the *Washington Post* with internal reports and allegations of misconduct.

"He had sort of broken the unspoken rule of how things worked," said one former TNC employee, who still works in the industry and didn't want to be named. "In the past, nobody would have thought of sending internal documents to the *Washington Post*. You circle the wagons. It was us against the world."

The *Washington Post* series charged the Conservancy with a raft of insider business dealings, unscientific decisions, and neglect of its mission. It disclosed McCormick's fringe benefit package and the questionable loans made to him and other senior staff members.

Among the most damaging information was that the Conservancy was conducting oil drilling at Texas City preserve, home to one of the last remaining flocks of the Texas state bird, the Attwater's prairie chicken. Not only did the Conservancy keep drilling after some of the birds died, the *Post* revealed that TNC had been embroiled in a lawsuit with another charity that owned the oil field next to its preserve. The Sage Foundation accused it of stealing its mineral rights in a nasty fight that ended with TNC paying a $10 million settlement.

"As far as I am concerned, it was criminal. They were stealing our oil," James Roane was quoted as saying to the *Post*. Roane was a co-owner of the parcel owned by the Sage Foundation.[12]

Other damaging disclosures included that TNC allegedly helped its members and other insiders take large and inappropriate tax breaks on conservation land bought from the Conservancy. Before selling the properties, TNC had added conservation easements, a legal framework for restricting land development that is TNC's signature tool. The easements also offered the landowners significant tax benefits because such development restrictions lower the real estate value of the land. The easements chronicled in the *Post* stories, however, were for parcels inside nature preserves that allowed the purchasers to build large homes complete with swimming pools, tennis courts, multi-car garages, and guest cottages, at the same time that they took steep tax breaks for agreeing to the so-called conservation limits.

There were also claims of questionable deals between TNC and the companies of its board members. Among others, the newspaper looked askance at "cause-related marketing" arrangements. It pointed out that TNC had entered into partnerships with corporations such as oil and gas and logging companies even after it held focus groups that sent a clear message that such companies were not appropriate corporate partners.

As it turned out, rather than economic green thumbs, TNC officials were all thumbs, so to speak, when it came to business. By 1999, the Center for Compatible Economic Development, an autonomous TNC operation that oversaw the Eastern Shore Corporation and the other for-profit ventures, had collapsed after blowing through millions of dollars in start-up capital. And other sustainable business ventures were failing, often in the wake of questionable business decisions like letting one of its executives live rent-free at one of its properties. The *Post* chronicled these travails too.

"Maybe a nonprofit is not the best to make those decisions," said Weeks, who presided over the failed TNC for-profit ventures. He says running a business that lived up to the highest conservation values was simply harder than they thought it would be.

The stories sparked a two-year congressional inquiry.[13] Investigators went back ten years, delving deeply into all aspects of the Conservancy's business from June 30, 1993, to June 30, 2003. The atmosphere inside the Conservancy grew so tense that the Senate Finance Committee ordered TNC officials to make a public, written pledge not to retaliate against employees who spoke with congressional investigators. When the report was released in mid-2005 it excoriated the Conservancy leadership and stopped just short of suggesting that TNC should lose its nonprofit status. The report echoed many of the allegations made by the *Post*, raising concerns that ranged from insider dealing with board members and donors to abuses of conservation easements.

Investigators concluded that the Conservancy had issued so many of these easements that it had failed to keep up with monitoring and enforcement responsibilities to make sure the owners respected the development restrictions they had agreed to. The report recommended that the IRS consider revoking the tax-exempt status of organizations that routinely fail to monitor and enforce their conservation easements and suggested that excise taxes should be levied against the officers and directors of organizations that failed to adopt and enforce policies to make sure easements were upheld. An accreditation system for conservation organizations was also suggested.

The organization had maintained its board members always recused themselves from voting on business that involved their own companies. But investigators uncovered proof that John Smith, the chairman of General Motors at the time, had voted to approve a plan in which his company purchased millions of dollars in carbon credits from TNC, despite reporting to the IRS that Smith had not voted on the matter. The revelation raised questions about possible wider-spread conflicts of interest between the organization and its board members.

The series had also resulted in an IRS audit of TNC's books late in 2003 that had yet to wrap up when the report was published, so investigators went out of their way to avoid statements they thought might influence the audit, though they alluded to actions by the Conservancy that could justify stern sanctions by the tax agency.

In keeping with its longstanding policy, the IRS never publicly confirmed or denied the audit made public in the course of the congressional hearings and investigation. But the tax agency followed up on concerns about TNC's operation by launching a crackdown on land conservancy organizations nationwide, searching for abuses similar to those alleged in the *Post* series. It also stepped up enforcement of nonprofits, adding additional reporting requirements for all nonprofit groups, and began a probe of executive compensation packages.

The scandal also prompted observers to urge regulators to take a closer look at the growing for-profit side businesses of nonprofit groups and crack down on conflicts of interest. But, to date, little has been done to rein in conservation groups bringing in millions of dollars for services that range from questionable consulting fees to renting their logos and mailing lists to their corporate partners.

Calls for More Oversight

These were difficult times for all professional environmentalists, not just those at TNC. Their lavish lifestyles and corporate excesses had increasingly attracted the attention of investigative reporters. In 2001, *Sacramento Bee* reporter Tom Knudson wrote a scathing multi-day series that took aim at a slew of environmental groups.[14] He lambasted the movement for the posh offices and high salaries of its leaders, wasteful and often misleading fundraising and marketing operations, the crisis mentality, runaway litigation, and a tendency toward vagueness that highlighted the potential for IRS tax abuses, among other things.

Conservation groups were also fielding attacks by indigenous rights advocates and others who objected to the organizations' often heavy-handed work in impoverished countries, where their hard currency gave them significant political clout. Meanwhile, closer to home, two young activists sent shock waves through the environmental world with their essay "The Death of Environmentalism," which declared that the movement was coasting on its past victories.[15] It had become fat and complacent and had "strikingly little" to show for years of work and millions of dollars spent on environmental causes. Authors Michael Shellenberger and Ted Nordhaus asserted that environmentalism must die in order to clear a path for a more visionary progressive movement.

These events ushered in an era of soul-searching, debate, consternation, and internal reforms. TNC scrambled to address allegations made by the *Post*. McCormick repaid the home loan and took a 5 percent pay cut, and the Conservancy called in loans made to other executives.[16] It also convened an independent panel to carry out an organization-wide review. The panel headed up by New York lawyer and business ethics expert Ira M. Millstein issued twenty-eight pages of recommendations. TNC made sweeping changes based on its recommendations a year before the congressional investigators completed their work.[17]

The suggestions TNC implemented included restructuring its board to add a new eleven-member executive committee, consolidating power previously spread among its thirty-six-member board. The organization also committed itself to more transparency, banned transactions with the companies of its board members, and put new rules in place to guard against insider deals, among other changes.

McCormick also bowed to public outrage, announcing TNC would stop drilling for oil at Texas City and other preserves.[18] But to this day TNC continues to log many of its conservation lands, a practice that the organization defends as a way to demonstrate to logging companies more environmentally friendly methods of forestry. But it's one that has prompted other environmentalists to disparagingly refer to TNC as the conservation world's biggest timber baron. Equally controversial have been the joint ventures established to show ranchers more conservation-minded methods

Its Montana green banking project, marketed as a way to reduce the amount of land ranchers set aside for grazing, has come under fire from both conservation and ranching quarters as untenable. "Once you stop, there is nothing to keep the landowner from going back to harmful practices or plowing it," author and ranching expert George Wuerthner told *The New York Times*. [19]

Despite the continuing criticisms, TNC recovered rapidly from its brush with federal investigators. The scandal doesn't appear to have taken a long-term toll. The organization earned high marks for its rapid response and has kept on posting record revenues. Insiders and admirers of the organization brushed off the *Post* articles as an unfair portrait that took a few bad deals and blew them out of proportion.

"On the whole, they way overstated these themes," says Weeks. "There were hundreds of people doing deals. Sometimes people do the wrong thing."

Regardless if that assessment is true or a modern-day rendition of the "circle the wagons" mentality from TNC's past, the need for more accountability is a theme that predated the TNC scandal and has continued. Before his death, Sawhill coauthored an essay on the Conservancy's work to establish "metrics" for measuring its successes that went beyond the old "bucks for acres" model.[20] In 2002, Steven Sanderson, chief of the WCS, made a case for independent scientific audits of international projects that would be subject to peer review.[21]

But establishing effective ways to measure success—not only in saving habitats and species but winning more public support of the cause—is still a work in progress. It is an intangible realm involving a wealth of factors, including many beyond a conservation group's control. Efforts also have to be enduring, a tricky business considering that conservationists count their victories in terms of things that don't happen—developments thwarted and forest clear-cutting averted, for instance. As the late David Brower once reportedly said, "All our victories are temporary and all our defeats permanent."

The uncertainty surrounding land preservation victories concerned Seth Neiman in the early 2000s, when TNC's California chapter pressed him for a large donation to help save woodlands rapidly disappearing to make way for San Jose's encroaching suburbs. The Silicon Valley venture capitalist wanted to know if his money would help TNC save the Mount Hamilton ecosystem not just for a few decades but for five hundred years. It was a question to which TNC officials had no response.[22]

So Neiman gave the Conservancy $500 million to pilot a new approach to monitoring and assessing its work. Realizing that conservation nonprofits have a history of failing to clearly measure their results, Neiman set out to help Conservancy scientists find a way to scientifically "audit" their work so they could learn from their successes and failures. They set out to adapt accounting methods common in the business world to TNC's scientific work.

"People don't realize it took hundreds of years to develop what we know as accounting. . . . The nonprofits are just beginning that process," say Neiman, who notes that nonprofit groups lack the business world's most useful feedback tool: the marketplace.[23]

"If [businesses] stop making money, they die, so well-run businesses try to get really good in telling themselves the truth. . . . It's up to the nonprofits to create their own measures," says Neiman, who applauds TNC officials for their courage to search for reliable performance measures that could potentially hurt its fundraising efforts by exposing weaknesses in its operations to the public, which it relies on for donations.

Since Sawhill's day it has become commonplace for big conservation groups to adopt business models, often claiming the approach as a way to improve operating efficiency or accountability. But it's a tough claim to prove. Not all environmentalists agree it's a good idea. Kierán Suckling, executive director of the Center for Biological Diversity, is among the environmentalists who reject calls for nonprofits to act more like businesses.

"I'm actually puzzled by this notion that if one pays close attention to the bottom line, one is following a 'business model,'" says Suckling, who points to TNC as an example of how becoming more businesslike doesn't necessarily improve operations or transparency. "As they had more businessmen running their organizations, they became vastly more inefficient. They started hemorrhaging money through bad decisions and poor governance. The whole notion that having a business model is associated with efficiency is just not well demonstrated."

Other observers note that as nonprofit groups have gravitated toward the business realm, adding for-profit businesses and joint ventures, the tax reporting requirements have not kept pace. Even after the reforms ushered in by the TNC scandal, nonprofits are required to disclose very little information to government regulators and the public. Despite the light disclosure burden, they are well known for filing incomplete tax returns. They seldom face serious penalties for submitting false or misleading information on those forms or on the marketing and PR materials produced for donors. In practice, there is more bureaucracy and paperwork but less accountability than ever and growing confusion about what constitutes success. As groups have developed a corporate mind-set, fundraising hallmarks are too easily confused with advances in saving species and landscapes.

Large international conservation groups generate reams of scientific documents, papers, and internal reports, but somehow lack key data. When a group of scientists sought to carry out the first independent audit of conservation spending in 2004, they planned to compare stated priority areas to actual spending by several conservation groups but found only three of the organizations—WWF, CI, and Birdlife International—had sufficiently detailed maps delineating their priority areas.[24] And "surprisingly," the researchers concluded that not one of the three organizations actually tracked their spending relative to their stated priorities. Three years later, another report examined audits of conservation projects carried out between 2003 and 2007.[25] It found most were well planned, but less than a third had rigorous monitoring and evaluating systems in place to measure effectiveness.

Conservationists are coming under increasing pressure to audit their efforts as funding for their work reaches new heights, along with criticism about how they spend it. And, yet, efforts to stave off extinctions have failed to keep pace with proliferating threats. The number of endangered species on the World Conservation Union's Red list has increased by 65 percent in a decade. Over the same time frame, a third of the world's mangroves and a fifth of the coral reefs have been destroyed. Experts predict the last of the old-growth forests are also heading toward extinction. Things would no doubt be worse if these groups had not existed. The more pressing question, however, is, why haven't they been more successful?

Joshua S. Reichert, director of the environment program at Pew Charitable Trusts and a former CI executive, says not enough attention has been paid to whether conservation groups have spent their money well.

"Big organizations are working in parts of the world where there is really no accountability and no external way to measure progress. What gets done is subject to interpretation," says Reichert, who laments that too few international projects are evaluated "at arm's length distance . . . to ask and answer the question: What has really happened here? . . . There's been a lot of money spent and effort spent. But how much of it has worked?"

Part Two

Chapter Six
Oil, Gas, and Conservation

Why are the dirtiest industries on Earth among the biggest contributors to conservation groups?

In exchange for their cash, some of the largest oil and gas companies supplying the U.S. market acquire public relations benefits that can come in handy when seeking drilling rights and after spills, explosions, and fires that leave people dead and the environment wounded. These companies are toasted for "leading the way" on nature conservation at the same time they are breaking records for willfully neglecting environmental and safety laws.

In the last decade alone, the Department of Justice has mandated billions of dollars of fixes at refineries owned by ExxonMobil, BP, ConocoPhillips, Chevron Corporation, Shell Oil, and other major oil companies. The government settlement orders were simply to bring them into compliance with the Clean Air Act that the companies had been violating for years. Energy conglomerates that make some of the highest profits in the world have paid hundreds of millions of dollars in criminal and civil penalties to a host of federal agencies for fatal

Oil and Gas Contributors to Conservation Groups

Company	CF	CI	ED	TNC	NRDC	WWF-US
ExxonMobil	•			•		
BP	•	•	•	•	•	
BG Group		•				
Chevron Corporation	•	•		•		
ConocoPhillips	•	•		•	•	
Shell Oil	•	•	•	•	•	

Relationships include donations, partnerships, programs, projects, joint councils, and advisory boards. Sources: Web sites and tax returns of the organizations and corporations.

workplace accidents and violation of clean air and water laws. They have been charged with shortchanging the federal government and Native American tribes in royalty payments for oil drilled on government and reservation land.

The cleanup is still not complete on the spill that triggered the largest fine in U.S. history—the $1.1 billion levied in the wake of the Exxon *Valdez* oil disaster off the coast of Alaska in 1989.[1] The millions of gallons of crude oil that spilled into the sea killed an estimated 250,000 seabirds, 2,800 sea otters, 300 harbor seals, 250 bald eagles, and 22 orcas, as well as millions of salmon and herring eggs. The uproar led to new federal legislation aimed at preventing and responding to oil spills. But, ExxonMobil's record has been far from clean since then. In 2007, the company settled a landmark Clean Air Act case involving all seven of its U.S. petroleum refineries in five states. The country's largest oil company agreed to pay $14.4 million in penalties and community environmental projects and make another $537 million in upgrades to reduce the amount of pollution produced.[2]

BP: The New Exxon?

These days, however, BP could be the new Exxon. It has the dubious distinction of being the oil company that most aggressively markets itself as a friend to the environment while at the same time it is the biggest environmental scofflaw in an industry of scofflaws.

In the space of two years in the mid-2000s, BP had—among a raft of lesser violations—the most deadly refinery accident and the biggest pipeline rupture, and was caught illegally cornering the U.S. propane market. The company is on probation until October 2010.

The Occupational Safety and Health Administration levied the largest fine in the agency's history against BP after the March 2005 explosion at its Texas City refinery that killed fifteen workers, injured 180, and sent harmful gases wafting through the surrounding community. OSHA referred the case to the Department of Justice, which brought felony charges. The company paid a fine of $50 million, the largest ever assessed by the agency for a Clean Air Act violation.[3]

U.S. Chemical Safety Board Chairman Carolyn W. Merritt testified before Congress that BP had ignored standard safety measures and allowed important equipment to decay to the point that malfunctioning start-ups became the norm. Budget cuts that had left the facility short on staff, training, and equipment maintenance laid the groundwork for the tragedy, she concluded. And "striking similarities" were present in the Prudhoe Bay, Alaska, pipeline rupture that took place a few months later, she told Congress. Though the company already knew the pipeline had corroded dangerously, according to its own internal audits, it did nothing to prevent the disaster, which dumped

200 million gallons of crude oil onto tundra and a nearby frozen lake. It was the largest spill ever recorded on Alaska's North Slope and disrupted the country's oil supply.[4]

The company pled guilty and agreed to pay a $12 million criminal fine and donate $4 million to the National Fish and Wildlife Foundation, a donation it later bragged about as part of its "environmental stewardship" efforts.[5] The company has also given lavishly to every major U.S. conservation group except WWF, ties it publicizes at every opportunity. Each year, BP produces several glossy publications and colorful Web pages touting its good corporate behavior. It translates its annual sustainability reports into Chinese, German, Russian, and Spanish.

While such attention to corporate social responsibility has become a hallmark of today's modern corporation, there is plenty of evidence to suggest some companies use these good citizenship reports to misdirect the public. Take BP's industry outlook section in its 2006 report: Despite its travails with U.S. regulators, it features a chart that shows fatalities and lost work hours due to accidents on the job declining steadily over the previous decade to just "0.47 per 200,000 hours worked—the lowest in our recorded history."[6]

Perhaps that's what Merritt, the government chemical safety inspector, was referring to when she noted, in her bruising congressional testimony after the Texas explosion and the Alaska oil leak, that "BP focused on personal safety statistics but allowed catastrophic process safety risks to grow."[7]

Enron and Corporate Responsibility

While it might seem ironic considering its 2001 collapse ushered in calls for more corporate oversight, Enron was an early adopter of corporate social responsibility reporting. But, in the aftermath of the scandal, the company's philanthropic endeavors were reinterpreted as part of an elaborate snow job aimed at making the company appear a successful and responsible corporate player.

Enron was well known in Washington for its largess with politicians on both sides of the aisle. Chief executive Kenneth Lay supported George W. Bush's 2000 White House bid and had used the company's relationship with the Clinton administration to lobby for tax credits and other legislation that would favor the company. Enron wielded its corporate philanthropy in a similar manner: to advance its business interests.

Of growing importance to the company in the late 1990s were wind, solar, and other alternative energy projects. Even then, these technologies were starting to attract attention. And, though they were dependent on government funding and subsidies, they promised big returns if the Clinton administration were to sign the Kyoto Protocol, part of the United Nations' Framework Convention on Climate Change, which called for industrialized nations to reduce their greenhouse gas emissions. If the United States were to ratify the pact, it would have created a new market in pollution credits that companies, especially power conglomerates that generate 60 percent of their energy from coal, could purchase to offset pollution they generate.

On the alternative energy front, Lay followed the lead of his colleague and friend Sir John Browne, BP's chief executive at the time. Browne had thrilled the green world and shocked his industry with speeches on climate change at Stanford University and in Berlin in 1997, much the way Wal-Mart's president H. Lee Scott would eight years later. Browne articulated a vision for making BP the first green energy conglomerate. Browne resigned in May 2007 after a scandal that revealed he had put company staff and resources at the disposal of his lover and later lied about it in a British court. But BP kept the green advertising. It also kept the green-and-yellow sun logo and the solar panels mounted—some said more for show than energy generation— atop thousands of its gas stations.

Both Browne and Lay became celebrated corporate executives, praised for their "21st century" business vision. But Enron's internal memos, leaked to reporters during its bankruptcy scandal, revealed other motivations.

An August 1, 1997, memo, a few days before Lay's August 4 Oval Office meeting with President Bill Clinton, Vice President Al Gore, and Browne, predicted a treaty capping carbon emissions would be good for Enron stock. It would, the memo stated, "do more to promote Enron's business than will almost any other regulatory initiative outside of restructuring the energy and natural gas industries in Europe and the United States."[8]

That December, Browne and Lay had another audience with Clinton and Gore. "Sir John," an internal Enron memo stated, "thinks there will soon be government regulation of greenhouse gases. And companies that have anticipated regulation will not only know how to use it to their advantage, they will also, as Browne puts it, 'gain a seat at the table, a chance to influence future rules.'"

Enron also had plans for using its support among environmentalists, who cooed over Lay and Browne. One internal communiqué thumped Enron's "excellent credentials with 'green' interests" at Greenpeace, WWF, NRDC, German Watch, the European Climate Action Network, and other groups. The company planned to use those friends to help open a carbon trading marketplace.[9]

Earlier that same year, Browne hosted four "off the record" forums that drew a range of environmentalists from Greenpeace to TNC to discuss how the company could improve its environmental record.[10] John Sawhill, TNC's president at the time and a longtime friend of Browne's, chaired the U.S. meetings. Those forums allowed the company to "road test" the environmental message unveiled at Stanford University in May 1997. Breaking with the rest of the industry, Browne acknowledged climate change and advocated for energy taxes and carbon emissions trading as policy options, the same business solutions Lay says Browne envisioned would make both companies a fortune.

Besides announcing plans to conserve energy in its operations and invest in cleaner technologies, the company used its environmentalist friends to strategic advantage: BP signed a deal with TNC to conserve three million acres of rainforest in Bolivia, a politically volatile country where BP had formed a joint venture that same year and would soon begin exploring for oil. It also cut a deal with ED that put the nonprofit to work developing policy recommendations on emissions trading and other options for turning pollution into a tradable commodity. No doubt any carbon trading scheme would have more credibility coming from a respected nonprofit group than from an energy conglomerate looking to score a lucrative new revenue stream.

The company also announced it was moving solar energy "up to the big table," on par with its exploration, oil, and chemicals businesses.[11] It soon embarked on what has been called both the most successful green advertising campaign ever and the biggest greenwash in the history of the world.

Greenwashing

Shortly after Browne's momentous speeches on global warming, BP hired the British advertising agency Ogilvy & Mather to launch the "Beyond Petroleum" campaign for a reported $200 million.[12] It aimed to "rebrand" BP as a clean energy company. Billboards, television, newspaper, and magazine ads boldly proclaimed statements like "It's time to turn up the heat on global warming" and "We were the first major energy company to take steps to reduce greenhouse gas emissions."

Sales rose and so did public approval and brand awareness. In the spring of 2007, BP led the field of energy companies in a survey of public views about corporate greening efforts. According to Landor Associates' "ImagePower Green Brands Survey," BP was not only considered the "greenest" of the leading energy companies; more than a third of respondents said they identified BP as a company that had become "more green" in the previous five years, despite the highly publicized Texas City and Prudhoe Bay accidents two years earlier.[13]

If the company had used some of the millions of dollars it spends on green marketing and gives away to conservation groups to replace corroded sections of the pipeline in Prudhoe Bay, it could have avoided the spill altogether. Such a preemptive act would have shown a quiet commitment to wildlife conservation but would have denied the company the public relations bonanza it receives from its association with environmental groups. It appears that BP finds greenwashing provides a better return on investment than actual moves to green its operations.

"Maybe their image insulated them from some of the outrage," says Steve Kretzmann, executive director of Oil Change International, a nonprofit group that challenges the oil industry.

By and large, though, he says there is far too little outrage about the oil industry's impact on the environment. "People, unfortunately, are used to spills, pipeline explosions, people dying, and the world just getting fouled as part of oil companies' general operating procedures," he says. "We are numb to it."

Ad Week concluded the campaign was a big success for the company. "Regardless of whether industry observers believe BP is truly 'green,' the company and its rebranding campaign have managed to convince the public that it is more eco-friendly than its competitors," the industry newspaper wrote in January 2008.[14]

None of the world's largest energy companies have "green" records that go beyond token gestures. And even the donations to nature conservation programs can usually be traced back to a drilling project requiring public approval or a public relations mess in the wake of an environmental disaster or human tragedy. BP's greenwashing campaign, however, is possibly the boldest.

"It's one of the greatest cons in recent history," says professor Kent Moores, of BP's Beyond Petroleum gambit.

Moores, an oil industry specialist at Duquesne University in Pittsburgh, says the environmental stewardship claims by BP and other oil companies should be taken with a grain of salt since they have resorted to such niceties as part of their all-consuming interest in keeping their stock prices high. "It's not something oil companies do because they like nature. It's always related to the bottom line," Moores says.

The quickest way to cut through the hype is to look at BP's balance sheet, where the company's advertised faith in "solar, natural gas, hydrogen, wind" loses power. Although Browne announced way back in 1997 that its solar energy operations would be on the same footing with its other core businesses, that never happened while he was at the helm of the company and has not happened since.

Of BP's $20.6 billion in total expenditures in 2007, it spent just $874 million on "gas, power, and renewables," the category in which BP lumps not just the solar operations but all of its Earth-friendly investments, representing about 4 percent of total expenditures. The company spent sixteen times as much—$13.9 billion—on exploration and production in 2007 than on gas, solar and wind power, and other renewables combined.[15]

But BP isn't the only oil company charged with greenwashing. Shell Oil had its hand slapped by the Dutch Advertising Authority in mid-2007.[16] The Authority ruled against an advertising campaign that touted a green energy initiative that uses carbon dioxide to help grow flowers. The ad, run in several European newspapers and magazines, showed flowers sprouting out of a refinery chimney and blowing away like exhaust. Friends of the Earth reported Shell to the Authority, which agreed that the ad was misleading because Shell was only piping a tiny amount of its carbon dioxide emissions into greenhouses. The ruling, however, was rare. The same complaint was rejected by Belgian advertising authorities.

Conservationist-Corporate Cooperation

Despite their environmental rap sheets, oil companies have no problem finding friends among the big conservation groups. CELB, CI's chief conduit with corporate America, convened the Energy and Biodiversity Initiative, known as EBI, in 2001. The oil company members were BP; Chevron; Enron, which dropped out after declaring bankruptcy; Shell; and Norway's

Statoil. Their nonprofit counterparts were CI; IUCN; TNC; Fauna & Flora International; and the Smithsonian Institution.[17]

In a National Public Radio interview broadcast in December 2004, TNC's lead scientist M. A. Sanjayan described the initiative as an effort to improve the companies' operating practices "to something slightly better."[18]

The radio host commented that it "doesn't sound terribly ambitious" and asked CI chief Peter Seligmann, who was also on the program, if he would agree with the assessment. Seligmann responded: "We are not looking for incremental changes; we're looking for very significant changes in the way that the energy sector operates."

In hindsight, Sanjayan's description was more accurate. Several of the oil companies involved said the collaboration led to improved corporate policies on drilling in a more environmentally gentle manner. But there was no independent evaluation of those claims. The only concrete success story was a partnership between the Smithsonian Institution and Shell Gabon to use the EBI frameworks in a project to manage the wildlife that coexists with oil wells in the West Central African country's national parks system, called the Gamba Complex of Protected Areas. The project produced a glowing review by the BBC, but the story failed to grasp the backstory: Shell's production at those Gabon oil fields had been declining for years. When Gabon's president Omar Bongo announced in 2002 that he was creating thirteen of the country's first-ever national parks, he shrewdly upped the pressure on Shell to find a socially responsible corporate exit strategy. Shell has oil fields inside the newly declared parkland that would make it harder for the company to pull up stakes without assisting the locals in finding alternative economic activities.

Like many other business–nonprofit alliances, the group seemed to exist largely to publicize itself. During its six-year run, EBI produced several reports and translated them into four languages. Group members held many meetings, made presentations, and distributed their reports at international conferences. They held workshops, created a Web site, and carefully monitored the number of visitors. But they weren't able to come up with another joint project before deciding to disband in 2007.[19]

My former colleague at CI Julian Teixeira blames such tepid results on the nonprofit leaders who fail to press the scofflaws for significant change. They work with the companies on narrow conservation projects while turning a blind eye to the areas where the same companies are ravaging the environment.

"In the environmental movement, we either keep our mouths shut or go 'the Greenpeace way,'" says Teixeira, referring to the widespread tendency he witnessed toward self-censorship for fear of offending the corporate benefactors.

About the time EBI was winding down, ED, NRDC, and TNC joined forces with a few other environmentalist groups and a couple of dozen corporations including leading oil, mining, power, and car companies to form the United States Climate Action Partnership (USCAP). The new organization was established to push for a U.S. greenhouse gas emissions trading program like the cap-and-trade system already in place in Europe. The alliance describes itself as "a group of businesses and leading environmental organizations that have come together to call on the federal government to quickly enact strong national legislation to require significant reductions of greenhouse gas emissions. USCAP has issued a landmark set of principles and recommendations to underscore the urgent need for a policy framework on climate change."[20]

"Urgent" changes but not too urgent, the world learned during the December 2007 UN climate summit in Bali, where the International Rising Tide Network duped several media outlets with a fake USCAP Web site and a press release. Activists, posing as USCAP representatives, announced its corporate members were committed to a 90 percent reduction in their carbon emissions by 2050 and an immediate moratorium on new coal-fired power plants.

Rising Tide's pledge was not far off the mark of what internationally esteemed scientists advocated as the only way to arrest rising global temperatures before it's too late. Only a month earlier, the intergovernmental panel on climate change had said reductions of as much as 85 percent of 2000 levels of carbon emissions would be necessary. A few months later, in March 2008, Ken Caldeira, senior scientist of the Carnegie Institution in Stanford, California, co-authored a paper concluding global carbon emissions must be slashed to near zero if the planet's temperatures are to be kept from rising dangerously. And, even the U.S. Congress has debated a 70 percent emissions cut.

Several newspapers and wire services had published Rising Tide's story before the real USCAP members caught on. The group had scheduled its own media event at an elegant Bali resort, but the hoax overshadowed those plans. The real USCAP ended up scrambling to deny the faux emissions targets, and reassert the coalition's considerably vaguer and less ambitious proposals calling for 60 to 80 percent reductions by 2050.

These corporate–conservationist alliances may not yield much in terms of environmental protection. But they represent the sort of "win-win" storyline irresistible to news organizations that have come under pressure from the public to report more optimistic news in the last few decades. More radical members of the international environmental movement are often not taken in, however. Irreverent activists have responded with pranks bent on exposing greenwashing.

Rising Tide had taken a page from "The Yes Men," the satirical performance artists/activists who have wreaked havoc at international trade meetings and industry conventions by impersonating corporate executives and public officials.[21] In June 2007, for example, the Yes Men's Andy Bichlbaum and Mike Bonnano infiltrated a Canadian oil conference posing as executives from ExxonMobil and National Petroleum Council.[22] They gave a keynote speech on the a fictional Exxon technology designed to capitalize on the growing numbers of natural disasters caused by climate change. Millions will die in increasingly frequent and devastating hurricanes, tsunamis, prolonged droughts, and diseases incubated in the rising temperatures. Millions more will perish in the subsequent economic and political upheaval as countries stagger under the weight of catastrophes, crops fail, and water becomes scarce. But they would not die in vain, the imposters assured the oilmen and women assembled for the speech. The new technology, they told the attentive audience, would turn millions of people who perish in climate-related tragedies into a new form of fuel oil called "Vivoleum." By the following day, the Yes Men's tongue-in-cheek Vivoleum Web site had been taken offline, but the hoax was thoroughly debated on the blogosphere.[23] Bichlbaum and Bonnano said they targeted Exxon and the Canadian oil industry to rap their investments in oil sands, an extremely heavy form of crude oil. It requires an open-pit mining process that destroys forests and uses a lot of water, making it even more environmentally invasive than old-fashioned oil drilling.

To remove the gooey tar sands from the ground in Canada's boreal forest, it's first necessary to clear stands of pine and spruce and muskeg swamps. Once they're removed, it takes three to five barrels of water to separate a single barrel of the molasses-like stuff from the clay and dirt. Turning oil sands into something you can pour into your car's gas tank is several times more energy intensive than processing conventional oil and contributes more than twice as much greenhouse gases.

Until recent years of oil price spikes and declining reserves, it was considered too costly—in financial and environmental terms—to extract oil sands on a large scale. Today every major oil company, including the biggest supporters of conservation groups, is vying for oil sand leases in Canada and elsewhere.

Shell's Environmental and Human Rights Record

Several members of USCAP have roared into the oil sands business, despite its harsh environmental toll. Shell, for instance, is working in the three main oil sands deposits in Canada's Alberta province. It's not the first time the company has talked like an enlightened environmentalist without actually becoming one.

Returning to Shell's partnership with Smithsonian Institution in Africa, the project gave the oil company a PR boost, allowing it to bask in the Smithsonian's prestige. At the time, Shell was in the midst of its own "rebranding," along the same lines of that which BP had already embarked upon and that Wal-Mart is currently pursuing. Shell was in dire need of a makeover after the bad publicity it had received during its dustup with Greenpeace over its plans to scuttle the Brent Spar oil platform in the North Sea and fallout from the execution of Nigerian writer Ken Saro-Wiwa.

While Shell has its share of "criminal" and "willful" violations of U.S. environmental law, its international record is hair-raising. Going back decades, Shell has been the target of divestiture campaigns led by activists who object to its relationships with brutal African regimes from apartheid-era South Africa to present-day Sudan, where the government is linked to the genocide underway in Darfur.

In Nigeria, Saro-Wiwa was executed by Nigeria's military dictatorship in November 1995 for leading the Movement for the Survival of the Ogoni People in the fight to shut down Shell's drilling operations, which had left a myriad of other environmental scars on the Ogoni people's tribal lands. Since Shell had started drilling there in the late 1950s, fertile farmland and coastal areas have been ravaged by oil spills and acid rain that has decimated fish stocks and other wildlife and traditional livelihoods, but local communities have received scant revenues from the drilling.[24] In the Niger Delta, Saro-Wiwa's execution immortalized him as a martyr to big-business interests. Anger over his death, the environmental degradation, and lack of community benefits continued simmering for years, eventually boiling over into a low-intensity rebel movement that disrupts Nigeria's oil fields to this day.

International outrage, directed not only at the regime, but at Shell, also simmered for years. As mentioned in the previous chapter, the company finally got a PR break in 1999, when TNC, which had received hundreds of thousands of dollars in Shell donations, gave the company a conservation leadership award. But many environmentalists and human rights activists reacted with outrage, calling the award a classic case of quid pro quo.

Shell isn't the only TNC "conservation leader" among the oil industry giants. Its corporate donors ExxonMobil and California's Occidental Petroleum Company have received them too. The latter is the same company involved in the Love Canal hazardous waste scandal of the 1970s. The canal had been a hazardous waste site in the city of Niagara Falls for decades when its original owner, the Hooker Chemical Company, decided to cover it with earth in 1953. The company sold the land-filled parcel to the city for $1, and homes and an elementary school were built on it. But within a couple of decades barrels of toxic waste started breaking open and leaking into backyards, forming puddles of noxious liquids and killing trees and gardens. Children received chemical burns. Before New York authorities started evacuating the community, residents discovered they had higher rates of cancer and their children were more likely to be born with birth defects. President Jimmy Carter declared a state of emergency after it became public that 20,000 tons of toxic chemicals were buried there. The person widely credited with bringing the Love Canal story to a national audience was Lois Gibbs, a local mother, who first questioned whether her children's health problems were related to the leaking chemicals in 1978. Gibbs became a formidable activist. The ensuing fight is often credited as inspiring a grassroots environmental movement that has spread around the globe, even to poor developing countries, where industrial activity often goes on amid looser environmental and safety standards.

Today, residents in more than a dozen Peruvian indigenous villages are embroiled in a Love Canal–style fight with Oxy, as Occidental Petroleum Company is often called. The activists from the remote Amazon region accuse the company of dumping toxic wastewater directly into rivers and streams, violating industry standards and Peruvian law, according to the residents whose U.S. lawyers have filed suit against Occidental in a Los Angeles court. The lawsuit charges that Occidental knew it was exposing the local people to serious health problems by discharging millions of gallons of wastewater into the tributaries but never warned them of the risks. Several people became ill and some died after drinking or bathing in contaminated river water, while others experience serious health problems. Two-thirds of the children living in the nearby villages have dangerously high lead levels, while nearly all residents have elevated levels of the carcinogen cadmium. The company pulled out of the region in 2000, after more than a quarter of a century extracting billions of dollars of crude oil. Since it left, the environment hasn't recovered either. A slew of heavy metals, radioactive compounds, and other toxins have seeped into their lands. The once-flowering papaya, cassava, and banana trees are dying and many locals are ill.[25] Crops have failed and fish and wild game have declined, according to the lawsuit, though the company denies the charges and plans to defend itself in court.[26]

The case has been called a hallmark of a new era: one in which local groups, even in the most remote rainforests, have the savvy and the technology to build alliances with international human rights groups that can amplify their grievances. As even the most marginalized members of the global village find their voices, corporations turn to big conservation groups for PR damage control. But the relationships aren't always enough to quell criticism in today's increasingly wired world where a group's size is not necessarily as important as its ability to get its message out.

Despite Shell's cordial relationships with some of the world's biggest conservation groups, it had to bow out of its sponsorship of the British National History Museum's "Wild-life Photographer of the Year" contest after a two-year campaign by scrappy British activists.[27] Shell, meanwhile, ended up selling a promising liquefied natural gas venture in Russia's Far East island of Sakhalin after Russian environmentalists dogged the company with allegations that it was polluting the feeding grounds of the endangered gray whale, in violation of Russian environmental law. The company sold the $22 billion project to the state-owned Gazprom gas company for $7.4 billion, the *Financial Times* reported.[28] While brouhaha over the photography contest illustrates how grassroots groups are lobbing increasingly successful greenwashing complaints at major corporations, the Russian drilling controversy is a more ominous sign for the companies: It shows how local watchdogs can get in the way of business deals.

It's a situation that is only likely to increase as the world's known oil and gas reserves dwindle and the Western giants find themselves competing for fields in places where increasingly savvy and internationally wired watchdogs have already established themselves.

These activist coups are often held up as signs of a changing global playing field, where corporations must involve communities or risk costly failures. But are these cases the rule or the exception? What about parts of the world with brutal dictatorships and an absence of civil society groups with access to a global audience? Chevron has rebuffed overtures from its activist shareholders to discuss its plans for its assets in Burma, where a violent military dictatorship has squelched the democracy movement. Even companies that claim to be reformed continue to run afoul of community activists around the globe. For instance, Shell, which has spent much time and money on writing lengthy sustainability and human rights policies, was forced to pull out of an offshore drilling project in Peru after public outcry. BP has been accused of reneging on promised social investments in communities surrounding its rich Tangguh gas field in the Indonesian province of Papua.

Back to the Future

One way to gauge how much things have changed is to look back at the 1980s, when corporate–conservationist partnerships were in their nascent stages. Secretary of the interior James Watt and his colleagues in the Ronald Reagan administration were attempting to roll back many of the landmark 1970s pollution, clean water, and endangered species protections. The situation appeared so dire that Bill Turnage, then president of the Wilderness Society, and Cecil D. Andrus, the secretary of the interior under the previous Jimmy Carter administration, set out to meet with the CEOs of the country's largest corporations. As Turnage recalls it, they weren't trying to raise funds. Rather, they hoped to present a reasonable face of U.S. environmentalism, one that could counter Watt's portrayal of the environmental movement as a bunch of "communists," while muting the rumblings of more militant groups like Earth First, which were advocating "monkeywrenching"—acts of environmentally motivated sabotage such as attacking ski resorts.

Among the CEOs they visited was Clifton C. Garvin Jr., chairman and CEO of Exxon Corporation from 1975 until 1986. Garvin, once described by *Time* magazine as "folksy but forceful," had guided the company through the 1970s energy crisis. At the time Turnage and Andrus came calling he was also the chairman of the Business Roundtable, composed of the leaders of the country's largest corporations.[29]

"We had a very good conversation," Turnage recalls of the meeting with Garvin. "He said, 'I think I understand where you all are coming from and I respect your sincerity. But I just have to tell you that, in my world, if we discovered oil in Yosemite National Park, I would do everything that I could to see to it that we drilled for it.'"

Fast forward a quarter of a century: ExxonMobil and its competitors have spent millions lobbying Congress for drilling rights in the Arctic National Wildlife Refuge. They also held a bidding war for exploratory oil and gas leases in Alaska's Chukchi Sea, despite concerns about the region's most famous resident, the beleaguered polar bear. The only difference: Today these companies also call themselves stewards of the environment.

Chapter Seven
Mining and the Environment

We could hardly imagine life without the metals used in our computers, cell phones, iPods, and automobiles, not to mention jewelry. In fact, mines supply raw materials to industries that contribute at least 16 percent of the national gross domestic product.[1] Mining companies, however, have racked up horrific environmental and human rights records—perhaps the worst of any industry.

There are more than one hundred thousand abandoned mines in the United States alone. Some of them are leaking mercury, lead, arsenic, and other toxins into the environment. Entire mountaintops are removed each year to get at valuable coal reserves underneath. The coal, which burns dirtier and creates more greenhouse gases than any other energy source, even oil, provides more than half of the fuel firing the nation's power plants. Together, those plants are a major contributor to air pollution that causes tens of thousands of deaths from asthma and other pollution-related illnesses each year.

Around the globe, mining companies have a long legacy of forced evictions and violent and sometimes deadly confrontations with the locals, who accuse them of poisoning water supplies, sickening livestock, ruining farmland, killing off fish stocks, and generally destroying lives and livelihoods. For centuries, no place has been off-limits to mining companies. Open-pit mines have been dug into lands sacred to native people, protected forests, and even UN-designated World Heritage Sites.

Open-Pit Impacts

Underground shafts worked by rugged men wearing hard hats topped with built-in flashlights—it's a familiar stereotype but one that is quickly becoming a quaint relic of a bygone era.

Most mining today goes on aboveground. Open-pit and strip mining are cheaper and less risky than the historic pickax-and-shovel approach. These modern techniques have made it profitable for companies to revisit historic sites where high-grade veins of ore were long-ago exhausted, leaving lower-grade quantities of gold, silver, copper, and other metals once ignored as uneconomical.

An open-pit mine is a massive affair. First the vegetation and top layer of soil, known as overburden, are removed. Then, miners use explosives to blast the ore apart. The pits are cut into the earth in concentric terraces. These mines can measure more than a mile across and nearly as deep. In the case of gold mining, trucks dump the debris from the mine on "leaching pads," where cyanide is sprayed on the heaps of rubble. After a few months, the cyanide bonds with the gold, allowing workers to separate it. Other valuable metals such as silver and copper are also gathered up, but that leaves a mind-boggling amount of "waste rock" behind. Experts estimate that it takes seventy-nine metric tons of mine waste to deliver one ounce of gold, according to Oxfam America and Earthworks, nonprofits working together to publicize environmental and human rights abuses in the industry.

The cyanide—the same deadly stuff of spy movies, known to kill instantly—is usually recycled for using again. But thousands of accidental spills have polluted streams and groundwater in the United States alone, causing wholesale die-offs of fish and aquatic life

And, that's just the scenic damage caused by mining for gold and other metals. Besides the toxins that run off into streams and seep into the earth and the groundwater, the industry's ill effects waft away on the breeze. In fact, the mining and metallurgic industry is the number-one source of pollution in the United States. It contributes more than any other industry to the fouling of our air, water, and soil, dumping more than one billion pounds of toxic substances into the environment each year, according to the EPA.[2]

Mining waste gets into the food we eat and impacts fresh water supplies.[3] Not only is it linked to deadly water contamination, mining can also lead to water shortages. It is known to change hydrological cycles, altering the water table and drying up wells. Wind causes erosion on the piles of excavated rock, known as tailings. The dust created blows away, contributing to air pollution and human health problems. Besides the dust, toxic emissions associated with mining also cause serious air pollution. Smelters used in processing the ore release arsenic, zinc, and palladium. Once in the air, they rain down on farmland and end up in the food we eat. Mercury is another byproduct, one that can have a particularly adverse impact on children and developing fetuses. Mercury exposure can cause neurological and developmental problems. It can impair vision, motor functions, and memory. It's been shown to lead to language problems and attention deficits.[4]

One of the most energy-intensive industries, mining plays a role in global warming, as well. According to estimates, worldwide mining operations use as much as 10 percent of the world's total fossil fuel consumption. The energy is needed both for extracting the raw materials and processing them into usable metals. Aluminum smelters, for instance, release two tons of carbon dioxide for every ton of aluminum produced. The smelting process, used not just for aluminum but for many metals, releases large amounts of nitrogen and sulfuric oxide and other substances that contribute to smog and acid rain.[5]

Acid Mine Drainage and Water Quality

While all those problems are serious, the most daunting type of mining pollution is water contamination that can last a thousand years or more.

The modern surface mining methods require enormous movements of earth. Open-pit mining creates nearly ten times more waste than underground mining. Mountaintop removal, meanwhile, which began in the 1970s as a variation of strip-mining techniques, usually involves dumping the excess dirt in valleys, choking rivers and streams. After more than a century of mining, there is an excess of one hundred billion metric tons of mine waste lying around the country's abandoned mines today.

Depending on its mineral composition, this waste rock, which probably hadn't seen daylight since it was created millennia ago, remains relatively benign or turns into a disposal nightmare. When it goes bad the process is called acid mine drainage. It occurs when mine waste, mixed with air and water, releases sulfuric acid, the same stuff in acid rain but many times more concentrated. The acid, in turn, leaches heavy metals such as arsenic, mercury, lead, and cadmium out of the stone, creating a rusty-colored slimy liquid that often finds its way into rivers and streams and seeps into groundwater.

While modern mining companies have come up with ways to contain this toxic sludge, there is no quick solution, especially given the enormity of today's surface mines and the monumental amounts of waste produced. There is no average estimate of how long it takes for mine waste to return to an "acid neutral" state and stop posing a threat to the environment. Sometimes it's expected to take hundreds of years. In other cases, experts calculate time frames that run ten thousand or even twenty thousand years.

"You are devastating big areas," says Stephen D'Esposito, Earthworks' president. "One of the biggest unknowns in mining is what the long term impact will be."

"There is no easy answer," adds Dan Randolph, executive director of Great Basin Mine Watch, a nonprofit coalition of environmentalists, Native Americans, and scientists based in Reno, Nevada. "Once the problem is created, it doesn't necessarily go away."

Experts have traced some damage in Spain's Rio Tinto mining district to acid drainage from mines that operated during Roman or Phoenician times.[6] In the United States, the same phenomenon—a legacy of more than a century of mining—has laid waste to several thousand miles of rivers and streams and hundreds of thousands of acres of land, according to the EPA.[7]

Inadequate Government Regulation

Nevertheless, mining companies continue to receive government permits to operate mines where they know acid drainage problems await. Newmont Mining Corporation's Phoenix Mine on the outskirts of Battle Mountain, Nevada, is one of these sites. Gold and copper was first extracted from the area more than a century ago, leaving a halo of low-grade reserves and a big water contamination problem. In the mid-2000s, Newmont sought to reopen and expand existing open-pit mines, estimating that it could extract as much as 450,000 ounces of gold a year worth many billions of dollars over the anticipated fifteen-year life of the mine.[8]

Since previous operations had already led to serious acid drainage problems, there was no question that the project would create more water contamination. The EPA had predicted the mine will become a SuperFund site, an abandoned hazardous waste site so onerous it ends up on the EPA list of cleanup priorities. The environmental impact study by the Bureau of Land Management (BLM), which oversees the mine, estimated that acid mine drainage could be an issue for tens of thousands of years into the future. BLM required Newmont to set aside a trust fund for the "perpetual treatment" of the waste to contain the problem—essentially a mitigation measure to last forever.

Still, the project moved forward. The only sticking point was the size of the trust fund. Randolph's watchdog group wanted a $40 million fund. The EPA pushed for $33.5 million, warning that the cleanup could become an "enormous financial burden" for taxpayers. But the BLM accepted Newmont's proposal of a $408,000 fund. The company executives had argued more money wasn't necessary because they did not agree with

BLM's assessment that the mine would require such long-term remediation measures. As a concession to critics, the company posted an additional $1 million bond in case the cleanup costs escalated. Even with the additional bond, however, the cleanup funds represented less than one percent of Newmont's estimated $200 million investment spent to reopen the mine in 2006.[9]

Environmentalists were outraged that the BLM did not require a bigger financial commitment from Newmont. But the Newmont trust fund was, nonetheless, a step forward in regulatory efforts to address long-term problems associated with mining. The industry has been subject to federal clean air, water, and other environmental laws since those laws were enacted a few decades ago. But, surprisingly, rules requiring companies to set aside cleanup trust funds have only been enacted in recent years. The Phoenix was the first mine on BLM land in Nevada to be required to make the financial commitment.[10]

Cleanup Efforts Questioned

Mining industry officials say modern mines use state-of-the art environmental safeguards that reduce the potential for long-term problems.[11] They have developed ways to dam up the tailings and eventually reclaim the earth. The rehabilitation involves capping waste dumps, then covering them with native vegetation to soak up moisture in the soil and prevent it from reaching and reacting with the mine waste.

Despite the safeguards, releases of waste rock, mine tailings, and smelter slags happen frequently. In the United States alone, mining companies report to the EPA hundreds of accidental spills each year. One of the largest occurred in February

2005, when a waste rock dump at Newmont Mining Corp.'s Gold Quarry mine in Nevada collapsed. The detritus seeped off Newmont's grounds and crept down State Highway 766 for the length of two football fields.[12]

Even when no accidents occur in disposing of the waste, there's no way to tell for sure what will happen hundreds of years into the future. The industry does not have a very long track record. While acid drainage problems linger for centuries or longer, large-scale open-pit mining has only been around a few decades. The attendant environmental cleanup and protection regulations are still evolving, which means there is very little certainty about the impact today's open-pit mines will have on the future of the Earth.

For mining companies that are no longer around to clean up after themselves, taxpayers foot the bill. The country is littered with abandoned mines dug during previous gold rush eras. BLM and the Forest Service do not even have a good idea of how many abandoned mines exist on the public lands they manage. One estimate puts it at 100,000, primarily in Arizona, California, Nevada, and Utah. But the Government Accountability Office (GAO) put the number higher: at 161,000 abandoned sites with more than 33,000 showing environmental degradation.[13] Other estimates suggest the country has as many as half a million abandoned mines.

Since the late 1990s, the Forest Service, EPA, and the Department of the Interior's Office of Surface Mining have spent at least $2.6 billion on reclaiming abandoned mines on federal, state, native, and private lands, according to the GAO. Most of the money went to address pollution caused by mines built in the distant past. But the GAO told Congress in March 2008 that cleanup funds committed by mining companies operating on federal lands continue to fall short today of the true cost of the cleanups. Since it often takes decades for contamination problems to become evident, failing to set aside sufficient funds now could lead to massive taxpayer-funded bailouts in the future.[14]

A Nineteenth-Century Legacy

The mining industry contributed more than $78 billion to the U.S. economy in 2005, according to the National Mining Association. While it's a large and modern industry, it is still governed by a nineteenth-century federal law passed chiefly to encourage settlement of the West. The General Mining Law of 1872, signed by President Ulysses S. Grant, not only fails to mention environmental protection, its wording has been interpreted to mean that the federal government cannot turn down any miner's claim to mineral deposits on federally owned lands. Not only must the government allow miners access to public lands, the transactions continue at 1870s prices: The law stipulates that miners will pay no more than $5 an acre, ridiculously low by today's standards.[15]

Over the years, there have been many efforts to reform the law. Most recently, bills have proposed barring mining of ecologically sensitive areas and adding protections for groundwater that are missing from current federal legislation. The reform efforts would also require mining companies to pay royalties for what they extract on public lands, as oil and gas companies do. So far, however, all have failed.

Today, mines—both historic and modern—figure prominently on the EPA's National Priority List of SuperFund sites. The EPA estimates it will take between $4 and $45 billion to clean them up.[16] While old underground mines prove a challenge to locate and restore, environmentalists say today's enormous open-pit mines promise unimaginable future water-pollution problems.

"We don't know what the long-term impacts of the large-scale mines are and we won't know for generations," Randolph said. "What we do know is the short-term impacts are very often worse than what was predicted for the long term."

Communities in Revolt

Over the last few decades, communities near the sites of open-pit mines and proposed mines have increasingly risen up to challenge them. The list of grievances against mining companies is too long to detail exhaustively here. But Peru, Chile, Argentina, Indonesia, Ghana, Papua New Guinea, and the United States are just some of the places that have seen controversy. While the geography changes, the stories fit a similar pattern: Community members say the prosperity they were promised when the miners arrived never materializes. Instead, the mines generate "boom-bust" economic cycles that create jobs for the lucky few. But since most mines employ only a fraction of the local population, the new jobs—which often pay considerably more than others locally available—often produce new class and social tensions in the community. Problems such as increased alcoholism, prostitution, and crime also arrive along with influxes of unemployed people looking for work. After a few years or a few decades the mine closes, leaving enormous waste dumps. When acid drainage has caused water-quality issues, locals may never be able to resume previous activities such as farming, ranching, or fishing.

At Barrick's Pascua Lama silver and gold mine, Chilean law-makers accuse the company of evicting local indigenous people and doing irrevocable damage to glaciers that play a crucial role in the region's agriculture and water supply. A 2002 report by the country's General Water Directorship found that three glaciers had lost at least half of their mass as a result of Barrick's mine prospecting activities such as building roads into the remote region.[17] The company maintains that the glaciers were already shrinking. But the conflict illustrates the increasing tensions over resources such as water.

At Barrick's Porgera Mine in Papua New Guinea, Newmont's Akyem facility in Ghana, and Ashanti Goldfields Co.'s Ghana operations, clashes with local residents have led to violence and several deaths.[18]

In some of the incidents, the local residents were engaged in "artisanal," or small-scale, mining. In many places, artisanal mining has long been part of the mix of activities rural people engage in to survive. While they may primarily rely on subsistence farming, digging up small quantities of metals might be the only way open to them to earn cash for paying school fees and doctor's bills or for buying medicines, their activists say. In other parts of the world, human rights activists maintain that subsistence farmers turn to makeshift mining after large-scale mines pollute their farmland and watersheds, leaving them with no other way to make a living. But, from the perspective of the mining companies that own the mineral rights, the local people are stealing from them.

Such conflicts with local people are all too commonplace. Half of all mines are on indigenous lands. Increasingly, however, indigenous people are moving to block mining companies from breaking ground. Barrick is fighting efforts to derail its Cortez

Hills project, which would build an open-pit mine on Nevada's Mount Tenabo, a sacred site of the Western Shoshone Native Americans.[19] Its mine near Lake Cowal in Australia has come under similar criticism for excavating at an aboriginal ceremonial site. In Canada, an Ardoch Algonquin First Nation activist has served jail time for defying a court injunction against a protest blocking uranium exploration in an area subject to a long-standing native land claim. Other Canadian activists of the Shabot Obaadjiwan and the Kitchenuhmaykoosib Inninuwug Nations have also faced legal action as a result of protests against mineral exploration on native territory, according to press reports.

In Papua New Guinea, the world's largest mining company, BHP Billiton, was slapped with a lawsuit in 2007 by villagers who live on traditional lands along a thirty-eight-mile stretch of the Ok Tedi River in the country's Western Province.[20] The thirteen thousand villagers are seeking about $4 billion to compensate for alleged contamination that their experts expect will take three hundred years to clean up. The company dumped so many mine tailings that the deep, slow-moving river turned into a much shallower, faster-moving waterway, making it difficult for locals to navigate. When it flooded, toxic sludge from the riverbed coated a wide floodplain used for agriculture. The mine waste also ended up in the Fly River, an Ok Tedi tributary. The combined effect of the dumping, the plaintiffs claim, makes it impossible to eat produce from their gardens, or the fish and other river wildlife that villagers traditionally rely on as major sources of food.

The mine has a long and troubled environmental history. In the mid-1990s, local landowners first sued BHP in Australia's Supreme Court charging that the mine had destroyed the environment and their traditional way of life. In 1999, BHP acknowledged major environmental damage from dumping about eighty thousand metric tons of mine waste into the river over several decades. The company agreed to pay $40 million in compensation to the landholders and to dredge tailings from the riverbed in an effort to contain future problems. Four years later, the plaintiffs returned to court, accusing the company of breaching the agreement by failing to fulfill cleanup promises. After BHP merged with British mining giant Billiton to form BHP Billiton, the company sold its stake in the Ok Tedi mine but signed agreements with landowners that traded financial benefits for consent to continued mining there. They released BHP Billiton from liability. But the villagers who brought suit in 2007 are members of clans that did not sign the agreements. They want the company to acknowledge that the mine had a more widespread impact. BHP and its co-defendants, however, say the claims cannot be substantiated and have sought to have the case thrown out of court.

The Ok Tedi case was filed in Papua New Guinea. But, increasingly, community activists abroad are taking their claims to U.S. courts, where non-citizens may sue based on violations of international law. Rio Tinto has spent the better part of the last decade defending itself from charges of crimes against humanity, among other things. The case was brought to U.S. District Court in San Franciso by a dozen Papua New Guinea landowners, seeking to represent thousands of civilians. It charges the world's third-largest mining company with war crimes, racial discrimination, and environmental damages at its Bougainville Island mine. It was one of the world's largest copper mines until it closed down in 1989 amid protests over environmental degradation and armed attacks on the mine itself. The plaintiffs allege Rio Tinto and the Papua New Guinea government colluded to brutally quell protests against the mine. The controversy sparked a decade of civil war, as Bougainville fought for independence. The Bougainville plaintiffs want the company to foot the bill for cleaning up the damage done by the mine. They also want to prove Rio Tinto was complicit in war crimes and crimes against humanity carried out by the PNG army.[21] Rio Tinto has said the claims are "wholly false and malicious" and sought to have the case dismissed since it was first brought in 2000.[22]

The conglomerates have also come under fire for building mines in biologically sensitive ecosystems and protected forests. Freeport McMoRan has operated an open pit on the edge of the Lorentz National Park in West Papua, Indonesia, that activists say has dumped tons of waste tailings a day into the Ajikwa River. The largest protected area in Southeast Asia, Lorentz was declared a World Heritage Site in 1999, but the designation came too late to save the area around Freeport's mine. By the time the ore is depleted, a few decades from now, a 230-square-kilometer hole in the forest is expected to be clearly visible from outer space, according to Oxfam America and Earthworks. BHP Billiton operates inside West Africa's Mount Nimba Strict National Reserve and hasn't ruled out developing its concession on Indonesia's Gag Island, which has been considered for World Heritage status.[23]

In early 2008 mining company Anglo American was embarrassed by environmentalists who convinced more than two dozen large retail chains including Tiffany & Co. and Wal-Mart not to carry jewelry made from gold taken at the Pebble Mine, an open pit that has not even been built yet. Pebble is a proposed mine in Bristol Bay, Alaska, that Anglo plans to build in a joint venture with a Vancouver company. The mine would sit between two national parks and could have an adverse effect on the world's largest sockeye salmon run, according to activists.[24]

Newmont's Travails

While each of the major mining companies has had its share of scandals, Newmont has been most frequently in the public eye during recent years. In 2004, the company and one of its top executives were tried in Indonesia for allegedly polluting the waters offshore from the island of Suluwasi, while massive street protests in northern Peru threatened to close down its most productive gold mine there, and residents in Ghana opposed the company's plans to build new mines in their communities.

Newmont and its regional director Richard Ness were facing criminal charges alleging the company had dumped dangerous amounts of toxic waste from its Mesel Gold Mine into Suluwasi's Buyat Bay, killing fish, sickening local residents, and damaging coral reefs. The company paid a $30 million settlement to the Indonesian government in 2006, but did not admit wrongdoing. Ness was facing a maximum of ten years in prison, but he and the company were acquitted in April 2007 and won a civil suit filed by environmentalists a few months later, clearing them of the pollution charges. The company had never tried to hide the fact that it dumped the waste in the bay, but has consistently maintained its deep-water storage methods were safe. Many activist groups, including Earthworks, say ocean dumping has not been scientifically proven to be safe. The international controversy over the practice is ongoing, even after Newmont's legal victories in Indonesia.

In Peru, Newmont also reassured local residents that its plans to expand its Yanacocha Mine in the north of the country would pose no threat to the region's water supply. But, when it moved in bulldozers to break ground on a mountainside known as Cerro Quilish, local residents scrambled to block the road.

In the mayhem that followed, teargas was lobbed at the pro-
testors. Women and children were among those arrested, and
several people were hospitalized after clashes with police. Quilish Mountain is an ancient sacred site of the local indigenous
people and an important watershed for the entire valley below
including Cajamarca, the provincial capital, with a population
of 135,000. After an estimated ten thousand people took to
Cajamarca's streets in protest, the company backed down. Newmont withdrew its bulldozers and took the Quilish reserves,
estimated at $2 billion in value, off its books.

According to a case study by the World Resources Institute,
Newmont was not always seen as a bad guy in Peru.[25] When the
mining company arrived in 1992, locals were hopeful that the
foreign investment would help lift the region out of poverty.
Within a decade, however, what had started out as a relatively
modest operation had turned into six open-pit mines spread
across five mountaintops and four watersheds. Yanacocha had
become Newmont's most important producer of gold. But the
operation had completely dwarfed all other economic activity
in the region. Tensions over the mine's pollution, enormous
water use, and other impacts had started to fester. The mine was
seen as undermining the region's pastoral way of life. Nearby
farmers and ranchers complained that Newmont's operation
was a water hog and that the company engaged in coercive land
purchasing practices that allowed it to amass huge landhold-
ings within its nearly 68,000 square mile government-issued
mining concession.

Newmont's relationship with the community took a turn
for the worse in 2000 after a truck leaving the mine accidentally
spilled 330 pounds of mercury on the highway, where children
scooped it up and played with it. Adults also collected it, think-

ing the substance was mixed with gold. More than a thousand people reported vision problems, vomiting, skin rashes, respiratory and nervous system disorders, and kidney problems. Some sued the company. The World Bank's International Finance Corporation, which had a small stake in the mine, investigated. It concluded that the company had contributed to the disaster by failing to implement standard policies for handling and transporting hazardous materials.

The public eventually became convinced the mine was contaminating its water supplies. So, when Newmont announced plans to expand to Quilish, the city of Cajamarca took defensive action. The mayor declared the mountain a protected area, off-limits to mining. The case went to Peru's Supreme Court, which ruled in Newmont's favor in 2003.

At the time, however, the Supreme Court didn't have all that much credibility in Peru. It's the same judicial body that had ruled in favor of Newmont three years earlier, in an unrelated dispute with a French mining company over a minority stake in Yanacocha. But the impartiality of that decision was later questioned after secret tape recordings surfaced of a meeting between Peru's infamous secret police chief Vladimiro Montesinos and high-ranking Newmont executive Lawrence T. Kurlander.[26]

Kurlander asked for Montesinos' help resolving the legal battle with the French company. Montesinos promised to intervene on Newmont's behalf. Weeks later, when the country's Supreme Court had voted three-to-three in the case, Montesinos met with the judge appointed to break the deadlock. He is caught on tape promising to help the judge obtain a coveted judicial appointment in exchange for his vote on the matter. Two weeks later the judge decided the case in Newmont's favor.

But later the same year, Montesinos' intervention became public when his secret stash of tape recordings was leaked to the press and aired on Peruvian television. The scandal brought down the Fujimori government, and landed both Montesinos and Fujimori in legal trouble for a variety of crimes from graft to extra-judicial executions.

Though Newmont eventually backed down from its plans to mine at Quilish, the public suspicion stirred up by the Yanacocha affair spread to other areas of Peru, where mining companies were seeking to invest. But Newmont was the hardest hit by the controversy. Despite rising gold prices, Newmont's stock lost 8 percent of its value in 2004, a development widely attributed to the company's "reputational" problems.

The next year, while company executives were still reeling from the bad press, Newmont struck up relations with CI. The miner and the nonprofit worked together to establish systems to "integrate" biodiversity conservation into the way Newmont mines. And, Newmont Ghana Gold Ltd., a company subsidiary, began a close relationship with CI's Ghana office and its local partners. According to both, the partnership was established to make sure biodiversity issues were taken into account at the company's Akyem and Ahafo mines.[27]

The Ahafo mine, which would become Newmont's first foray into mineral-rich Ghana, was near completion, while the Akyem project was still on the drawing board.

Both had garnered considerable local resistance and criticism from national groups about mining in national forests, among other issues. A campaign by the country's National Coalition on Mining, made up of nonprofit groups including Friends of the Earth Ghana and mining communities, had also mobilized to protest against violent conflicts between local residents and international mining conglomerates. Among the incidents the group decried was a November 2005 confrontation at Akyem. According to the activists, gunshots were fired and two people were killed after farmers had gathered to protest the mine and seek compensation for its alleged impact on their lands. But in all the literature produced to promote the relations between Newmont and CI, there is no mention of the community dissent. In fact, the project's reports and brochures give the impression that local people are working happily together with the mining company and the nonprofit.

Besides its ties to CI, Newmont also signed up for the Business and Biodiversity Offset Program (BBOP,) a public-private organization created in 2004 by CI and Forest Trends, another U.S. nonprofit group. BBOP was established to experiment with carbon credit schemes to fund conservation projects. Newmont has pledged to bankroll one of BBOP's first offset programs.

It is an initiative that offers some insights into what the nonprofits and the mining company mean when they talk of "integrating" conservation into mining operations. An open pit, by its very nature, involves clearing large swaths of land. And, its enormous waste dumps, tailing ponds, and cyanide leaching pads create the prospect of accidental spills that could annihilate wildlife far beyond the confines of the mine. Given these constraints, one cannot help but wonder how a mining company would "integrate" biodiversity conservation into its operations. At Akyem, the situation is particularly sensitive because a portion of Newmont's mining concession is located inside the Ajenjua Bepo Forest Reserve, 130 kilometers northwest of Accra.[28]

As it turns out, the BBOP project involving the Akyem mine won't attempt to minimize the biodiversity damage to the Ajenjua Bepo Forest. Instead, the plans call for the company to pay BBOP to carry on conservation work in the Mamang Forest Reserve, another protected area to the south of the mine. Conservationists would use the Newmont funds to hire more forest rangers charged with keeping the local people from invading the reserve, cutting down trees to plant crops and hunting the forest's fauna for bushmeat, a staple of their diets. While the funding may improve the health of the Mamang reserve, it will not change large-scale impacts from Newmont's open-pit mine nearby. And, it is destined to exacerbate local residents' resentments against Newmont, as well as the conservationists for limiting their rights to the forests. Essentially, Newmont has purchased its "conservation steward" credentials by bankrolling enforcement efforts aimed at kicking local people out of the forest. And, it still gets to build the 3,665-acre open-pit mine.

Controversy and Conservation

Newmont is certainly not the only mining conglomerate to purchase its status as a "conservation steward." Of the dozen or so multinational companies that dominate today's mining industry, they all take ample credit for preserving the biodiversity surrounding the open pits they blast into protected areas and other ecologically sensitive landscapes. Barrick even lists its conservation work as a selling point in efforts to recruit new executives.

By this standard, even coal mining outfits and the power companies that they supply are "conservationists." Due to industry consolidation in recent years, they are often the same companies. For instance, Rio Tinto and BHP Billiton, major global gold miners, also supply Asian markets with coal via their Australian mines. The two companies helped fund a study by WWF's Australian branch examining options for weaning the economy off warming fossil fuels.[29] But there is little reason to believe they will be getting out of the coal mining business any time soon.

Coal is experiencing a resurgence. As international oil and gas reserves decline and prices skyrocket, coal, one of the world's most plentiful energy sources, has become a popular global commodity fueling rapid growth rates in China and India and providing robust export markets for a dozen countries, including the United States, which has the largest coal reserves in the world.

Coal already provides nearly two-thirds of U.S. electricity. The world's coal consumption has seen double-digit growth in recent years, far outpacing any other source of energy. While growing public concern over climate change has helped derail dozens of planned U.S. coal plants in the last few years, the world appears to be gearing up for a big expansion of coal power. Some analysts predict coal usage will double by 2030.[30] As the dirtiest of all the fossil fuels, however, it contributes more than its fair share of greenhouse gases. Globally, coal provides about a quarter of energy consumption, but contributes 39 percent of the industry's carbon dioxide emissions. Besides the fears of global warming, the surface mining techniques used to get the coal out of the ground have a host of environmental problems similar to other forms of mining, including acid mine drainage issues.

Consol Energy Inc., one of the biggest U.S. coal producers, has donated land to CF and TNC and won a slew of environmental awards. But it also removes entire mountaintops and dumps the debris in valleys through the Appalachian Mountains despite public outcry by local environmental and community groups.[31]

American Electric Power (AEP), one of the country's largest electric utilities and another generous giver to CF and TNC, agreed to the single largest environmental enforcement settlement in history in October 2007. The company was required to pay $75 million and invest $4.6 billion in reducing sulfur dioxide and nitrogen oxide pollutants at sixteen plants in five states. The deal sprung from a 1999 enforcement action brought by the Clinton administration, nine state attorneys general, and more than a dozen activist groups. The company fought a bitter eight-year battle against the settlement, possibly waiting to see if the George W. Bush administration would succeed in its efforts to nix the Clinton rules on which the enforcement action was predicated.[32]

Despite all that, AEP devotes much space on its Web site to its "stewardship of our natural environment." It touts its efforts to develop new, as yet unproven technology that stores carbon dioxide underground instead of releasing it into the atmosphere. While that's all good, it held out for years against an investment that would give millions of residents downwind of its plants immediate improvements in air quality by reducing sulfur dioxide and nitrogen oxide causing smog and acid rain.

The company's plants are also big mercury polluters, according to the Environmental Integrity Project, a Washington, D.C.–based nonprofit that analyzes federal government emissions data for more than a thousand coal-, natural gas-, and oil-burning power plants. The Project ranked five of AEP's plants among the fifty biggest mercury polluters in the United States in 2006. The worst offender is the company's Pirkey, Texas, plant, which had the worst ratio of power produced to mercury released: It releases more than one thousand pounds of the neurotoxins for every five million megawatt hours.[33]

In all, U.S. power plants increased their emissions of carbon dioxide by nearly 3 percent in 2007, the largest annual jump in nearly a decade, the Environmental Integrity Project reported. The biggest producer of carbon dioxide in the country was the Scherer coal-burning power plant, operated by Georgia Power, a big donor to CF. The plant spewed about twenty-seven million tons of pollution into the air, an increase of two million tons over the previous year. In an interview with the Associated Press a spokesman for the company attributed the increase to booming demand for energy in the state. Georgia Power's parent, Southern Company, operates all three of the top carbon dioxide–emitting plants in the country. But you wouldn't know that to visit Southern's Web site, where the top news is the "Change a Light" award Georgia Power won from the EPA and the U.S. Department of Energy in 2008. What did it do? Something to reverse its upward-trending greenhouse gas emissions? Perhaps it installed wind turbines? Solar energy panels? Nope. The company won the award by giving away 200,000 compact fluorescent light bulbs.

Speaking of greenwashing, Alcoa, the world's leading aluminum producer that was one of the first companies to cozy up to big conservation groups more than two decades ago, has gotten lots of good press for its eco-efforts. But its aluminum smelters are big air polluters. While aluminum is energy-intensive to produce, the company's pollution record is worse than it needs to be. Federal regulators have taken the company to task for dirty and inefficient plants; the EPA named three of its four Rockdale, Texas, plants the dirtiest in the nation. And in 2003 the Department of Justice ordered them shut down. Alcoa promised to spend $330 million to modernize pollution controls at the plants under the terms of a consent decree. But the company kept operating the dirty plants for three more years and only shut them down after federal officials returned in

2006, slapping the company with $9.2 million in fines for continuing to violate clean-air standards.[34] The company's Warrick County, Indiana, plant is another notorious polluter. Nevertheless, Alcoa has resisted upgrades, possibly waiting to see if it could purchase carbon offset credits from other states, according to the Environmental Integrity Project. The Project ranked it as the third least-efficient power plant in the United States in 2006 because it produces more than thirty-two pounds of sulfur dioxide for every megawatt hour generated.

Alcoa's Wagerup refinery in Australia, meanwhile, has also been hit with fines for air pollution and industrial accidents since it opened a quarter century ago. Local residents in the town of Yarloop in Western Australia have hired Erin Brockovich, the legal researcher who led an environmental fight against PG&E that was later dramatized in a movie staring Julia Roberts.[35] They believe pollution from the refinery has caused respiratory problems, skin irritation, sore throats and eyes, nosebleeds, cancers, and organ failure. The plant refines bauxite into fine white powder called alumina, which is used to make aluminum. The company has denied the charges but Brockovich plans to take Alcoa to court in Pittsburgh, where it is based. Activists in Iceland and Trinidad have also rallied against Alcoa's plans to open plants there.

Mining and Power Corporations Tied to Conservation Groups						
Company	CF	CI	ED	TNC	NRDC	WWF-US
AEP	•			•		
Exelon				•	•	
Entergy	•					
USX	•					
PG&E				•	•	•
First Gen		•				

Company	CF	CI	ED	TNC	NRDC	WWF-US
CONSOL	•			•		
Alliant				•		
Duke Energy				•	•	
NRG Energy				•	•	
PNM				•	•	
FPL Group				•	•	
AES Corp.						•
USX Corp.	•					
Freeport MacR.		•				
Alcoa		•		•	•	•
Rio Tinto		•		•	•	
BHP Billiton		•		•		
Barrick		•		•		•
Newmont		•				

Relationships include positions on boards of directors, donations, partnerships, programs, projects, joint councils, and advisory boards. Sources: Web sites and tax returns of the organizations and corporations.

Sustainable Development and Greenwashing

Mines have decimated scenic landscapes, discharged toxic waste directly into streams and oceans, and thrown people off their lands. The industry has left such a devastating legacy that companies have come under enormous pressure in recent years, facing increasing scrutiny as communities learn how to take their grievances to the world and activist shareholders step up campaigns to enact reforms from within. Because mining is one of the world's most polluting industries, growing concern about global warming has added even more urgency to the debate. The companies are particularly big targets due to industry consolidation in recent years that has left standing a small number of mega-corporations.

Facing a proliferation of protests, mining companies have embarked on ambitious efforts to green themselves, or at least their images. The result has been a dramatic turnaround in corporate rhetoric in a very short space of time. In the last few years alone, they have written sustainability reports and policies, and retained the services of big conservation groups to help them with their image problems. Unprecedented local and international pressure has led to some remarkable self-imposed reforms in an industry with a long and barbaric history of human rights and environmental abuses around the globe.

In 2002, Rio Tinto shocked the world when it became perhaps the first mining company to ever apologize for forced evictions.[36] The company expressed "regret" for removing people from their homes to make way for the Kelian Gold Mine, in East Kalimantan Province of Indonesia. While it is true that Rio Tinto only apologized after the country's National Commission on Human Rights investigated the company's record there, it was still a watershed event. It marked a turning point in an industry that has been involved in similar human rights violations probably for as long as mining has existed. To move beyond this legacy, Rio Tinto and its competitors among the large international mining corporations have enacted human rights policies.

Concern about "blood diamonds" led to the Kimberly Process, an international certification program that has made it harder for governments and rebel groups to use the precious stones to finance civil wars in Africa. In 2008, Anglo American and Rio Tinto announced that they would not move forward with joint ventures with Chinese companies in Africa unless Chinese executives agreed to comply with "Western" environmental and human rights standards.[37]

After BHP Billiton was called to task for polluting the Ok Tedi River in Papua New Guinea, the company pledged to never again dump mine tailings directly into any river.

In 2003, for the first time a group of fifteen of the largest mining companies in the world pledged to stop blasting apart World Heritage Sites. The move came three years after the World Parks Congress made a public request for the industry to stop mining operations inside protected forests that hold the most critically endangered wildlife. While the companies declined the wider ban, the move was the single most significant environmental policy reform ever made by the mining industry.[38]

At Newmont, management decided to support a shareholder resolution authored by Christian Brothers Investment Services, a faith-based institutional investor. The proposal called on the company to establish an independent board to review its global operations and suggest ways it could improve its relationships with communities. In April 2007, 93 percent of shareholders voted in favor of the proposal, making it the resolution to receive—by far—the highest approval rate of any shareholder proposal that year.[39] The company invited a Christian Brothers representative to take a seat on the independent panel.

"That would not have happened five years ago, I guarantee you. It's because they thought their reputation was tarnished," says D'Esposito, the president of Earthworks, which also has a seat on the panel.

All of these companies today trumpet "sustainable development" as one of the cornerstones of their operations. And, their environmental and human rights records are a whole lot better than they were even a decade ago. But the question remains: Can mining be done in a way that is environmentally sustainable?

Even the activists say yes. But a sustainable industry would look much different that the one we have today.

First, mining companies and regulators would need to be honest about where mines should and should not go. Allowing mines to set up in areas with conditions known to cause long-lasting water contamination should not continue.

Not all mines have acid drainage problems. In fact, a 2006 study commissioned by Earthworks took a close look at 25 modern U.S. mines and found only a little more than a third—36 percent—of them developed acid mine drainage.[40] But eight out of the nine mines that developed problems had assured government regulators that the possibility was low or non-existent. The companies must improve their ability to honestly assess the potential for problems or government regulators should step in to play the role for them. And, the companies should have to foot the whole bill for cleanup costs. Anything less essentially amounts to an industry subsidy, activists say.

If the environmental toll of the mining industry were incorporated into the bottom line, it would likely push the price of metals higher. But it would encourage more recycling, too. Metals are one of the most recyclable products. If we were to use more of what's already been pulled out of the ground, Randolph argues, we could dramatically reduce the need for virgin ore.

Besides recycling more, consumers could play a role in deciding when the environmental toll is too great to warrant some finished products. For Jeffrey T. S. MacDonagh, portfolio manager at Domini Social Investments, it comes down to utility versus vanity. While he doesn't rule out investing in mining companies, he says few of the gold mining behemoths could meet the firm's standards for worthwhile social investments.

CI founders on retreat at Bethany Beach in 1987, the same year the organization was formed. **(Photo courtesy of Sumner Pingree)**

CI board meeting in New York, October 1988. Left to right: Charles Hedlund, Andrés Marcelo Sada, Spencer Beebe, Louise Emmons, José Sarukan, and Jack H. Vaughn. **(Photo courtesy of Spencer B. Beebe)**

Conservation International's headquarters is located in this Crystal City, Virginia office building. **(Photo by Christine MacDonald)**

President Jimmy Carter meeting with John Sawhill, Deputy Secretary of Energy, on August 27, 1980. Sawhill later led The Nature Conservancy. **(Photo courtesy of the Jimmy Carter Library)**

Huey Johnson during his tenure as Secretary of Resources for the State of California from 1976 to 1982. **(Photo courtesy of Huey Johnson/Resource Renewal Institute)**

The Nature Conservancy's headquarters in Arlington, Virginia, a suburb of Washington, D.C. **(Photo by Christine MacDonald)**

Russell E. Train during his swearing in ceremony as EPA administrator in September 1973. Left to Right: William D. Ruckelshaus, former EPA administrator; Aileen Train; her husband Russell Train; and John Quarles, deputy EPA administrator. **(Photo courtesy of the National Archives, photo no. 412-6-12-2163)**

World Wildlife Fund's Washington, D.C. headquarters. **(Photo by Christine MacDonald)**

Russian oak, birch, and pine logs await transport at a Chinese rail yard just across the border in Suifenhe, China. (Photo © Environmental Investigative Agency)

Logs on their way to the market.
(Photo © Environmental Investigative Agency)

A logger removing trees inside the Tanjung National Park in Indonesia.
(Photo © Environmental Investigative Agency)

Furniture aisle of a U.S. retail store.
(Photo © Environmental Investigative Agency)

After a 2007 landslide at the Bellavista gold mine in Costa Rica.
(Photo courtesy of EARTH-WORKS, credit: CEUS del Golfo)

Left and below: A March 2004 rally in Esquel, Argentina, against a proposed open pit gold mine. Public opposition propelled the government to pass a three-year moratorium on mining activity in this region of Patagonia in 2006.
(Photo courtesy of Payal Sampat/EARTHWORKS)

Aerial shot of a mountaintop removal coal mining site between Rawl and Buffalo mountains in Logan County, West Virginia. **(Photo courtesy of Appalachian Voices and SouthWings. Credit: Kent Kessinger)**

Aerial shot of Buffalo Mountain, West Virginia, where the mountaintop has been removed to excavate the coal underneath. **(Photo courtesy of Appalachian Voices and South-Wings. Credit: Kent Kessinger)**

Brazilian activist Judson Barros, president of Funaguas, which has been fighting Bunge in court over its use of firewood and other practices.
(Photo by Christine MacDonald)

Three satellite images showing growth of the Yanacocha gold mine in northern Peru from 1989 to 2001:

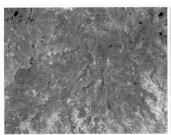  

1989 satellite image of the Yanacocha gold mine.

1996 satellite image of the Yanacocha gold mine.

2001 satellite image of the Yanacocha gold mine.

(Photos courtesy of SkyTruth, www.skytruth.org)

Two satellite images showing downstream impacts of mine waste flowing from Freeport-McMoRan's Grasberg mine in Indonesia into the Aghawagon, Otomona and Ajkwa rivers, eventually discharging into the Arafura Sea:

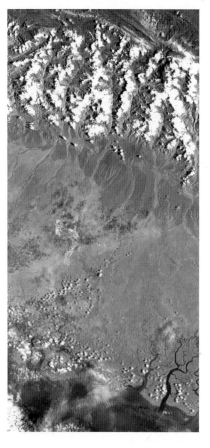 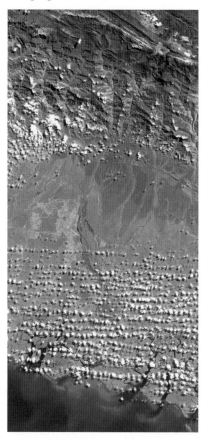

Above left: Satellite image February 21, 1988.

Above right: Satellite image May 29, 2003.

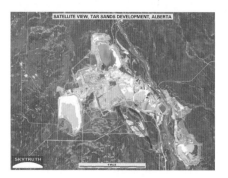

Landsat satellite image on May 14, 2002 showing impact of oil sands mining near Fort McMurray in Alberta, Canada.

"At least when you are mining for industrial metals you get some kind of economic utility out of these things, but precious metals, out of all the metals, are the most frivolous," MacDonagh says. When using a cost-benefit analysis to determine the best investment, MacDonagh says decimating the environment to make jewelry simply doesn't add up.

By its very nature, mining is a one-time activity; the very opposite of a "sustainable" endeavor. "It's not like you are growing corn. You're not going to grow another crop next year," D'Esposito says. Nevertheless, D'Esposito acknowledges that society, which relies on minerals for so many things, is not going to give up mining any time soon. This reality makes mining practices that cause the least environmental harm all the more imperative.

"One part of the question is how do they dig holes better?" says D'Esposito, referring to today's open pit mines. "The other part is how do they meet society's needs sustainably?"

Several of the industry's leading companies have made strides in improving their mining and reclamation efforts and have come around to the idea that they need "a social license," or community agreement, before breaking ground on a new mine, he says. But standardized, binding commitments are still lacking.

"We're not looking for saints; we're looking for a system. The leadership of companies changes, so we're more interested in a series of certification systems, so you can evaluate each company," D'Esposito says.

But it remains to be seen if the mining industry will adopt such concrete measures. Operations around the globe continue to be controversial. Newmont, which has done so much in recent years to change the tenor of its conversation with communities, could expand its Yanacocha mine to Quilish Mountain yet. Alberto Benavides, the chief executive of Newmont's Peruvian partner Cia. de Minas Buenaventura, told the *New York Times* it was only a matter of time.

"We have the concession, and we have the land," he said. "I do not understand what social license means. I expect a license from the authorities, from the minister of mines. I expect a license from the regional government. I don't expect a license from the whole community."

Chapter Eight
Wal-Mart:
Corporate Villain or Hero?

It's getting so I can't go to a Wal-Mart without images of disappearing forests dancing in my head. Visions of leopards, tigers, Himalayan black bears, and other so-called "protected" species come to me while I wander the aisles. Their former habitat is everywhere: in the baby cribs and picture frames. Even the Popsicle sticks are made from wood removed—possibly stolen—from one of the world's last great old-growth forests.[1] The oak toilet seats may be the last souvenirs we'll have of Russia's once vast Far East woodlands, home to the Siberian tiger, the world's largest cat. There are only about 500 of these felines left in their dwindling forest home that provides not only for the tiger but, scientists believe, has also long supplied the planet with a buffer to global warming.

With nearly two hundred million customers, its low-price mantra, and ten-thousand-mile supply route, Wal-Mart is implicated in large-scale deforestation. And Wal-Mart and other big-box chains are under fire for trampling places closer to home as well.

Despite the company's celebrated "green awakening" and multimillion-dollar contributions and "partnerships" with green

149

organizations, Wal-Mart has a dismal U.S. environmental track record. The company stands accused of contributing to urban sprawl, air and water pollution, and the destruction of the natural habitats surrounding its stores, not to mention its impact on human communities. It has paid millions of dollars in fines for violating the Clean Water Act and hazardous materials storage and air pollution laws.

But the company's environmental sins were hardly a public relations issue when it surprised the world in late October 2005 with its unlikely entrance into the environmental movement. It had much bigger problems with labor unions, which decried the poverty-level wages and crummy health benefits, and Wal-Mart's union-busting ways. Lawsuits by former employees, called "associates" in Wal-Mart-speak, had sullied its all-American image with allegations of forced overtime without pay and lawsuits over sex and racial discrimination. Its sales growth had slowed, its stock price stalled. And increasingly, communities around the country were waging successful campaigns to keep it from opening up new stores in their towns. Wal-Mart, the world's largest retailer and the second most profitable company in the United States, was mired in deep image problems.

Green Beginnings

The groundwork for Wal-Mart's environmental awakening was laid earlier in the decade when CI's chief executive Peter Seligmann had a mutual friend introduce him to Wal-Mart's chairman S. Robson "Rob" Walton, son of the late founder Sam Walton. For the next four years, Seligmann took Walton and his two sons on exotic adventure-vacations. They dived among the unique wildlife of the Galápagos Islands, hiked Madagascar, and cruised Brazil's freshwater wetlands. Then one day, during a ten-day trip to Costa Rica, Seligmann finally popped the question: He asked for a meeting with H. Lee Scott Jr., Wal-Mart's president and chief executive.[2]

Walton wasn't sure it was a good idea. He told *Fortune* magazine in a rare interview that "we are really, really careful about mixing personal interests and the business." But he set up a meeting. Seligmann and a couple of his top lieutenants met with Scott in a conference room at Wal-Mart's Bentonville, Arkansas, headquarters in June 2004. As a result, Wal-Mart hired the company of a friend of Seligmann's, a former river-rafting guide named Jib Ellison, to measure Wal-Mart's environmental impact, according to *Fortune*.

By October of the following year, Scott made a speech titled "21st-Century Leadership" that shocked the world. In it Scott promised to move the company toward self-sufficiency by reducing the energy its stores use, improving the fuel efficiency of the country's largest fleet of trucks, streamlining product packaging, and nudging its suppliers to "green" their operations too. Scott said Wal-Mart would invest $500 million in technologies to reduce greenhouse gases and expressed a desire to steer the company toward total dependence on renewable energy sources one day.

Environmental campaigners trekked to Bentonville to see the Wal-Mart conversion first-hand. ED set up an office there. Even Greenpeace sent an emissary. Carl Pope, executive director of the Sierra Club, a board member of Wal-Mart Watch, a prominent critic of the retailer, had tangled with Wal-Mart over construction of its big-box stores. But even Pope urged critics to give the company a chance to prove it was serious.

Scott later admitted to *Fortune* that it started as "a defensive strategy" but has grown into a passion for him. The company adopted a credo that goes like this: "Wal-Mart is taking the Lead on Environmental Sustainability. At Wal-Mart, we know that being an efficient and profitable business and being a good steward of the environment are goals that can work together. Our environmental goals at Wal-Mart are simple and straightforward: To be supplied 100 percent by renewable energy; to create zero waste; and to sell products that sustain our resources and our environment."

Regardless of whether Scott was sincere, the PR value of Wal-Mart's ecological conversion was on prominent display in the company's 2007 progress report.[3] It only got mixed reviews from environmentalists, who pointed out that the company had, for the most part, only tackled the easiest of its environmental implications: reducing its carbon footprint, thus cutting back on its greenhouse gas emissions. Wal-Mart, too, admitted there was a lot left to be done. But it used the report to do a whole lot more than recount its successes on the environmental front. Wal-Mart also put a happy face on issues that were its real problems in 2005 and that continued to draw criticism: It gave itself high marks for what it characterized as improvements in areas like worker pay, health insurance, and diversity, despite the ongoing lawsuits and labor union campaigns against it.

The company also responded to its chief environmental critics. The report stated that Wal-Mart tries hard to lease or sell old stores before moving out, addressing criticism that abandoned big boxes blight the landscape. It also touted its $35 million "Acres for America" program with the National Fish and Wildlife Foundation, which requires the company to pay for the permanent conservation of at least one acre of critical wildlife habitat for every acre its stores inhabit.

The last point spoke to the Sierra Club and other environmentalists who have campaigned against big-box expansion whenever the new stores are seen as threats to ecosystems. Besides the more than one million square feet the average supercenter takes up, the gargantuan parking lots have been cited repeatedly by environmental protection officials around the country for allowing storm water contaminated with gas and other petroleum products to run off into surrounding ecosystems, damaging wetlands and killing fish. By promising to set aside an equal amount of land for environmental conservation, the company was speaking to critics who see Wal-Mart's aggressive expansion as dooming the country to a future with end-to-end strip malls.

The company acknowledged that it should perhaps do a better job of building bridges with communities before it breaks new ground. And the chain, once criticized for giving too little to charity, bragged about being recognized by the *Chronicle of Philanthropy* as the largest corporate cash contributor in America that year. Its makeover to good corporate citizenship seemed complete.

Not everyone was convinced, however.

Critics theorized that Wal-Mart was trying to split the alliance of labor and environmental groups that had formed to block the opening of some new stores and push for legislation that could limit the size of future supercenters and hurt its profitability. Its stores have more than doubled in size in the last few decades. While the company has scores of new stores on the drawing board, it has publicly committed to building only a tiny fraction of them to meet environmentally friendly standards. And, while the company says it tries to unload its abandoned supercenters, there are still hundreds of Wal-Marts sitting empty across the country at any given time.

They also pointed out that Wal-Mart's entire business strategy is predicated on people driving to their stores and purchasing cheap goods that quickly wear out and will end up in landfills, initiating the process all over again. Indeed, Patrick Jackman, a Bureau of Labor Statistics economist who studies Wal-Mart's prices as part of his job calculating the country's consumer price index, says the very disposability of its products has twice the negative effect on the environment than, say, sturdier products since it requires more raw materials to replace items that die young and more landfill space to hold all the defunct products.[4]

Writing in the online environmental journal *Grist* in March 2007, Stacy Mitchell called Wal-Mart's plans worse than greenwashing: "This cannot be dismissed as greenwashing. It's actually far more dangerous than that. Wal-Mart's initiatives have just enough meat to have distracted much of the environmental movement, along with most journalists and many ordinary people, from the fundamental fact that, as a system of distributing goods to people, big-box retailing is as intrinsically unsustainable as clear-cut logging is as a method of harvesting trees."[5]

While she lauded the company for owning up to its carbon footprint, Mitchell, a senior researcher at the anti-sprawl Institute for Local Self-Reliance, believes Wal-Mart's contribution to global warming goes far beyond what the company has calculated. The proliferation of the super chain across the landscape is a major factor fueling increases over the last few decades in the amount of time Americans spend in their cars, Mitchell argues. Along with the gasoline the cars guzzle is a massive amount of greenhouse gas emitted by Wal-Mart shoppers that the company hasn't even begun to contemplate in its carbon footprint, she says.

Big-Box Impact

To be fair to Wal-Mart, it's not the only big retailer with a harsh impact on the planet. Costco, Home Depot, Lowe's, IKEA, Macy's, and other big retailers have also been named by activist groups and journalists as accessories to environmental crimes.

Researchers from TerraChoice Environmental Marketing published a study in late 2007 examining the environmental claims advertised on the labels of more than one-thousand consumer goods sold at six leading big-box retail chains. They found all but one misleading or flatly untrue.[6]

Nearly 60 percent of the products were guilty of "the hidden trade-off"—they touted one environmentally friendly attribute but ignored other unfriendly considerations that cancelled out the positives. For instance, paper towels and other paper products touted their recycled content, but glossed over the air and water pollution and global warming impacts of their manufacturing process.

More than a quarter of the products offered no proof of the environmental claims made on the labels, while 11 percent made such broad claims researchers concluded they would likely be misunderstood by consumers. Other products advertised themselves as free of certain environmentally damaging chemical compounds, but failed to mention those chemicals had been illegal in this country for nearly three decades. Some cited certifications and standards that don't exist or misrepresented existing ones. Then, there were items that confused organic with environmentally friendly, the study concluded.

While organic farming may be gentler on the Earth, it has been linked to the destruction of natural habitats in some places. Because of the boom in demand for organic produce coupled with a certification process that requires farmers to prove their fields have been free of chemical pesticides and fertilizers for years before they are eligible to sell their products under the official "organic" label, organic farmers haven't always been the best conservation stewards. In parts of the United States, Latin America, and South Africa, some farmers have cleared previously untouched natural areas on their properties to increase acreage and reap immediate profits off the growing organic market.

Sustainable farming and fishing—other buzzwords among today's environmentally conscious consumers—have their own complications. As part of its eco-makeover, Wal-Mart has announced plans to supply its North American stores with wild-caught fresh and frozen fish that meets Marine Stewardship Council standards. But, as we've previously discussed, some observers say there are simply not enough MSC-certified fisheries to meet Wal-Mart demands, while others question whether the MSC standard is tough enough to ensure true sustainability of fish stocks.

The company also got into trouble with its farmed shrimp, a product not covered by the MSC, which only certifies wild-caught seafood. Wal-Mart and other giant retailers in the United States, Europe, and Japan get much of their farmed shrimp from Thailand. But the Thai industry has been plagued by environmental and human rights allegations. The shrimp farms have a record of destroying mangroves and polluting waterways,[7] as well as using child labor and employing Southeast Asian refugees in slavelike conditions in their operations.[8]

Apparently seeking to distance itself from the industry's problems, Wal-Mart helped create a new farmed-seafood certification process. It participated in drawing up new standards for shrimp farming by the industry-backed Global Aquaculture Alliance. Working with Conservation International and other environmental groups, the company pledged to certify all of its shrimp suppliers within eighteen months.

Thai shrimp—which started out as a public relations fiasco—is now listed as a "sustainability success story" on a Wal-Mart Web site. But concerns over greenwashing persist. John Hocevar, an oceans specialist with Greenpeace, and Jennifer Lash, of the Living Oceans Society, blasted the company for endorsing a standard that sets the bar too low.

"We're very concerned that with Wal-Mart being such a huge driving force in the market, there will be a rush to meet the lowest possible standards in order to feed the Wal-Mart machine," Lash told the *Financial Times*.[9]

Hocevar, who had traveled to meet with Wal-Mart officials shortly after their sustainability announcement, was also quoted in the story. When I called him later to ask about how Wal-Mart executives had responded to his critical view of the GAA, he told me that he received a phone call from Wal-Mart vice president Peter Redmond, an official he had met in Bentonville, the day after the article ran. Redmond thanked him for the feedback and promised the company would continue improving its sustainability record.

"That was the best of all worlds, we were sitting at the table with them and directly giving them our input but still feeling free to speak our mind and speak the truth," Hocevar says.[10] But the overtures haven't necessarily improved Wal-Mart's practices.

"They've come out very publicly saying they want to be a sustainable company and sell sustainable seafood. They also want to continue to sell lots of shrimp because they are making a lot of money off of it. So they want to find a way, at the very least, that makes it sound like they are exercising due diligence and doing the best they can," Hocevar says. "But when a large company like Wal-Mart is basically telling certifiers that 'we want to sell fifty million pounds of certified product,' there is an awful lot of pressure to cut corners—to sell things as they are—rather than to change the status quo much."

On the other end of the "sustainability" debate, the Thai shrimp farm industry didn't react well to Wal-Mart's greening efforts. They protested in the streets after publication of a *Wall Street Journal* article headlined: "The New Wal-Mart Effect: Cleaner Thai Shrimp Farms." The Thai business owners didn't appreciate allegations that their operations were not up to international environmental and social standards.[11]

Greening the Supply Chain

Greening the supply chain was the first things on the Scott's agenda in 2005. He laid out his vision in a speech to suppliers at a business conference on October 20, four days before he unveiled the rest of the company's sustainability plan: "The factories in China are going to end up having to be held up to the same standards as the factories in the U.S. There will be a day of reckoning for retailers. If somebody wakes up and finds out that children that are down the river from that factory where you save 3 cents a foot in the cost of garden hose are developing cancers at a significant rate so that the American public can save 3 cents a foot, those things won't be tolerated and they shouldn't be tolerated," Scott told them before announcing that he would be getting on a plane to Shanghai to talk with the company's suppliers and Chinese government officials to encourage environmentally sound manufacturing practices.[12]

Wal-Mart has more than sixty-eight thousand suppliers. It doesn't say how many are in each country, but several watchdog groups allege that the bulk of Wal-Mart's merchandise is made in small Chinese factories. For corroboration, they point to Xu Jun, Wal-Mart-China's director of external affairs, who told the *China Daily* newspaper in November 2004 that "if Wal-Mart were an individual economy, it would rank as China's eighth-biggest trading partner."[13] But the country's atrocious environmental and human rights record is also widely known.

The changes Scott promised have, so far, not been as far reaching as promised. Within six months of the announcement, he appeared to be backing away from the commitment. When asked if it wouldn't require rethinking the entire ten-thousand-mile supply chain to achieve sustainability, Scott demurred.[14]

"You know I think clearly there will be challenges there. But today I will tell you our focus is more on the size of the products for the moment, which has impacts on the energy intensity of our supply chain," Scott said, launching into the story of how the company had convinced reluctant laundry detergent makers to move to smaller, more concentrated products that clean the same amount of loads but take up half the packaging.

The shift to smaller bottles requires fewer trucks to transport them from factory to store, at a significant reduction in greenhouse gas emissions. The smaller packaging had been widely praised as an example of the company's willingness to convince manufacturers to join them in adopting a more sustainable mind-set.

But what about the thornier issues with suppliers spread out across the globe? As globalization has led multinational corporations to source their products from increasingly far-flung locations, activists have called on them to be more responsible global players.

Oxfam International has named the world's largest grocery retailers such as France's Carrefour, Adhold of the Netherlands, and Wal-Mart as part of the commodities crisis and challenged them to match their practices to the corporate social responsibility rhetoric.[15] The international relief organization linked depressed commodities prices paid to poor farmers in developing countries, where millions survive on less than one dollar a day, to consumers in rich countries, who ultimately buy those commodities in the form of cappuccinos, chocolate bars, and cotton T-shirts. Noting that Wal-Mart and other multinational retail food chains control a large and growing slice of supermarket sales around the world, Oxfam said it was up to them to use their market clout to ensure farmers were paid fairly and that factory workers enjoy labor conditions that comply with international standards.

Another report commissioned by Friends of the Earth Netherlands and two other Dutch organizations connected European supermarkets to rainforest removal and human rights abuses such as forced labor—modern-day slavery—in the Brazilian interior. The report traced soybeans grown on former rainforest and savannah land in the Amazon and Cerrado regions of Brazil to European poultry farms, where the beans ended up in the chicken feed. The chicken ended up on Dutch dinner tables.[16]

The Environmental Investigation Agency, meanwhile, posed as foreign buyers and met with Wal-Mart's Chinese wood product suppliers—the same companies Wal-Mart two years earlier promised to green. The result was a scathing report accusing Wal-Mart of turning a blind eye to suppliers who use timber removed illegally from several of the world's last great forests.[17] While the company has adopted a strong policy against the use of illegally and unsustainably logged timber, EIA investigators concluded company executives didn't really want to know where 83 percent of their wood products hailed from. This "no questions asked" behavior had emboldened suppliers to ignore the company's environmental standards, at the same time they cleaved closely to price and quality requirements, which Wal-Mart executives did not neglect.

China has finished off much of its own forests, leading to devastating environmental catastrophes such as the 1998 Yangtze River deluge that left more than three thousand people dead and fourteen million homeless. Now, Chinese manufacturers have turned to shady foreign wood suppliers, fueling deforestation in Russia, Indonesia, Papua New Guinea, and elsewhere. "China's sources for hardwood log imports reads like a 'Who's Who' of countries with problems with illegal logging," concluded one study commissioned by the American Forest & Paper Association.[18]

In only about a decade—the same period in which Wal-Mart dramatically expanded its foreign product sourcing—China became the world's leading importer of logs and other raw wood and the world's largest exporter of finished wood products. They end up at Wal-Mart and other big-box retailers largely in the United States and Europe.[19]

In example after example cited by EIA, Wal-Mart showed special attention to the cost and quality of items produced in China, demanding inspections of eight in every ten products at one factory. Despite the company's policy against the use of illegally begotten logs, several Chinese manufacturing executives told EIA's undercover investigators, posing as potential buyers, that Wal-Mart never asks where the wood comes from.

At a factory in southern China, the exporter told EIA representatives that the company had explored purchasing raw wood from Pennsylvania, but pressure to keep costs down killed the deal. So the company continues to get its wood, with few questions asked, from the Suifenhe, a timber hub on the Chinese border with Russia. The owner of a company that sends two cargo containers a month of Popsicle sticks to stock Wal-Mart craft aisles told investigators that even by keeping costs low by using birch of questionable origin from a Russian mill, she has struggled to turn a profit under the terms of her long-term fixed price contract with Wal-Mart. When EIA's undercover agents pressed one executive at a Chinese baby crib manufacturer about the origin of the raw materials, she said Wal-Mart has never asked about where the wood came from— her response was: "No, no, never, never." She said the factory kept no records of the wood's origins and it had never been an issue with its customer. "We already made many many pieces for Wal-Mart, so we know the standard."[20]

Wal-Mart was contacted and given the opportunity to comment on the EIA allegations. In response, the company provided the following statement, first published in the wake of the nonprofit's December 2007 report:

"Sustainable wood sourcing is important to our business and our customers. We have and will continue to encourage and advise our supplier partners to source from sustainable and ethical sources. Earlier this year, Wal-Mart published guidelines for our Wood Furniture Supplier Preference Program. These guidelines encourage all of our suppliers to embrace transparency for wood fiber and raw materials by 2010. Through this program, Wal-Mart already gives preference to suppliers who can verify their use of sustainably harvested and recycled wood fiber. When we discover sustainable sourcing or factory issues, we are committed to seeking alternatives, or even removing products from shelves. This was the case when we let our suppliers know that we would stop buying cypress mulch—bagged or forested in Louisiana—because of concerns around the loss of cypress forests along the coasts in that state. We have reached out to our supplier community for further insight."

The Big Cost of "Low Cost"

Given the company's public commitment to finding ways to address global warming, it seems ironic that Wal-Mart is implicated in abetting the disappearance of the world's last great natural forests, which scientists believe play such a crucial role in removing carbon from the atmosphere. The company trumpets its switch to compact "double-roll" toilet paper, a move that saves 31,000 trees a year by reducing shipping and packaging impacts. But critics charge that it has given little thought to the toilet seats being carved out of oak and ash taken under suspicious conditions from Russian forests.

The company has also been criticized for selling Chinese-made toys and other products that allegedly caused the deaths and injuries of babies. Newspaper reports have also chronicled the existence of lead in jewelry, tainted wheat gluten in its private-label doggie biscuits, and salmonella in snack foods made in China and sold by Wal-Mart. After the toy scare, Wal-Mart announced it would start conducting independent testing of its products. Undercutting that move, however, were newspaper reports in several states that Wal-Mart continued to sell some recalled products.

In all those cases and many other controversial issues facing Wal-Mart, the common denominator is its low cost, low price mantra. The company accused of driving the world's poorest farmers deeper into poverty, fueling deforestation that could finish off the world's forests, and risking the lives and well-being of its customers, is the same one that says a $2-an-hour pay increase to help lift its employees above the poverty line would decimate its profit margin.[21] This seems a curious stance from one of the most profitable companies in the United States with net profits of more than $10 billion for each of the last several years, making it second only to ExxonMobil. In 2007, the company posted a net income of $12.7 billion on $375 billion in sales.

Scott and other top executives make millions of dollars in annual salaries plus millions more in company stock. In 2007, Scott's total compensation came to nearly $30 million. Sam's heirs, meanwhile, have been called "America's richest family." According to *Forbes* magazine, their collective wealth reaches $65 billion. That's not counting the $1 billion used to endow the Walton Family Foundation, a move that marked a major turnaround after years in which social critics complained about the stinginess of the Walton family.

But improving the company's environmental and labor records would not necessarily take a bite out of any of those fortunes. Such improvements could actually be good for its business and its stock price. A New York consulting firm that studies reputational issues says changing its bad reputation could bolster Wal-Mart's bottom line. Communications

Consulting Worldwide, a boutique consulting firm that studied Wal-Mart's stock at the request of *Business Week* magazine, charted its press coverage and stock price performance, then compared the results to rival Target Corp.[22] The consultants concluded that if Wal-Mart could improve its reputation on par with that of Target, its stock would be worth 4.9 percent, or $2.35, more a share, translating into an additional $10 billion in market capitalization.

Some argue it matters little how much of Wal-Mart's new "green" awakening is true and how much is PR hype, because the rhetoric alone signifies a huge shift in attitude as environmental consciousness goes mainstream. While there may be some truth to that, it won't resolve the real environmental threats at our doorstep. Wal-Mart must do more than just press its suppliers on price. It must go beyond the policy statements and take steps to ensure its suppliers abide by international environmental and labor standards. Reducing its carbon footprint is a worthy goal, particularly for a company as large as Wal-Mart. But those efforts will hardly make up for finishing off the world's last great forests, which provide a natural bulwark against climate change. Once the old-growth forests are gone, which some experts say could happen before the end of this century, they are gone for good. There will be no more endangered-timber baby cribs, toilet seats, and Popsicle sticks. One way or another, Wal-Mart and the rest of the world are going to have to come up with another way.

While the company provides forceful rhetoric about the importance of environmental sustainability, there are many indications that it has so far fallen short on putting its corporate values into action. Perhaps even the company's own executives aren't sure if their efforts are truly green or merely greenwashing. As is the case at many corporations that have taken up the sustainability mantle, there seems to be internal debate raging inside the company.

"Working with Wal-Mart is a little like dealing with Dr. Jekyll and Mr. Hyde," Michael Marx, executive director of Corporate Ethics International, told the *Washington Post* after helping Wal-Mart complete its eco-critique in the fall of 2007.[23] "Environmentally, I really believe it wants to do the right thing. The Mr. Hyde Wal-Mart often turns around and does terrible things to totally undercut all its good work."

Chapter Nine

Green Building or Greenwashing?

In 1999, Centex Corp., one of the country's leading home-builders, struck a deal with TNC that netted the group $35 for every house Centex built. Since the company builds nearly forty thousand homes a year, TNC made several million dollars. And, it later bestowed conservation leadership awards on Centex in 2000 and again in 2002. The homebuilder, for its part, advertised the relationship with the country's largest land conservation organization as proof of its stature as a "green" company.

But what about two of the biggest threats to the environment: deforestation and urban sprawl?

In recent decades, U.S. metropolitan areas have seen land developed at twice the pace of population growth, faster in some places. Centex subdivisions from New York to California are the very definition of sprawl. If after buying a new Centex home atop land that was once a forest, the lucky homeowners head to Lowe's for home improvement purchases and fill the new abode with wooden furniture from IKEA or Wal-Mart, they are very likely contributing to decimation of some distant rainforest, as well.

The environmental impact of human consumption patterns is not lost on many companies. In its 2007 sustainability report, Wal-Mart puts it succinctly when it says "an area of forest the size of a football field is cleared every second. That's 86,400 football fields a day. In the tropical forests, it's estimated that 50,000 species become extinct each year because of deforestation."[1]

To allay customer concern over environmental degradation, the largest retail giants strive to establish reputations as "green" companies. Home Depot has donated to CF and partnered with TNC, as has its rival in the home improvement market, Lowe's. IKEA claims WWF as its "cause-related marketing" partner. Wal-Mart has a bevy of relationships with CI, ED, NRDC, and WWF. Centex has given millions of dollars to CF and TNC since 1999. Its competitor, Pulte Homes Inc., is on TNC's International Leadership Council, as is Plum Creek Timber Co., which engages both in logging and homebuilding. Every one of those retailers has been implicated in selling wood products derived from the violent and corrupt international timber smuggling trade. Each of the homebuilders, meanwhile, has built its business on urban sprawl.

Since 1990, sprawl has consumed an average of two million acres of rural land a year, an area equal to the size of Pennsylvania.[2] Sprawl's impact on ecosystems is clear: More than two dozen different types of ecosystems have virtually disappeared since European settlement of North America. Today, nearly two thousand species are on federal threatened or endangered species lists.[3] Low-density housing developments and roads that cut across migratory corridors have led to the breakdown of once thriving ecosystems, leaving species homeless. While we most often hear the aesthetic objections to sprawl—the cookie-cutter subdivisions and the ugly strip malls—it is easy to forget its victims all over the country, from the Florida panther to Arizona's ancient ironwood, from the creosote bush to the saguaro cactus. New England's tiny piping plover has lost much of its Atlantic Coast nesting grounds. The hawksbill sea turtle is in decline in the Gulf of Mexico. The nocturnal lynx is disappearing from its northwestern U.S. habitat. Urban sprawl is one of the primary culprits in the gradual demise of the tallgrass prairies that once covered portions of fourteen states from Texas to Minnesota. They have been reduced to a tiny fraction of their former landscape, according to TNC, which has established a preserve in Oklahoma to assure this unique American landscape doesn't slip away entirely.

The extinction rate has sped up exponentially, largely due to habitat degradation and destruction, according to research conducted by TNC even as it was making money off Centex's building boom. Ironically, fears about the effects of sprawling new suburbs on once pristine landscapes was one of the reasons TNC was established more than half a century ago. Things have undoubtedly grown worse since then, creating debate and dissent inside the organization about its direction at the same time its leaders were raking in the Centex dough.

"Sprawl is without a doubt the most pervasive threat. Failure to recognize and address this threat on all levels, not just buying land, will result in a mission-critical policy failure," wrote one TNC scientist in a 2001 survey, obtained by the *Washington Post* and published in the paper's scathing 2003 series on TNC, in which it took the nonprofit to task for, among other things, its partnership with Centex.[4]

Sprawl's Impact

One of the factors propelling the spiraling outward of the country's metropolitan areas is that it's cheaper and easier for corporations like Centex to build new homes on undeveloped land than to wrangle with city planners and feisty community groups in older urban areas, where strict rules and savvy constituents tend to keep a tight rein on builders. That's not to discount the urban renewal transforming the centers of many U.S. cities in recent years. Older cities like Boston, San Francisco, Chicago, and New York have seen a renaissance that has turned blighted neighborhoods into expensive and trendy new urban villages. However, much faster growth has occurred in areas increasingly far from city centers.

The suburbs are home to six in every ten Americans. Nearly half of those suburbanites live in the "exurbs," bedroom communities sixty or seventy miles from metropolitan centers. With the country's population expected to grow by 50 percent, adding 130 million people by mid-century, more sprawl seems on the horizon.[5]

Exurb growth has often been seen as a boon to local economies. But that's short-sighted, critics say. Unbridled housing development also drains public finances by requiring new roads, schools, and sewer systems. Sprawling suburban developments are also notorious for their traffic woes. Bulldozing of wetlands, parklands, and woods, meanwhile, is linked to declining air and water quality, flooding, and erosion, not to mention the loss of recreation areas and scenic vistas with their intangible but important aesthetic and even spiritual value.

Habitat destruction, however, isn't the only negative environmental effect of sprawl. A third of all carbon dioxide emissions in this country come from vehicles. As suburbs have spread farther and farther from city centers, where most of the jobs are, the nation's commute times have steadily lengthened. According to the U.S. Census Bureau, more than half the U.S. workforce crosses county lines to get from home to work these days. The number of people spending more than three hours a day commuting has increased 95 percent since 1990.

Sprawl has locked many Americans into a car-centric lifestyle that is cooking the planet.

The more our communities sprawl, the harder it will be to combat global warming, argues Ryan Avent, an economist and blogger who writes on public policy issues. In other countries, policymakers are already implementing ways to charge people based on how much they drive.[6] London has a congestion pricing fee for drivers who take their cars into the city's center on weekdays. Since the 1990s, Mexico City has combated its dangerous air pollution problem with the "one-day-without-a-car" program which requires drivers to keep their vehicles off city streets once a week or face stiff fines. Commuters, living in U.S. exurbs, with scant public transportation options and ever increasing prices at the pump, would likely resist similar efforts to curtail carbon emissions since it would further increase their commuting costs, Avent argues.

Construction and Logging Companies Tied to Conservation Groups						
Company	CF	CI	ED	TNC	NRDC	WWF-US
Centex	•			•		
Home Depot	•			•		•
International Paper Co.	•			•		
IKEA						•
Pulte Homes				•		

Company	CF	CI	ED	TNC	NRDC	WWF-US
Kiewit Pacific Co.	•					
Coyote Springs Investment	•					
Lowe's				•		
AFPA*	•					
Consolidated Paper	•					
Baskahegan						•
Georgia-Pacific				•		
MeadWestvaco				•		
Temple-Inland				•		
Weyerhaeuser Co.		•		•		
Plum Creek Timber				•		
Domtar				•		

Relationships include donations, partnerships, programs, projects, joint councils, and advisory boards. Sources: Web sites and tax returns of the organizations and corporations.
*American Forest & Paper Association

Endangered U.S. Timberland

The United States has lost more than a quarter of its forest cover since the times of the Pilgrims' landing, according to the U.S. Forest Service.[7] A vast swath of the country remains forested today, but most of it has been heavily logged. Not even public lands have been spared. Under an antiquated forest law, private logging companies have been harvesting timber inside the nation's forests for decades at a cost of more than a billion dollars a year in federally subsidized logging roads and other taxpayer-funded services to the timber industry. And, the figure does not include the environmental and biodiversity losses.

In addition to the public forests, more than half of the country's remaining 750 million acres is privately owned timberland. Many of the private forest owners are older people, nearing retirement age, according to one Forest Service study, which has raised the prospect of dramatic turnover in forest ownership as it is inherited by a younger generation, perhaps less tied to the land.

The nation's industrial forests, which make up about 13 percent of the total, have already experienced such a "land rush." Between 1995 and 2006, approximately three-quarters of the country's industrial forests—nearly fifty-one million acres, equal to more than twice the size of Maine—changed hands according to U.S. Forest Capital, an investor advisory firm that specializes in forestry.

Among the timber companies that cashed in is International Paper Company, once the country's largest timberland owner. International Paper has long professed its conservation values, sits on TNC's International Leadership Council, and labels its products with the logo of the Sustainable Forest Initiative, a certification and marketing program that claims to adhere to sustainable forestry standards, though questions have been raised about the veracity of those claims. When it sold nearly all of its U.S. forestlands in 2006, it negotiated partnership agreements with TNC and the CF. The deal preserves nearly three hundred thousand acres of ecologically rich land, including the last old-growth longleaf pine forest in the country, in exchange for $383 million.

While the company was toasted for its conservationist ethos, the rest of its vast holdings that spanned more than a dozen states face a more uncertain fate. The same year, International Paper sold more than five million acres of forestlands, nearly its entire holdings, for more than $6 billion. Most of the land went to Resource Management Service LLC, one of a new breed of timberland investment management firms that buy, sell, and manage land for institutional investors and other clients. Unlike the old timber companies that managed the forest as a source of raw materials over the long term, the objective of today's timber investment firms is to maximize shareholder profit. It's such a new phenomenon it's hard to say what kind of stewards these new forest owners will turn out to be.

For now, International Paper continues to log many of its former holdings under long-term agreements with the new owners. Whether those lands remain timberlands will depend on profitability, says Steven Chercover, a senior research analyst at DA Davidson & Co. in Portland, Oregon. Chercover notes that the new owners have already sold off portions of the nation's working forest. The subdivisions often end up as "the private playgrounds" of wealthy individuals. One casualty will be public access to the land. While logging companies traditionally allowed people to hike and camp on their timberlands, new owners, whether they be investment firms or wealthy individuals, are less likely to continue the tradition, he says.

"These companies have even less incentive to keep it as forest than the logging companies did," Chercover says of the new owners, who are legally bound to put shareholder value first. "There are zero guarantees that the land is going to be better managed than it was twenty years ago."

That's an alarming thought, considering the environmental complaints against logging companies like International Paper.

Scot Quaranda, a spokesman for the Dogwood Alliance, an umbrella group of environmental organizations working to stop the destructive practices of the forestry industry in the South, the most heavily logged region of the country, says the company is the worst actor in the industry. Not only has International Paper continued to convert natural forests into tree plantations where only a fraction of the former biodiversity can survive, its use of harmful chemicals and large-scale clear-cutting belies its conservationist rhetoric. "As far as we can tell, it's all talk and no action," Quaranda says.

Logging companies have long been the archenemies of environmental groups like the Dogwood Alliance. But there is another growing threat to the nation's timberlands. In areas with rising real estate values, International Paper and other logging companies are selling out to housing and resort developers and getting into the real estate business themselves. Grassroots environmental activists worry the future may look like Plum Creek Timber Company's fight in Maine's North Woods.

One of the country's largest timberland landlords, with nearly 8.2 million acres in eighteen states, Plum Creek is a member of TNC's International Leadership Council and professes a conservation ethos. It calls itself a timber company, but it is really a real estate investment trust (REIT) that both logs its timberland and converts choice tracts into residential and vacation homes. It's a lucrative business. For one thing, REITs pay much lower taxes than logging companies. And, there are other advantages: For instance, the company purchased land near Moosehead Lake in Maine in 1998 at timberland prices, considerably less than the company stands to gain if it gets approval for its plans to turn twenty thousand acres of forest into two resorts and nearly one thousand house lots.

Since Plum Creek first unveiled the idea in 2005, public outcry has shot down bids for approval from Maine's Land Use Regulatory Commission. The state's two largest environmental groups, Maine Audubon and the Natural Resources Council of Maine, have mounted an all-out campaign against the plans that they say would triple the number of people living in the area, seriously damaging wildlife habitat and the state's natural beauty.

Taking a page from the activists, the company launched its own petition drive in favor of the development and teamed up with regional business leaders and snowmobile clubs to form the Coalition to Preserve and Grow Northern Maine, a one-note organization created expressly to build community support for the Plum Creek plan. While the fight rages on, the company also lavished donations on area community groups and the local hospital, and has given scholarships to college-bound high school grads.

Such community courtship is now a staple in multimillion-dollar development fights. Centex raised eyebrows in 2006 when it offered the town of Warrenton, a northern Virginia suburb of Washington, D.C., a $22 million payment in exchange for approving plans to convert farmland into three hundred luxury homes. Industry specialists called the deal a bribe, though Centex defended it as "the cost of doing business."

It's an insightful comment when one considers that Centex has spent a total of $6 million on nature conservation efforts with TNC and CF since 1999.[8] Seen in the light of the Warrenton arrangement, the company purchased its "green" reputation for a mere fraction of what it was willing to pay to push through a single residential construction project.

But the Warrenton money turned out not to be such a good deal, after all. A few months later, the real estate market nose-dived. The company reneged on the offer and gave the town an ultimatum: If they wanted to keep the money, the community would have to approve a higher-density plan that members had already rejected. It called for building so many houses it would increase the town's population by nearly third.[9]

Greenwashing the Banks

While the giant homebuilding and retailing companies have proved able to respond quickly when specific evidence surfaces that could threaten their public images, they have shown reluctance to take more comprehensive action to improve their environmental footprint. Once stung by the wrath of a more militant group, instead of making substantive changes to their business practices and supply chains, corporations usually follow a familiar pattern: They buy a little "reputational insurance" from a high-profile conservation group. Besides the immediate PR windfall, they know the next time they end up in a fight with uncompromising environmentalists they can count on having a conservation heavyweight in their corner. For decades, militant environmental groups have fought with logging companies whenever chainsaws threatened endangered species. Those campaigns often sent lumber companies into the arms of the big conservation groups, as well.

Financial institutions have also been implicated in bankrolling illegal logging and residential sprawl. Besides joining the ranks of the partners, sponsor, and "stewards" of the conservation movement, some banks have made impressive environmental mea culpa gestures in recent years. Citigroup, for instance, has pledged $50 billion over a decade in investments and project financing to reduce global carbon emissions. The announcement in May 2007 wowed business and environmental circles and was interpreted as yet another sign of the U-turn corporate America has made to embrace environmental sustainability. Still, many activist groups remain wary, pointing out that the money represents a tiny fraction of the bank's total lending. Besides, the investment is not an act of charity but a foray into the emerging clean-energy industry that could pay off handsomely for the company, in addition to distracting critics from the fact that the bank—and its rivals for the "environmental steward" moniker—hasn't done much to "green" its lending portfolio. Citigroup, for instance, is helping to finance a BP oil pipeline project passing through the pristine Borjomi Nature Reserve in the country of Georgia, and a Brazilian tree plantation and pulp mill operation named for contributing to the destruction of that country's Atlantic Forest, among other "dodgy deals" monitored by Bank Track, an international network of people and nonprofit groups that keep tabs on large corporate deals.

Among Bank Track's contributors is the Rain Forest Action Network (RAN), the San Francisco–based environmental group that has orchestrated protests against new coal power plants outside the local branches of several large U.S. banks providing financing. RAN, smaller and more aggressive than the conservation outfits like WWF and TNC, started out a few decades ago by opposing rainforest destruction one logging operation, oil field, open pit mine, and agribusiness expansion at a time. Eventually, the group realized they could have a wider impact by targeting the banks, says Rebecca Tarbotton, RAN's global finance campaign director.

"If you follow the money, it actually comes back to a small number of banks that are bankrolling all of it," she says. "And the banks have customers," in cities and towns across America who tend to react with dismay when they learn their savings accounts are being used to finance the Amazon deforestation and other environmentally damaging corporate activities, she says.

Increasingly banks have adopted due diligence guidelines meant to help them steer clear of projects that could potentially damage their reputations. But even banks with written policies have been involved in scandals. The U.K.-based human rights groups Global Witness and the Forest Peoples Project have denounced the British bank HSBC for violating its own forest sector guidelines by providing investment banking services to the Malaysian timber company Samling in 2007. HSBC, together with two other banks, handled Samling's offering on the Hong Kong stock exchange that year, despite long-running allegations that the company is involved in illegal logging. For nearly a decade, Global Witness has dogged Samling with allegations of illegally taking timber from tropical rainforests. The British human rights group alleges that Samling has decimated forests in Cambodia, Papua New Guinea, Guyana, and Malaysia. And, the Forest Stewardship Council revoked the sustainable forestry certification of Samling's subsidiary Barama in Guyana in 2007. Samling has denied it is involved in illegal logging. Despite losing the FSC certification, a Samling spokesman told the BBC, the company is moving in the right direction.[10] The activists, however, say, if HSBC had been following its tough due diligence policy, the allegations alone should have derailed the deal.

As it dawned on banking executives that their institutional reputations were on the line, many have banded together to create new initiatives such as the Equator and Carbon Principals. So far, however, the commitments haven't gone much beyond paying lip service to the problems, says Tarbotton. RAN and other activist groups complain the banks that adhere to the Equator Principal, which governs project financing in the developing world, have been reluctant to publicly report enough information about the projects they finance to evaluate whether they are following the rules. Meanwhile, the Carbon Principals, drawn up by banking officials with the help of NRDC and ED, lack binding obligations that could lead to meaningful reductions in carbon dioxide and other greenhouse gas emissions by the banks' clients which include the nation's largest power companies, Tarbotton says.

Nevertheless, the banks that have "engaged" environmental groups in recent years deserve credit, for taking steps—albeit small ones—in the right direction, Tarbotton says. Many other financial sector companies have simply refused to examine questions involving the environment and human rights.

The same praise could be offered of all the companies that donate to big conservation groups and have publicly identified themselves as environmentalists. Their willingness to go public with their values is commendable, but whether those values are reflected throughout their operations is the real test. Today, sadly, too many self-professed environmentalist corporations have shown reluctance to put their values fully into action.

The International Illegal Logging Trade

In developing countries, sprawl looks a lot different than it does in the United States. The megacities of Africa, Asia, and Latin America have certainly burst out into surrounding countryside in the last half century. In poor countries, however, sprawl is not just a suburban—or even an exurban—phenomenon. It also involves the gradual transformation of once impenetrable forests first by timber, oil, or mining prospectors. Once the roads are opened, agriculture expands and urbanization follows.

Just about anywhere with remaining forest stocks—the South American Amazon, the Russian Far East, the equatorial region of Africa—is being stripped of its timber today. Not all the unsustainable forestry is being done illegally. Much of it is sanctioned by governments motivated by development aspirations or just plain corruption. But illegal logging, controlled by violent and organized criminal syndicates, is an international blight responsible for shocking environmental and human rights abuses on several continents.

The World Bank has estimated developing countries are facing as much as $15 billion a year in lost assets and revenue due to illegal logging.[11] As much as 60 percent of Russian hardwoods are leaving the country illegally, while nearly half of Brazilian exports may be illegal, and all of Indonesia's log and more than half of the country's plywood exports are likely of illegal extraction, according to another study commissioned by the American Forest & Paper Association.

In recent years, leading industry groups like the forest association have issued policies condemning illegal logging. And U.S. and European lawmakers have begun to debate how best to arrest outlaw deforestation. In fact, in the spring of 2008 the U.S. Congress was working on landmark legislation that would make the United States the first country in the world to ban the importation and sale of illegally logged timber. Individual companies have also started to change their practices. After being hammered by environmental activists, Home Depot spent two years researching the origins of all the wood products on its shelves and now says it can vouch for the legal origin of every broom handle and piece of lumber it sells. The company carried out the same type of supply chain audit IKEA has said it lacks the resources to undertake. Today, however, there are few legal obstacles to selling blatantly stolen timber in E.U. markets.

Even measures taken to combat the smuggling have shown less than stellar results. Undercover agents working for the non-profit EIA tracked more than two shipments a day of Indonesian sawn timber into the United States, despite a ban on those products that should have kept the wood out of the country. In all, EIA reported 1,570 shipments of the Indonesian wood during a two-year period ended in November 2006.[12] According to the nonprofit investigators, 10 percent of U.S. annual imports come from illegally logged timber. It's a $3.8 billion annual trade in this country alone, says EIA. As much as half of the European Union's timber imports are at risk of being illegal, Friends of the Earth asserts. As previously noted, the retailers themselves acknowledge that products made from illegally acquired timber end up on their shelves.

EIA, Greenpeace, and Friends of the Earth have published detailed reports tracing timber from illegally logged rainforests to manufacturing operations in China, then on to the United States and Europe, where most consumers are unaware they are buying products tainted by theft, violence, and murder. Such coveted wood as Central and South America's big-leaf mahogany, for instance, has spawned an illegal industry that uses forced labor. Unsustainably harvested teak coming out of Burma, meanwhile, helps fund the country's brutal military junta.

Smugglers use a variety of methods to escape detection. Some have been caught forging documents. Others have been observed loading containers in the Indonesian forest to escape scrutiny. Many U.S. and European retailers are either unaware or unwilling to take responsibility for the problem, activists say. When Greenpeace questioned Netherlands retailers, only four of three hundred timber traders and flooring retailers could prove their wood was logged legally. The national trade association representing the flooring dealers defended their members by arguing that they were not responsible since they bought the wood through middlemen.[13]

The Economics of Stolen Rainforests

Stolen timber is a booming business because of the profits to be had. Illegally cut merbau from Indonesia's Papua Province, for instance, was worth $120 per cubic meter at port in 2005. By the time it reached China it was worth twice as much. It sold for $2,200 in the solid-wood flooring aisle of a U.S. retail store, according to one report by EIA.[14]

But the illegal trade also hurts timber dealers wherever it's sold by depressing wood prices across the board. Suppliers, who play by the rules, lose out on sales because their wood costs more. It is more expensive because of the environmental regulations, taxes, tariffs, labor standards, and other costs of doing business that the smugglers avoid.

Because of inadequate legislation outlawing the importation of illegal timber, once it enters the country a retailer's biggest nightmare isn't the police; it's crusading environmental activists. Groups like Rainforest Action Network and EIA have gone this route from time to time. Corporations, fearful of having public opinion turned against them, are often quick to make concessions. Home Depot and Lowe's took dowel rods from illegal Indonesian ramin and merbau flooring off their shelves after EIA contacted them with information about the illicit origins of both products. Several big-box chains have made public pledges—amid much PR fanfare—to sell only legally logged wood and shift their purchasing toward sources that are certifiably sustainable, only to quietly backpedal years later when they failed to meet their own timetables.[15]

The sustainability of those eco-labels has been hotly debated, anyway. But, what about more philosophical objections: Do we really need to use mahogany, redwood, and cedar, among the most majestic, ancient, and towering trees in their respective forests, as flooring and backyard decks, and for even less illustrious uses? Cedar, for instance, is sold as gerbil bedding and as a natural deodorizer for dresser drawers and golf shoes—rather ignoble ends for trees that can live a thousand years.

Violence and Murder
Associated with Illegal Timber Operations

When forests are cut down, loggers leave behind wasteland where diverse primary rainforest plants and animals once lived. After the habitat becomes pasture or plantation land, few of those creatures can survive. Most of the local people, usually indigenous tribes who have lived off the land for millennia, are also left without a livelihood. At their own peril, they often become outspoken. Many have paid with their lives for standing up to organized crime and politically connected timber barons.

While they hail from different parts of the globe, their stories are disturbingly similar. Kelesau Naan, the headman of a Malaysian indigenous tribe and outspoken leader in the community's battle against the logging of the Upper Baram Penan rainforest, was found beaten to death in January 2008. His was the latest in a series of extra-judicial killings and other human rights violations against illegal-logging opponents in the region. Members of the Honduran grassroots Environmental Movement of Olancho faced a similar campaign against their efforts to save their forest. At least five activists have been killed and other members have received repeated death threats, according to EIA. In Mexico, a Greenpeace activist was killed in May 2007 while gathering information on logging gangs. In Brazil the same year, a group of young Greenpeace activists were attacked by a mob of loggers and threatened with lynching. Earlier in the decade, Indonesian journalist Abi Kusno Nachran was hijacked by a gang that attacked him with machetes, hacking off several fingers on both hands, nearly removing his right arm before leaving him for dead. His assailants were widely believed to be doling out payback for a notorious timber baron, according to EIA. Several of the logging kingpin's illegal timber shipments had been seized by Indonesian authorities after Nachran exposed his role as financier to illegal loggers.[16] These are only a few of the documented atrocities being committed to bring us cheap plywood, dining room tables, and wooden toilet seats. The assault against Nachran led to international outrage, but experts say such violence is all too common against those who challenge powerful illegal logging interests.

Illegal crime syndicates, local police, and military officers have all been implicated in the illicit forest trade in many countries. From the Russian Mafia, said to be running operations in that country's Far East forests, to law enforcers in Papua New Guinea, illegal logging operations often use forced labor, political intimidation, and violence. Bribery and impunity, however, make it hard to stop the problems at their source.

In the western region of Papua, Indonesia, the Knasaimos people have faced similar struggles with intruders intent on stripping their forests of internationally valuable timber. According to the testimony of Frederick Sagisolo, traditional chief of the Knasaimos people, the loggers first arrived in 1999 looking for meranti, a wood comparable to oak and used in general construction, flooring, furniture, and cabinetwork. Three years later, when all the meranti was gone, they started cutting merbau trees, with the backing of a local military officer. Sagisolo says when his community complained about the illegal extractions, the local government issued a map that gave the outsiders rights to log even in areas sacred to the Knasaimos. "We asked 'why do you do this?' and the company said it was allowed because of the map."[17]

The operation was finally halted in 2005 by an Indonesian government crackdown, Operation Forests Forever, the biggest enforcement action against the timber robbers in Indonesian history according to Jago Wadley, an EIA forest campaigner. The police action resulted in 180 arrests, including the heads of the provincial forestry offices in Papua and West Papua and timber company bosses and senior police officials. More than 1,500 law enforcers were sent into the illegal logging epicenters of the country. They seized half a million cubic meters of logs, seriously reducing the international supply of timber by halting illegal log exports overnight, according to Wadley.

Still, much damage was already done. Today, merbau is on the IUCN's Red List of endangered species.[18] According to Friends of the Earth, the island of New Guinea is the only place left that still has enough merbau to warrant commercial logging, the rest having been ripped out of the forests in other parts of the region only in the last decade. That's how fast ancient rainforests can disappear. Today, merbau survives mostly as exterior doors in the Netherlands and expensive flooring in other parts of Europe and the United States, according to Friends of the Earth and Greenpeace, which have both investigated the illegal trade.

In the Knasaimos region, the military officer protecting the operation on Knasaimos lands left the area after the government crackdown and the company was forced to stop, according to Sagisolo, who later teamed with EIA and its Indonesia partner Telapak to make a film about the effects of illegal logging.

Sponsored by EIA, he traveled to Belgium to talk to European Union officials about the problem.

"However it was not all good," Wadley says. "Illegality still takes place and involves many of the same people, including enforcement and other government officials." He says today smugglers have changed operating procedures, substituting logs for sawn timber. They often take the wood to other islands in Indonesia before exporting to throw investigators off their trail, and take other evasive measures "to hide the goods."

No one arrested in the operation was ever convicted. And, much of the timber that had been seized was sold at auction to the same companies charged with illegally removing it from the forests—leading many to assume the auctions had been rigged. Meanwhile the communities, which had been among the first to try and stop the illegal timber trade, had their traditional logging rights revoked by the government, says Wadley.

Carbon Emissions and Sequestration

Beyond the human rights atrocities, there's plenty of reason why those of us living in the comfort of the developed world should care about what goes on in the forests of Indonesia and the Amazon. These last large forests provide the planet with important climate regulation "services" that we need in order to live. Besides removing harmful carbon dioxide for the atmosphere, healthy forests play a crucial role in maintaining fresh air, water, and soils, and stable climates.

Worldwide, deforestation is responsible for nearly a fifth of global greenhouse gas emissions annually.[19] Besides the impact of cutting down the trees, the construction of logging roads and settlement activity that follows increase emissions. According to one study on the effects of logging in the Democratic Republic of Congo, building the roads, milling of the logs, and other activity involved in removing the timber from the forest created 2.5 times the carbon emissions caused by the initial logging.[20]

As the world warms, conservationists are bracing for increased extinctions of species that fail to adapt to changing climate conditions and find themselves with no place to go. Their last refuges, the world's national parks and other protected areas, are bracing for dramatic changes. More than half of the protected areas worldwide face climate changes. In some places the climates will be completely different by 2100. A few will experience conditions previously unknown to Earth.[21]

What is hard to reconcile is that the organizations most concerned with the impact of climate change on endangered species are the same groups taking millions of dollars from corporations that are major players in deforestation and urban sprawl.

Executives at the big conservation groups have frequently gone on record arguing that their partnerships with loggers have made the timber barons more conscious of their impact on endangered species, led them to reduce clear-cutting, build fewer access roads, and make other eco-sensitive changes to the way they work. But their counterparts at the state and local levels hold markedly different points of view.

Weyerhaeuser Company is a Washington State–based timber conglomerate that has given millions to nature conservation efforts. The company is on TNC's International Leadership Council and CI's Business & Biodiversity Council but, as we've already established, that is not necessarily an indication of green business practices.

The Seattle Audubon Society and Weyerhaeuser Company have clashed in court over the fate of the endangered spotted owl and feuded over the role clear-cutting may have played in December 2007 floods in southwest Washington State, where mudslides rode down heavily logged mountain slopes, sweeping debris on communities downstream of the Chehalis River. The Seattle environmentalists also tried to get Weyerhaeuser kicked out of the Sustainable Forests Initiative (SFI), a green labeling organization it helped set up.[22]

Maine environmentalists made a similar move against Plum Creek Timber. In the separate cases, local groups accused the companies of pretending to be "green" and demanded they lose their rights to use the initiative's label. But, so far, the Sustainable Forests Initiative has declined to oust them from the certification program.[23]

The brouhaha highlights complaints about the growing proliferation of so-called sustainable labels.

Certification Confusion

Two-thirds of the wood consumed in the United States each year is used in home construction and renovation. Much of the rest of the world's timber goes into paper and pulp. Both are eligible for the growing number of sustainable forestry certifications. The top contenders are the SFI and the older and more respected FSC label, the Forest Stewardship Council certificate (Chapter Three). The Council was formed by a coalition of environmental groups and logging companies in 1993, a year ahead of the SFI. It has more stringent rules than SFI, which has been widely criticized as a creature of the logging industry.[24]

The SFI was established by the American Forest & Paper Association. And, while the SFI claims to be independent, executives of four of the country's largest logging companies—including Weyerhaeuser and Plum Creek—have seats on its board of directors. Besides letting the loggers make up the certification standards, one of the principal complaints about the SFI is that it allows logging companies to replace biodiversity-rich primary forests with tree plantations that increase the value of logging land but ecologically impoverish the planet.

The FSC was created by an industry-environmental joint venture with the hope of closing down the illegal timber trade and encouraging all logging companies to adopt more sustainable forestry practices. But it's come under fire for allowing companies with dubious track records to use the label. It also angers critics for allowing logging in the few remaining old-growth forests that provide homes for many endangered species.[25]

FSC hasn't been very successful from a business standpoint either. Companies including Home Depot and IKEA that publicly pledged to buy more of the council-certified wood say there is just not enough of it around to meet their super-sized demand.[26]

Green Building Standards Challenged

Similar controversies follow green building certifications such as Energy Star and LEED, which stands for Leadership in Energy and Environmental Design. The proliferation of such environmental certification programs—rather than safeguarding against unsustainable business practices—allows companies to game the system, certifying even the most gargantuan trophy houses and McMansions, according to a chorus of critics.[27]

Behind this seemingly schizophrenic position of the housing industry—which wants to be green and build McMansions too—is the schizophrenia of the U.S. consumer. Here are a couple of diametrically opposed facts: Americans want bigger houses and, increasingly, they want those homes to be environmentally friendly.

It's hard to underestimate how good things have gotten for most Americans in the last few centuries. In Colonial times, seven or eight family members typically shared an abode that would be considered tiny by today's standards. In 1775, the average house consisted of four rooms arranged around a central fireplace. Today the space would hardly suffice as a master bedroom.[28]

The biggest gains in personal space have come in the last few decades. The average home size has grown by two-thirds since 1970, from 1,500 square feet to 2,500 in 2008, according to the National Association of Home Builders. So has the amount of energy (and cash) needed to heat, air-condition, and keep the lights on in today's average suburban showplace. And, as electric bills have increased, so have the country's carbon emissions.

The green housing market is also registering remarkable growth. Green homebuilding has entered the mainstream, representing 6 to 10 percent of the market in 2008, according to the National Association of Home Builders.[29] Homebuilders large and small have entered this market niche. By 2013, the association expects market share to have doubled to between $40 and $70 billion annually.

These facts illustrate that the real choices are in the hands of the consumers, not the corporations. As consumers, we need to decide what's more important: a few extra square feet or clean air and a stable environment. Most timber products today go into homebuilding. But as Tim Hermach, the founder of the Native Forest Council, points out, most homes around the world are made from materials other than wood. My personal favorite is adobe. Used by the indigenous people of Meso-America for centuries, adobe is a natural insulator that keeps a home warm in cool temperatures and cools it off when it gets hot. While adobe may never entirely replace homes built from wood, it could be one of a new diversity of homebuilding materials that could take some pressure of the planet's remaining timber stocks. The problem is that many alternative building products remain prohibitively expensive. If consumers demand sustainable and economical housing options, the market will likely follow. We just have to hold them to their promises—which, as illustrated here, is no easy task.

Getting back to Centex and its $35-a-house plan with TNC: The company ended that arrangement a few years ago, after unflattering press coverage, and switched its allegiances to CF. Today, Centex advertises its Land Legacy Fund with CF as a sign that it has made land conservation a priority.[30]

Chapter Ten

Conservation Dictators and Refugees

A radiant native girl running through a lush rainforest with a pale-pink flower in her hands; a Brazilian cowboy, traditional straw hat shading his brow as he rides his horse alongside a river in the Pantanal, the world's largest wetlands; African fishermen preparing their nets before taking to the sea—smiling natives in colorful garb are among the most common images illustrating the annual reports and donation brochures of the world's largest conservation groups. They portray "harmonious" relationships with indigenous tribes and other impoverished people. However, critics of these groups say the images are merely a distraction from more unsavory alliances.

Far from their friends, the inhabitants of the forests often view conservationists as allies of oppressive governments and environmentally evasive corporations. Relations have frayed over oil, gas, mining, logging, and pharmaceutical company activities in and near remote communities. And indigenous groups have not taken kindly to lost rights to fish, hunt, log, and forage on ancestral lands turned nature preserves.

The industry ties yield large donations. Good relations, even with bad governments, help conservation groups operate abroad. But they hurt the environmental movement's credibility by fueling complaints of a double standard, in which the world's poorest residents must bear the brunt of the conservation burden, while the rich and powerful are immune.

It is undeniable, however, that indigenous and other poor, rural people often pose a threat to the Earth's rapidly disappearing biodiversity. In a constant struggle to survive, they empty forests of flora and fauna and practice the environmental crime of slash-and-burn agriculture. How to create alternatives that allow the poor to survive without destroying nature is a dilemma facing conservationists working in the developing world, home to the vast majority of the planet's biodiversity. Attempts by conservation groups to nurture development projects that are also environmentally sound have mostly failed. Critics both inside and outside the global movement say scientists and international administrators often create unnecessary friction by ignoring local concerns, culture, and expertise.

Conservation Refugees

Today a tenth of the world's landmass has been set aside in protected areas.[1] The vast majority of these national parks and reserves were created in the last few decades.

Conservationists have traditionally downplayed the human presence in these "wildernesses" and "last great places." One good example of this subterfuge can be found in the literature of the Wildlife Conservation Society. WCS has invested heavily in the West African country of Gabon, where a parks system covering 11 percent of the national territory was established in

2002 by presidential degree. WCS has described half a dozen of Gabon's parks as sparsely populated before the conservation restrictions went into effect. The reality is that thousands of native peoples were evicted to make way for the area's new protected status. In Lope National Park, for instance, WCS claimed "no villages existed within the park when it was created," when, in fact, two thousand Pygmies were expelled and have lost their ancestral rights to the place.[2]

WCS chief executive Steven Sanderson, the second highest-paid conservationist in the United States, is a political scientist and has lived in Mexico and Brazil. He has expressed deep concern about the plight of poor rural people and how to involve them in nature conservation. "How do people live in fragile ecosystems? How can impoverished populations contribute to conservation?" he once wrote in the group's magazine. While such conciliatory rhetoric is common among Western conservationists, Sanderson has also defended his group's operations abroad, saying the global environmental movement has been "hijacked" by advocates for indigenous peoples. "Forest peoples and their representatives may speak for the forest. They may speak for their version of the forest; but they do not speak for the forest we want to conserve," Sanderson has said, making him one of today's more candid conservation leaders.[3] But Africa is not the only place Sanderson's group has run into trouble. Indigenous groups in India and South America also accuse WCS of disparaging their role in remote ecosystems and calling for their evictions from ancestral lands.

Scholars say this is not a new phenomenon. They trace it back at least as far as William the Conqueror, who evicted thousands of Saxons and established a nearly 100,000-acre hunting preserve on their lands after evading England and leading a Norman army to victory in the Battle of Hastings in 1066. The Shoshone people were forced out of Yellowstone National Park in 1872—and the list goes on up to the present day as developing governments have decreed new parkland, bowing to international pressure and the promise of foreign aid dollars.[4] The trend has led activists to coin a new phrase: the conservation refugee. These are not refugees fleeing civil wars, hurricanes, earthquakes, or other natural disasters; the conservation refugee is kicked off the land to protect endangered plants and animals.

People have been evicted from their traditional homelands on every continent. Rodolfo Stavenhagen, the United Nations' special rapporteur on the human rights and fundamental freedoms of indigenous people, has denounced forced displacement as one of the biggest threats facing indigenous people in dozens of countries.[5] In Africa alone the evictions induced by conservation efforts are estimated in the millions of people. Oftentimes their homes, fields, and grain stores are burned and they are forced to move into villages, with no compensation for their losses and minimal assistance creating a new means of survival.

Conservation refugees often are thrust into precarious lives outside the forest. Evictions leave already vulnerable communities in dire straits. Even if they are provided new homes in settled areas, the refugees' difficulty adapting to an entirely different lifestyle leaves them at high risk of ending up homeless, hungry, and unable to take care of themselves.

In one case described to foreign researchers by a tribal leader: "White men came to tell us that the forest is protected and that we can no longer live there. They told us to stop hunting and go to live in a Bantu village outside the forest. . . . We had no choice, because they told us that they will beat and kill us, if they find us in the forest. They still treat us badly. We have no land, no food, nothing. We have to work on the farms of the Bantus or use the small plot the Catholic mission has given us. Some young men still go to the forest and look for food [meat and plants] but this is very dangerous. If the game guards catch them, they will take everything and beat them and ask the family to pay money. And these are even the lucky ones. They have killed many Baka from our area."[6]

The speaker and his family were among the nearly eight thousand Pygmies expelled from the Dja reserve in Camaroon in the mid-1980s to make way for a conservation plan funded by the European Union.

Critics point fingers at international nonprofit groups such as WWF, TNC, WCS, and CI as the villains behind these evictions. The groups and their supporters deny the accusation, pointing out that only governments have the power of eminent domain. And clearly conservation is not the only thing on the minds of the government officials in countries with the most brutal eviction legacies. Officials sometimes justified forced relocations as attempts to bring indigenous people the benefits of the modern world or to protect national economic interests such as tourism.

In Zambia, Tourism, Environment and Natural Resources deputy minister Todd Chilembo announced in January 2008 plans to evict "illegal land settlers" near game parks so that it could restock the parks with wild animals. "These animals definitely bring foreign exchange and also create job opportunities for local citizens. Our country has a vast land but it's unfortunate that some people still want to incline themselves near unsafe areas like Game Parks with animals around," Chilembo told the *Times of Zambia* newspaper by way of defending the move, expected to leave seven thousand Zambians homeless.[7]

In the case of the Botswana Bushmen, evicted from a game reserve in the mid-2000s, the government argued it was both protecting the park and the people: It wanted to bring health services and education to tribe members, who had to leave the reserve anyway because they were endangering its wildlife with their livestock and hunting practices. But indigenous activists maintained the government was actually bent on controlling what diamonds might be found inside the park.[8]

While it's true that governments may sometimes use conservation as a convenient stand-in for murkier motives, international conservation groups no doubt play a role in this particular refugee phenomenon. International groups do not often officially sanction the forced removals, but their in-country representatives have been known to be supportive of government eviction plans. Any tacit agreement or even help given by the international group's local players is easily overlooked in the home country thousands of miles away. The arrangement advances conservation goals while retaining plausible deniability, say scholars who have studied numerous cases.[9]

I had an opportunity to see this first-hand in my second week on the job at CI. Every spring, the heads of its twenty-some country offices converge on Washington for two weeks of planning meetings. In a gathering in May 2006, the director of CI's Liberia office Alexander Peal complained that he hadn't been given the public relations support he had requested of Washington a few months earlier when the Liberian government evicted squatters from the country's Sapo National Park, at CI's urging. The protected area had become a refuge for Liberian civilians during the long and brutal civil war that ended in 2003. Some inhabitants had set up illegal mining and logging camps inside the park. The arrangement had taken a toll on wildlife. Tom Cohen, media relations director, a veteran Associated Press foreign correspondent who had spent years stationed in Africa, explained the lack of media support was no oversight. He said he had intentionally decided not to publicize CI's role in the evictions, fearing the government actions could leave people dead and create a public relations debacle for the group. Cohen chose to preserve CI's plausible deniability.

Even when they play no role in the evictions, TNC, CI, and WWF have stoked controversies by taking on management responsibilities in the parks shortly after the forced removals. Such cases, even if unrelated to the evictions, leave local people with the impression that government forces merely did the dirty work for the foreigners.

Daniel Brockington and James Igoe, in their 2007 survey of conservation-induced relocations at 180 protected areas around the world, observed:

The unpopularity of protected areas has come as an unwelcome shock for many conservationists. For years conservation has enjoyed the moral high ground. It was saving the planet, rescuing species from extinction, and taking a stand against the rapacious consumption of resources by one virulent species. This image of "global good guys" is not only an important part of conservationists' own self-perceptions, it is also essential to the image of large conservation organizations in their fund-raising appeals. Now these same organizations find themselves engaged in publicity battles, the negative consequences of which could be particularly damaging to their institutional wellbeing. This situation has provoked a great deal of anguish. "Conservation scientists" are anguished over the perceived "hijacking" of their agendas. Those who would hijack those agendas are anguished by conservation displacements.[10]

Dictators and Oligarchs

Beyond refugee cases, there are a myriad of troubling stories and scandals regarding Western conservation groups working around the globe. International conservationists—once perceived as watchdogs guarding the public's interest—are now widely seen as members of the elite, insiders invited into the backroom dealings between governments and corporations and therefore unwilling to speak out against them, even when species and landscapes are at stake.

Equatorial Guinea is known as one of the most repressive and corrupt countries in Africa. But the government's dismal human rights record was no obstacle to CI executives, who provided technical assistance to convert more than a third of the central African nation's territory into protected areas in an attempt to improve its foreign investment prospects. "Doing this kind of thing for nature is a way to convey a different image. It's a kind of rebranding," Olivier Langrand, the head of CI's Center for Conservation and Government, told Reuters in 2006.[11] In return for ignoring the excesses of autocratic regimes, CI and other groups gain powerful allies in parts of the world with little or no rule of law, often at the expense of relatively powerless local residents.

CI is not alone in dealing with notoriously undemocratic regimes. WCS's partner in Gabon is one of the world's longest-serving heads of state: President Omar Bongo, whose four-decade lock on power has been tarnished by allegations of electoral fraud. And the list includes China, which has become the latest darling of conservationists, despite its environmental and human rights woes.

Weathering PR Maelstroms

Aside from partnering with dictators, big conservation groups have been criticized for close ties to the World Bank and other multinational financial institutions and aid agencies. These institutions have become important sources of conservation funding in recent decades. But they dedicate exponentially more financing to road, dam, and economic development projects with devastating environmental impacts. By taking their money, these groups have sold off the moral high ground they once inhabited as critics of misguided mega projects.

One instructive scandal unfolded in Papua New Guinea in 2003 after an internal WWF memo detailing plans for a forest management summit was leaked to the press. The summit had the lofty goal of building support for environmentally friendly forest management in the region. But WWF planned to seek funding from the World Bank, while keeping the bank's role "invisible" to the public.[12] Anger at the World Bank had been simmering since the previous year when five people were killed in protests against land reforms the government was being pressed to adopt. Papua New Guinea is home to one of the world's largest tracts of forests, historically held in "customary" or communal ownership by the island nation's five million inhabitants.

Critics blamed the World Bank for the land reform push. They feared the privatization plans would lead to large tracts ending up in the hands of logging and agribusiness interests, threatening communal culture and food security.

Several Papua New Guinea rights groups also accused WWF of keeping off the agenda a key topic—corruption in the forest sector—so as not to offend the high-level politicians and government officials from Papua and neighboring countries it hoped would attend the meeting. For those who believe the international conservation groups have gone soft, WWF's squeamishness was yet another example. It seemed to illustrate how the big groups have grown more concerned with kowtowing to powerful interests than advancing their own mission to preserve nature.

WWF and other groups weather such PR maelstroms because of their deep pockets. But it doesn't mean locals forgive and forget. CI withstood an even bigger scandal in Papua New Guinea in 2006. After several million dollars went missing from a community marine center in Milne Bay, investigators sent in by one of the project partners, the UN Development Programme, concluded that CI's mismanagement led the project to run out of money and halt activities a year before schedule. CI denied any wrongdoing but its reputation was sullied by revelations of serious management flaws and lavish spending by foreign managers from Australia, who quickly earned hostilities both inside the organization and in the community.[13] The provincial governor ordered all CI employees to leave the country. But when he was swept from office in the next election, CI's big problems were over and it could continue working in the country.

But it's not likely the class and cultural rifts CI's project leadership caused will soon be forgotten. Even before they were ordered out of the country, the UNDP accused CI managers of padding overhead costs and squandering money on expenses unrelated to the community center. Among other things, the Australian managers spent funds earmarked to save sea turtles and other species on "visa runs," international trips for themselves and family members to renew their visas.

The project was designed to reduce the threat to the local reef system, part of the "Coral Triangle," considered one of the world's best-preserved barrier reef systems. Conservationists arrived with plans to educate local residents about the importance of conserving the natural habitat and help them adopt new farming, eco-tourism, and fishing methods to take the pressure of the overexploited marine ecosystem.[14] Common in the region are practices such as dynamite fishing, which involves setting off explosions, then scooping up the stunned fish that float to the surface. From the outset, however, the locals complained that the CI field staff was arrogant, ineffectual, and out of touch. They set up the project office in the fanciest, most expensive part of town and installed a satellite dish that provided the only high-speed Internet access in the province.

The UN investigators noted that more than a dozen people they spoke with made statements to the same effect: "Big cars, fancy office, lots of talk but nothing to show for it." Other local observers complained that part of the funding shortfall could be blamed on CI's unwillingness to involve the community and instead engage in "empire building."[15]

At the time, CI had launched an in-house campaign to boost staff morale called "The Values of CI." The campaign chiefly consisted of thousands of posters extolling its organization's self-proclaimed values, such as passion, optimism, courage, and respect. One of these posters decorated a wall in the

Milne Bay office, where the Australian leadership was known to shout down local staff members, raising sniggering questions about just how institutional the group's "institutional values" really were.

The big contradictions of big conservation are causing a lot of pent up resentment in developing countries. Oftentimes, these aren't simple conservation issues. They are usually knotted together in broader "north–south" debates about national sovereignty, imperialism, and economic development. The stark pay differentials between staff members at Washington-area headquarters and field countries like Papua New Guinea are also a source of anger tied to historic north–south inequities. The tension between development and conservation; respecting the rights of people and the rights of nature; and private versus public good get mixed up and twisted, making for all sorts of strange bedfellows and counterintuitive alliances and enemies. Indigenous groups and nature conservationists seem like natural allies, as do small local nonprofits and large international groups. Instead, they often end up enemies, while big industry groups and big conservation groups that seem like logical rivals end up in alliances, partnerships, and pacts.

Sometimes frustrations lead to conspiracy theories. For instance, CI has been accused—among other things—of spying on the Zapatista Rebel group in southern Mexico for the U.S. and Mexican governments. Although unsubstantiated, such reports have been published in the Mexican press. In the Pacific, meanwhile, cargo cults that have more to do with the local historical and cultural perspective than fact have been constructed to explain the actions of the big conservation groups. Even these tall tales are grounded in very real frustration in the poor countries that resent foreign conservationists for calling the shots—and often not in the most diplomatic of terms.

International conservationists have also lost face for siding with powerful business interests, whose objectives conflict with their mission. Over the years, groups have faced a deluge of criticism from their colleagues in dozens of countries for corporate wheeling and dealing.

Partners Linked to Slavery

Many of the stories involving large corporations told elsewhere in this book have disturbing human rights elements. One of CI's partners, the agribusiness conglomerate Bunge, has worked with a Brazilian company charged with forced labor. Brazil is no dictatorship; the country has a democratically elected government. But grinding poverty and illiteracy, and rampant unemployment, particularly in rural areas, has fueled well-documented slavery and other rights abuses plus impunity for the powerful. Similarly, international human rights advocates charge suppliers of raw wood that end up on Wal-Mart's sales floors with engaging in a slew of human rights violations. While multinational corporations like Bunge and Wal-Mart are not directly involved, their supply chains are implicated in shocking abuses. Members of the Western Shoshone have fought with mining companies intent on destroying mountains and other places throughout the American West that the Native Peoples consider sacred.

Methods Questioned

In a newer development, conservation scientists around the world have joined in the criticism. In August 2007, a group of twenty-one respected conservation scientists from eleven countries compared big NGOs to corporations in a critique titled

"Globalization of Conservation: A View from the South" in the magazine *Science*.[16]

The authors characterized conservation agendas such as CI's Biodiversity Hot Spots and WWF's Global 200 Ecoregions as mere "branding" strategies, casting doubt on claims that the work is "science-driven." These branding strategies have proved highly successful for fundraising. But, the authors said, dramatic increases in spending by the international groups had been both a blessing and a curse. On the plus side, the money has helped fill the void created when US AID sharply cut its conservation budget during the George W. Bush administration. As the groups have opened new beachheads around the globe, however, their presence has been interpreted as a threat to national sovereignty. In Bolivia, there have been calls to "nationalize" protected areas. In fact, those areas are already in government hands, albeit with management help from groups such as WCS and CI. Instead of nurturing conservation movements, the authors charged the international groups with hogging financial resources and jeopardizing local conservation successes with misguided "global agendas."

A few years earlier, anthropologist Mac Chapin published a watershed critique in *World Watch* magazine.[17] Chapin threw down the gauntlet at three big international groups—TNC, CI, and WWF—charging them with putting their corporate sponsors before indigenous people.

After the Chapin assault, the groups issued lengthy responses, denying many of the specifics of the article, but agreed that they could do better to strengthen indigenous communities and give them a seat at the table.

Despite their tepid promises to do better, Chapin's rebuke emboldened critics, who keep heaping logs on the fire. In a showdown on public radio shortly after the article debuted, Armstrong Wiggins, director of the Indian Law Resource Center, took on representatives of the big three groups.[18] First, Wiggins, who is a Miskito Indian originally from Nicaragua, complained that WWF had abandoned Nicaraguan conservationists in a fight to stop a Korean company from clear-cutting the Awas Tingni people's lands. He alleged that WWF feared losing favor with the Nicaraguan government that backed the Korean deal.

Next Wiggins rounded on Peter Seligmann, CI's chief, for professing to respect indigenous peoples' rights but excluding them in his group's dealings with big oil companies that often drill on indigenous lands.

One of the most notorious cases involving conservationists and oil companies took place in the late 1990s. Like the forestry conflict in Nicaragua, WWF, along with Friends of the Earth, Amazon Watch, and other NGOs were outspoken critics of a plan by Enron and a Shell subsidiary to build a natural gas pipeline through pristine rainforest connecting Bolivia to Brazil. But WWF, the WCS, and the Missouri Botanical Gardens and a couple of Bolivian groups dropped their opposition after cutting a deal with the oil companies that involved a $30 million side agreement to do conservation work in the region. Friends of the Earth, Amazon Watch, and other environmental and human rights groups denounced the organizations, accusing them of being bought off. WWF had led the negotiations with Enron and Shell on the side deal. But, apparently stung by the criticism, WWF did an about-face and ultimately opted not to participate in the conservation work. WWF leaders said in a letter that the group had decided to pull out because the agreement lacked transparency and had excluded "local stakeholders," such as rural indigenous communities. WCS and the

Missouri Botanical Gardens and their local partners went ahead with the project without WWF.[19]

Other examples of conflict with local people abound. Chapin noted rebellion against the three groups in Mexico, Guatemala, Peru, Ecuador, Venezuela, Guyana, Suriname, Papua New Guinea, and the Congo Basin, among other places. In one case, angry villagers in the Laguna del Tigre area of the Guatemalan Petén set on fire a CI research station, fed up with the bitter feud between CI and a local NGO it had created.[20]

In 2006, villagers on the Indonesian island of Sumatra threatened to lynch several of World Wildlife Fund's local staff.[21] Resentments had simmered since the Fund convinced a Singapore timber conglomerate to stop letting impoverished locals use the company's ferry to take logs to market. The residents of the Tesso Nilo rainforest had long relied on meager income from selling a few logs at a time. But the practice—which contributes to deforestation—is illegal under Indonesian law. In contrast, the Singapore conglomerate, Asia Pacific Resources International Holdings Limited, known as APRIL, is deforesting the area at a much faster pace under a legal logging concession from the Indonesian government. The Fund initially embarked on a public campaign denouncing APRIL but cut a deal with the company instead. In the arrangement, the logger agreed to protect a core area of ancient forest in exchange for WWF's silence on its plans elsewhere. When the company stopped letting locals use its ferry, at WWF behest, they became incensed over what they viewed as WWF's hypocrisy. While WWF touted the project as a victory for biodiversity, locals saw the group siding with a powerful and environmentally devastating company at the expense of poor residents with a much milder impact on the local ecosystem.

CI's relationship with Newmont Mining Company in Ghana has prompted similar cries that CI is helping Newmont greenwash its image at the expense of the local people.[22]

This sort of incident, which has played out around the globe, illustrates how affluent conservationists from the first world—who spend most of their time in cushy Washington-area homes and offices—are out of touch with the hand-to-mouth reality facing many rural people in the places where they work. As a foreign correspondent in Mexico earlier in my career, I heard my local colleagues used the word *paracaidistas* (parachuters) to refer disparagingly to foreign reporters who would fly into the country for a few days before jetting back to more luxuriant lives elsewhere. They'd get the story without getting too mixed up in the messy local reality. Decision-makers at international conservation groups do the same kind of "parachuting" into and out of countries. When I worked for CI, my colleagues and I would sometimes complain that we spent more time in international airports than in the countries we visited. Just like many of the conservation-induced evictions—where people's homes, food stores, and forms of livelihood were callously taken from them—the events in Tesso Nilo underscore the anger, desperation, and occasional violence that can result when conservation plans do not include people who are as much a part of the landscapes as the endangered fauna and flora.

Sadly, WWF's deal with APRIL has not panned out as expected. Dialogue over ballyhooed plans to expand the size of APRIL's protected forest has dragged on for years but has failed to move beyond the talking stage. In 2004, despite objections from WWF, the company built an access road leading right up to the edge of forest block both sides had been talking about protecting. As expected, the road made it easy for peasants to move in and squat illegally on pristine forestland, which they cleared to plant palm oil, rubber, and cassava trees.[23]

"Once it's open, you can't stop encroachers from coming in," WWF campaigner Desmarita Murni told Agence France-Presse in 2007.

The Sustainable Development Dilemma

The need to help ecologically and economically strapped developing countries find new ways to make a living is not lost on the leaders of international conservation organizations. Over the years, there have been many different attempts to develop alternative livelihoods for local communities. Ecotourism, handcrafts, nut collection, tree oil tapping, and other "non-timber" activities are underway in rainforests at this very moment. But even when these projects work, they work on such a small scale that they rarely can stave off major threats to the forest.

After so many failed attempts at finding ways to make it pay to save the forest, conservation leaders now seem to be throwing up their hands and going for the simple payoff. In the last few years conservation organizations paid country governments and indigenous groups to preserve their forests. The African countries of Madagascar and Gabon and the Chachi and Kayopo indigenous tribes of South America are among those that have cut deals, usually involving endowments to make sure the money is there for them in the future.

Despite the payoff element, it's perhaps the best option on the table. By paying for the preservation of those ancient forests, conservationists are buying time to let the world catch up with what they already know: Forests are valuable commodities. They are going to get more valuable in time, as global warming sets in and the world becomes better acquainted with a whole range of healthy environmental "services" they provide the planet. We just need to buy a little time until the global real estate market for intact forestland surpasses the market values for its other uses. And paying the inhabitants of the rainforest to preserve it is certainly no departure from a capitalist worldview.

After all, indigenous people, who have always counted on the forests to hunt and forage, have been conservation's biggest losers. David Pearce, in his economic perspective on the conservation refugee phenomenon, calculated that the local community living on the shores of Lake Mburo National Park in Uganda lost a total $470,000 in income in a single year after the area acquired protected status. It's not that the new park didn't generate any new revenue; Pierce calculates that the community made $230,000 due to the park's presence but lost much more, an estimated $700,000.[24]

There is one important caveat to the new forest saving programs, however: There is no guarantee that the countries and tribes will opt to keep those forests intact forever. One day, they could opt to end the reserves and sell out to loggers or make other development decisions. Nevertheless, the days when it was easy to exclude indigenous people from the decision-making are drawing to an end, says Stephen Corry, director of the U.K.-based indigenous rights organization Survival International.

Indigenous people, increasingly savvy and connected to international allies, have already pushed conservationists to take the first step and acknowledge them. But until conservationists drop their "nineteenth-century colonialist views" and accept indigenous rights to their ancestral lands, Corry says they will increasingly find themselves confronted by their organizations and allies.

"Indigenous peoples are becoming more powerful," Corry says. "They are less willing to simply roll over and accept what someone who is coming from outside with a lot of money, a lot of machinery, and a lot of power is saying to them. The conservation organizations are not able to operate with the kind of carte blanche they once had."

Chapter Eleven
Carbon Credits and Critics

As concern over global warming has finally reached the mainstream, there has been a groundswell of tradable commodities and consumer products that promise to make a buck while saving the planet. It sounds like a great idea. But not all the plans deliver both good solutions and good business. Choosing the ones that do both is one of the bigger challenges before policymakers, corporate executives, and the average consumer. We've got carbon credits, biofuels, alternative cars, and forest saving schemes, to name just a few of the market-oriented options advertised as potential planet savers.

The goal, laid out in great detail by the Intergovernmental Panel on Climate Change in November 2007, is to keep temperatures from increasing more than 2.4 degrees Celsius. A rise of that order will leave roughly three in every ten plant and animal species on the planet at greater risk of extinction but would avert even more dire consequences from rising temperatures and sea levels. To meet the goal, it will require that global emissions peak by 2015 and then decline 50 to 85 percent from 2000 levels by 2050.[1]

Governments, the World Bank, nonprofit groups, private companies, and even farmers are hard at work developing new

markets to help solve the warming problem. The instruments
are taking the form of government tax credits, publicly traded
derivatives, and bank-issued bonds. There are wetlands and species mitigation banking, biodiversity offsets, and many other
options. But most fall into one of four main categories: efforts
to improve energy efficiency; finance renewable energy; change
land use such as reforesting marginal farmland; or reduce emissions from deforestation and degradation. For instance, U.S.
farmers have banded together to package and sell units of environmental benefit on the Chicago Climate Exchange (CCX).
Among the new "commodities" they sell is carbon sequestration involving soil, forestry, and wetlands projects. The farmers
have also found a climate market for rotational grazing, growing switchgrass that can be used for biofuel, and maintaining
native grass rangelands.

Climate exchanges that trade pollution credits—also called
carbon credits—have taken off in the last few years and are
expected to go higher as more countries roll out mandatory "cap-
and-trade" systems that place a ceiling on the amount of carbon
dioxide and other greenhouse gases industries, and particularly
companies, may legally emit. Those that exceed their "caps" may
purchase credits on an emissions market to bring their carbon
footprints into compliance and avoid fines from government
regulators. The Chicago exchange pioneered this marketplace
starting in 2003. While it has experienced dramatic expansion,
its growth and carbon prices have lagged behind the European
Climate Exchange (ECX), which, since 2005, has catered to the
European Union, where a "cap-and-trade" system established
under the rules of the Kyoto Protocol is already in place.

With global industrial activities spewing more than twenty-
seven billion metric tons of carbon dioxide emissions into the

atmosphere each year and more countries expected to impose mandatory carbon caps, pollution commodities trading is emerging as a lucrative business.[2] New exchanges have opened or are on the drawing board in Canada, the United States, Hong Kong, India, and New Zealand.

Ecosystems Services

While carbon credits are among the best-known financial instruments available on emerging climate exchanges, experiments are underway to "monetize" different aspects of nature. In conservation lingo, these newly valuable offerings are known as "ecosystems services."

Ecosystems services are not those measures humans are taking to protect nature; they are the services nature provides that we would be hard-pressed to live without. And, they go well beyond taking carbon dioxide out of the air during photosynthesis. While carbon sequestration is one essential service provided by forests, savannahs, wetlands, and other landscapes, these natural systems do a variety of other things for us as well. They help to regulate climate, reducing extreme weather. They hold back soil erosion, keep water plentiful and fresh, and provide habitat for wildlife we rely on in a variety of ways. They are essential to agriculture. For instance, honeybees, which have been mysteriously disappearing from their hives in recent years in a phenomenon that is worrying and perplexing scientists, play a big role in the agricultural industry. They pollinate crops and seeds that grow into more than $14 billion worth of fruits, vegetables, and nuts in the United States alone each year, according to one Cornell University study.[3] Forests, meanwhile, cover only 6 percent of the Earth today but more than half of all species live in them.

A quarter of our pharmaceuticals were developed from forest species. Without these ecosystems services, our world would be a very different, inhospitable place.[4]

Charging for "services" societies have long taken for granted may sound radical. But the rationale is pure capitalism: The price of keeping ecosystems healthy should be viewed as just one more cost of doing business, proponents say. Companies, which are the target markets for many of these new product offerings, already pay for raw materials, labor, electricity, transportation, and so on. Why shouldn't they be required to factor in the costs of maintaining those natural systems their businesses also rely on? After all, without them, the costs to industries and humanity would be even higher. We already pay hidden costs for environmental degradation in terms of dwindling fresh water supplies, the spread of deserts, declining productivity of agricultural lands, and human ailments tied to pollutants in the air, water, and food chain.

Saving the Forests

One important development on the forest front took place at the UN Climate Change Summit in Bali in December 2007, one month after the Intergovernmental Panel on Climate Change issued its report. Delegates from 180 countries set in motion a plan to combat tropical deforestation called Reducing Emissions from Deforestation and Degradation (REDD.) The report opened the door, for the first time, to monetary incentives for developing countries with large forests. It was one of the few concrete achievements of the meeting, ushering in the prospect that countries like Guyana and Indonesia could be paid to keep their forests healthy and intact.

Efforts to protect the world's remaining stands of forests and reforest degraded landscapes is already a major draw for carbon offset dollars and is likely to become an even bigger recipient of eco-investments in the future. The world's forests are in tough shape and their fate is inextricably linked to global warming. Forest degradation and loss is the second leading cause of global warming, contributing nearly 20 percent of total greenhouse gas emissions.[5] In countries like Brazil, with rampant deforestation, it outpaces any other source of global warming emissions. If current trends continue, the world's forests, which have been around for more than a hundred million of years, could be completely gone before the end of the century. Each year, thirteen million hectares of forests are lost to logging or cut down to make way for agriculture, mines, oil rigs, and urban expansion.[6] The countries with the largest remaining intact forests are the ones experiencing the biggest losses. More than one billion of the world's poorest people, who live in forests, have the most to lose. But the rest of us will also suffer if we allow them to slip away. Just as the loss of forest cover is fueling warming trends, preserving intact forests could play an important role in turning things around.

World Bank Carbon Finance Programs

The World Bank made its first foray into carbon offsets in 2002 with the Prototype Carbon Fund. Since then the Bank has gone on to manage more than $2 billion in ten global carbon funds for governments and private companies.

The new Forest Carbon Partnership Facility was launched at the Bali conference, with $160 million in seed money pledged by six European countries, plus Japan, Australia, and TNC, the only nonprofit, which put up $5 million. The facility is expected to grow into a $300 million fund that will help twenty developing countries prepare to participate in what the bank is expecting to be a large-scale carbon marketplace one day.[7] The money is earmarked to help countries reform their forest sectors with the objective of turning those forests into attractive investments once a market emerges.[8]

Today rampant illegal logging, corruption, and inadequate law enforcement is the norm in many countries with the biggest forests. A lack of well-trained and -equipped forest rangers has contributed to the rapid decline of even legally protected national parks. The trend has prompted critics to label many of the world's protected areas as mere "paper parks" with legal protections worth less than the paper they were written on. Unless their governments can get those problems under control and prove their commitment to protecting and restoring the forests, any carbon credits they may offer risk losing credibility that could derail the market before it even gets started. Once the countries have made the necessary improvements to forestry management, the Bank plans to select a few demonstration projects that could entail incentive payments. The payments may be tailored for protecting ecosystems services, changes in land use, or creation of new protected parks, for instance. The money could be earmarked for government or even local indigenous communities, with most payments made only after results are independently verified.

Private companies are also getting into the carbon offset business. An Australian forest investment management firm called New Forests PTY Limited cut a landmark deal with the state government in Sabah, Malaysia, to develop a wildlife habitat conservation bank serving the Malua Forest Reserve.[9] The company said it was the first ever government–private conservation business arrangement; more are expected to follow as developing countries seek to turn forest preservation into new sources of hard currency. As the project is designed, New Forests would pay for restoring and protecting the forest reserve, which covers about 34,000 hectares on the island of Borneo, home to orangutans, the clouded leopard, the pygmy elephant, and other endangered species. It will offer units or credits of biodiversity protection for sale to palm oil developers, energy conglomerates, and other companies.

Mitigation Banking

The Kyoto Protocol spurred many of today's emerging products. But precursors to carbon credit schemes can also be found in earlier environmental protection efforts. Since the early 1990s, the EPA has run a cap-and-trade program that has significantly reduced acid rain–inducing sulfur dioxide emissions and improved human health in the process. The EPA estimates that the $3 billion to be spent on the program in 2010 will produce $122 billion worth of health benefits.[10] Wetlands and habitat credits markets, meanwhile, were created by clean air and endangered species laws.

Mitigation banking has become a standard part of the permitting process required for construction projects on ecologically sensitive lands. Like many of today's offset programs, the mitigation banks function on the concept of no net loss of habitat or biodiversity by requiring developers and smaller landowners who cannot avoid destroying a protected ecosystem in one place to replace it somewhere else. The Clean Water Act's wetlands protection has given rise to an entire wetlands mitigation banking sector made up of both private firms and nonprofit groups, while endangered species protections have created similar wildlife banking initiatives. These programs usually work one of two ways: Mitigation banks pay to restore a degraded habitat and apply to the government for official recognition of the work. Then they sell the credits to developers, who need them to move forward with building projects. Nonprofit environmental groups have also come up with offerings, in which developers fulfill their legal requirements by paying the groups to carry out habitat restoration elsewhere at some future date.[11]

The Department of Agriculture has also contemplated expanding conservation offsets—tax breaks for farmers who practice good conservation stewardship. Some suggest agricultural subsidies that have been challenged as illegal under international trade laws could be replaced with conservation credits that would have far more beneficial impacts on ecosystems, while aiding farmers, as well.

Follow the Money

The threat of global warming has been well known for more than two decades, but many conservation groups have only recently started to publicly link the Earth's warming trend to their effort protecting endangered species. For years, they shied away from speaking out. Some say they were afraid of sounding like Chicken Little with apocalyptic pronunciations. Others suggest they were afraid of offending corporate sponsors from the oil and gas, mining, and power industries that are among global warming's prime movers. Their position started to change in 2006, a few months before the intergovernmental panel went public with its warning that the situation was reaching a tipping

point and the window was rapidly closing on human intervention to cushion the impact. Soon it became clear that global
temperature changes were going to have a huge impact on
endangered species living inside thousands of protected areas
that represent the biggest achievement of the international conservation movement. And efforts to combat global warming
moved to center stage.

But concern over the impact of global warming wasn't the
only thing driving this dramatic shift in appeal. The virtually
overnight increase in public alarm meant carbon offset offerings—both for people and corporate donors—were shaping up
as lucrative new funding opportunities. They have become a
new centerpiece of fundraising and marketing efforts.

The polar bear quickly became the biggest "ecocelebrity"
of all endangered critters. Organizations that had spent decades
saving tropical species bedecked their Web sites and appeal literature with bears adrift on melting ice floats, their cuddly cubs
looking lost. For years, these groups had focused on the places
on the globe with the highest numbers of unique and threatened species. The frozen artic—while important to the planet
for other reasons—simply does not qualify as one of these most
biodiverse places, which was evident as the conservation groups
struggled to remain relevant with a public now focused on melting polar ice caps. In the fall of 2006 the organization where I
worked, for instance, had only one photograph of a glacier in
its enormous image archive and had to scramble to add shots of
artic ice floats and portraits of wintry "ecocelebrity" species to
its collection.

While toasting the polar bear may highlight the extent to
which groups will wander away from their core missions in
search of donor dollars, the groups could be easily forgiven for

calling attention to global warming. Unfortunately, they have brought the same accommodating manner that governs their other relationships with corporations into their climate change initiatives. The result: ill-conceived carbon-busting plans that corporations love but that are not always in the best interest of people and the planet.

One of the more misguided projects is called the Business and Biodiversity Offset Program. As mentioned in Chapter Seven, Conservation International and Forest Trends formed BBOP in 2004 along with an advisory board comprised of corporations and nonprofits including TNC, WWF, IUCN, WCS, and Greenpeace.[12] Like the World Bank initiative, BBOP set out to develop good biodiversity offset policies and create a portfolio of demonstration projects. In practice, the conservation projects are largely the same types that have received conventional donations and foundation grants in the past. BBOP is just a new fundraising mechanism for the groups involved.

One of the BBOP demonstration projects is planned for Qatar, the oil-rich Arab emirate in the Persian Gulf. The desert landscape and marine habitat to benefit from the project is obviously not a priority area of Forest Trends, nor does it fall under CI's stated regions of main concern. CI has published lists of biodiversity hotspots, wilderness areas, and seascapes that it has identified as crucial to its work; Qatar isn't on any of them. And, by the BBOP's own description, the waterfront and offshore areas the project encompasses are not unique or critical in any way.

The nonprofits clearly have no strategic reasons to invest their limited resources in Qatar. But CI's corporate patron Shell Oil needed to offset the environmental footprint of its gas production and pipeline operation in Qatar to meet the company's own environmental standards and improve relations with Qatar environmental regulators. Shell is not only a big corporate contributor to CI; the company is on the BBOP advisory committee along with mining giants Newmont and Anglo American and several other corporations.[13]

Other BBOP projects are helping Newmont and Anglo American develop conservation components to projects in Ghana and South Africa. In Ghana, Newmont is paying the organization to do conservation work near its Akyem open-pit gold mine the company is building inside the Ajenjua Bepo Forest Reserve, as discussed in greater detail in Chapter Seven. The project has the stated purpose of helping Newmont improve its relationship with environmental protection authorities but makes no mention of community opposition to the mine that has roiled the region for several years.[14]

While those two mining projects raise questions, BBOP's most onerous undertaking is slated for the island of Madagascar. The organization is helping a mining consortium in its quest to convince government authorities, local residents, and investment banks to support construction of the Ambatovy nickel mine and pipeline inside a primary forest.[15]

Madagascar is one of the world's largest islands. It separated from the African continent thousands of years ago, which led to the evolution of unique species seen nowhere else besides the forests that once blanketed the island. It is considered one of the most "mega-diverse" places on the planet. But its wildlife is also under enormous pressure. Today, Madagascar's forest cover has shrunk to less than 15 percent of its territory. BBOP's stated mission is to preserve what's left of the world's biodiversity. Those goals simply do not jibe with nickel mining that holds the prospect of devastating pollution damages, some of which could linger for centuries, endangering some of the country's little remaining primary forest—or old-growth forests formed naturally over many thousands of years leading to a richness of biological diversity that can never be recaptured. Once the ancient forest is cut down, many plants and animals do not come back, even after the area is replanted with new trees.

BBOP's draft consultation paper written for review by the United Nationals Environment Program states: "In order to secure a license to operate in an area of high biodiversity the company needs to merit the trust and support of the regulatory authorities and people of Madagascar. Further, the banks that are providing the capital to the Ambatovy Project have subscribed to the Equator Principals, which subscribe to biodiversity offsets in some circumstances, and are deeply concerned about maintaining their image."

The authors refer to the environmental protection principals many large banks have agreed to support in response to activist campaigns against them for financing environmentally devastating projects such as this one. The reference to the banks' deep concern about "maintaining their image" reads like a dig against the banks. But one has to wonder why CI, Forest Trends, and the various nonprofit groups sitting on the BBOP advisory committee are not more concerned about tarnishing their own images with projects such as this one.

Seeing the Forest for the Trees

Another option popular with conservation groups is reforestation campaigns that companies finance as a means of paying down their "pollution bills." From 1999 to 2002, for instance, General Motors paid TNC $10 million in an early carbon credits experiment. GM's money went for planting trees in Brazil's Atlantic Forest. In return, the company acquired "credit" it could put toward its greenhouse gas "debt" whenever the U.S. government got around to setting up a cap-and-trade system.[16]

The problem is there is no scientific consensus about the role trees play in the global carbon cycle. While there is no doubt that trees store carbon, figuring out just how much carbon dioxide a forest stores is not a straightforward equation because forests give off and soak up different amounts of carbon at different times in their life spans.

According to one controversial study, many tree-planting efforts are a waste of time and could actually lead to more warming. Ken Caldeira, an ecologist at the Carnegie Institution of Washington in Stanford, California, co-authored a study that shook up the climate change debate with its assertion that only trees growing in the tropics, near the equator, have the ability to cool the planet.[17]

Around the rest of the globe the trees may actually increase temperatures, according to Caldeira. Trees have long been known to use carbon dioxide for photosynthesis, which pulls the carbon dioxide out of the atmosphere. But forests also absorb sunlight. This is particularly true at higher latitudes. Temperate forests warm the planet because their dark canopies actually absorb more heat than, say, grasslands, which tend to be lighter in color. And in winter they obscure snow cover, which would otherwise deflect the sun's rays.

The key to the tropical forest's cooling influence is evaporation, according to Caldeira's research. Lots of water evaporates from the trees in the tropics, increasing the cooling cloud cover. When you cut down those trees you break the age-old cycle of rain, evaporation, clouds, and more rain. The result is less cloud cover and higher temperatures, among other things, according to the study.

"The idea that you can go out and plant a tree and help reverse global warming is an appealing, feel-good thing," Caldeira says. "To plant forests to mitigate climate change outside of the tropics is a waste of time."[18]

If he is right, a ballyhooed carbon credit project launched by Ducks Unlimited earlier in the decade and thousands of similar ones may have unwittingly misled investors. The organization recruited private landowners and twenty-five energy companies. The companies bankrolled the planting of thousands of hardwood seedlings to restore a forest of sweet gum, bald cypress, green ash, oak, and tupelo on hundreds of acres of marginal farmland in the Lower Mississippi Valley of Arkansas. Ducks acquired the right to sell carbon credits and traded them to the energy companies, which got bragging rights as "conservationists." For their part, the farmers agreed to one-hundred-year conservation easements. Over the life of the project, Ducks estimated 180,000 tons of carbon dioxide sequestration. For the companies, paying to plant trees was much cheaper than actually reducing their carbon emissions by that amount.[19] But if Caldeira's findings are accurate, those trees and similarly situated projects by TNC and other groups might actually be exacerbating global warming.

Not all scientists agree with Caldeira's finding. But there are other reasons to doubt that it's possible for newly planted trees alone to stave off dangerous warming. As the world warms, forests will be vulnerable to massive die-offs due to insect infestations, fires, and other ills. Forest fire is already a major contributor to global warming. While there is no doubt of the importance of preserving the world's remaining forests and that reforestation has a role to play in putting the brakes on warming, experts say we simply cannot plant enough trees to take care of the entire global warming problem.

Carbon Trading: The Fine Print

Other criticism of offset programs runs the gamut from philosophical to administrative. During the Senate Finance Committee's probe of TNC, its carbon credits program was one of the areas congressional investigators flagged.[20] The initiative—a precursor to the carbon credit marketplace that went into effect a few years later under the Kyoto Protocol—earned $34 million for a Conservancy program to save Latin American forests. But congressional investigators had a number of problems with it. Had the corporations paid a fair value for the right to continue polluting? Didn't it run counter to TNC's mission to champion a credit system that, at best, permits the participating corporations to maintain pollution levels, or, at worst, enables companies to increase their greenhouse gas emissions at the detriment of the global environment?

As for wetlands mitigation banking in the United States, it has provided revenue to nonprofits and spawned hundreds of mitigation banks. The boom has not managed to stem the loss of the nation's wetlands, however. It's too easy to game the current system, critics say.[21]

Under the concept of "no net loss" of ecosystem, developers today simply have to replace wetlands acre-for-acre. Some say a better plan would be one that would take a look at what services were provided by each wetland and make sure mitigation measures replaced each one in the same geographical area. For instance, Wal-Mart has promised to protect an acre of natural habitat for every acre used by its stores. While the pledge has its big-picture value, it doesn't do anything for the human, plant, and animal communities living near a new store, which will gobble up a lot of land including a gargantuan parking lot where storm water mixed with motor oil and other contaminants runs off its asphalt into surrounding natural areas. Even if Wal-Mart contributes to the health of a far-away natural area, the ecosystem where the new store is built will suffer.

And there are other criticisms. Though the regulations have spawned new economic activity, studies show mitigation money doesn't always find its way to wetlands restoration. Environmental groups often take the money for future restorations that never materialize, experts say. Or sometimes the initial work is completed, but the land is later developed or allowed to degrade.

As communities sprawl, there is no guarantee wetlands protections will hold. There are many examples of development on land once protected through mitigation. In those cases, the developer may be required to pay for protecting wetlands someplace else. This just leads to segregating wetlands far from human communities. Not only does this impoverish our everyday lives by further removing communities from nature, it's bad urban planning since eliminating wetlands often leaves residential developments vulnerable to flooding. These marshes, swamps, and bogs—once dismissed as mosquito-infested wastelands—are also important in preventing shoreline erosion, filtering water, and providing habitat.

Another controversial practice is called "stacking," in which the biodiversity or wetlands value of a particular parcel is sold once to a developer for its mitigation value. Later the carbon sequestration value of the same parcel could be sold to a company looking for a carbon emissions offset. Some observers see this as an efficient use of offset policies, while others say it could lead to misleading conclusions about habitat saved, since the same lands could be counted twice.

Other critics say there's too much uncertainty because the market could fall out of offset projects if better methods to deal with the planet's warming problem become available in the decades to come. Besides, these projects require constant monitoring and enforcement, which adds a layer of cost and uncertainty. An IRS crackdown on nonprofits that provide conservation easements in the mid-2000s found many groups neglect to follow through to make sure property owners respect the deed restrictions. Since many emission offset schemes involve conservation easements, this is likely to be an area of continuing concern with regulators.

Some organizations, hip to the backlash, have come up with new ways to describe carbon offset initiatives. For instance, the British bank HSBC is donating $100 million to WWF, the Climate Group, Earthwatch Institute, and Smithsonian Tropical Research Institute in a setup that resembles many carbon offsets. But the bank and its grantees have taken pains not to describe it as such. Instead, they refer to it simply as "the largest ever corporate donation" aimed at combating "the urgent threat of climate change by inspiring action by individuals, businesses and governments worldwide."[22]

Defensive Action

Stung by the criticism, conservation groups have gone on the defensive. WWF commissioned an independent study of carbon offset certification programs, which, perhaps not surprisingly, concluded the "Gold Standard" certification it uses is the best of the dozen or so "seals of approval" available for carbon credit offerings. Most offset programs aren't certified at all, but an official stamp of approval is becoming increasingly desirable.[23]

TNC, since its drubbing by congressional investigators, devotes an entire Web page to convincing potential donors that its offset program meets the highest standards.[24] The benchmarks developed by TNC and several other groups address many of the same points: To warrant a big thumbs-up, projects must exhibit permanence, proof they will be around long enough to fulfill the mission of capturing and storing the carbon. They should also demonstrate "additionality," meaning the investment wasn't already in the works but actually adds to existing global warming prevention measures. They call for measurement, monitoring, and verification as well.

The groups have also sought to address concerns about "leakage," when the avoided emissions simply shift global warming impacts someplace else. Take illegal logging; "leakage" occurs when progress reducing deforestation simply prompts loggers to shift timber taking to somewhere else in the world. In countries without good baseline data on true forest cover and deforestation rates, measuring a net increase in trees is no easy matter. Say you plant a million trees in one place; how can you know if two million won't be chopped down elsewhere in the region? Planting the trees may have many positive benefits. But the question is: Should companies that fund those projects get credit for "offsetting" pollution when there is no clear indication that the goal has been met?

The Biofuels Factor

Biofuel development is another type of offset project that hasn't lived up to its hype. Though Congress has endorsed them, biofuels, whether made of corn, sugarcane, palm oil, or other crops, have serious drawbacks in the realms of pollution, deforestation, and food security.[25]

It's important to think about land-use when thinking of biofuels, say scientists who have studied their impact. Because most of these fuels are made from crops, a massive shift to fuel production means converting wilderness into farmland or diverting harvests that people rely on for sustenance. In Brazil, deforestation of the Amazon has been fueled, in part, by farmers expanding soybean and sugarcane crops to supply biofuel makers. In Mexico, the price of tortillas skyrocketed due to spikes in international commodity prices for corn caused by the biofuels craze. In Africa and elsewhere, social commentators have raised the prospect that the poor could go hungry if other staples such as palm oil, a readily available and inexpensive part of many diets, were to gain more value as a fuel source. Rising grain prices have already sparked food riots in Haiti, Yemen, and Morocco and hoarding in other countries. In the United States, federal officials have suggested growing switchgrass for biofuel on conservation land the government currently pays landowners to keep as native grasses. It's another very bad idea, say environmentalists, who say it would undermine the federal program to protect wildlife on those lands.

TNC and the University of Minnesota published a joint study finding that many biofuels emit more greenhouse gases than gasoline, due in great part to the industrial activity involved in clearing land and planting and harvesting the additional crops. And there are other problems. Corn, for instance, is vulnerable to drought and disease, contributes to soil erosion, and has a several other downsides. Growing corn requires an enormous amount of nitrogen fertilizer and pesticides, which have their own unsavory environmental effects. In the Gulf of Mexico, the runoff from cornfields along the Mississippi River has created a huge "dead zone," where the chemicals have spawned excessive growth of algae that deplete the water of oxygen, making it impossible for aquatic life to survive.

Personal Carbon

Besides the growing number of corporations and the occasional rock band who buy their way free of the pollution they generate, you and I can also write off our personal "carbon footprints." We can each buy credits going to finance clean energy, tree planting, and nature conservation projects just like the ones attracting corporate dollars.

For just $49.95, the carbon offset provider TerraPass gives people who feel bad about their role in global warming a way to "remove" the ten thousand or so pounds of carbon dioxide a car emits while traveling 12,000 miles, the mileage racked up by the average American each year.[26]

TNC has a carbon calculator on its Web site and invites people to offset their own personal responsibility for global warming by investing in the organization's projects such as the Tensas River Basin restoration project, its first voluntary carbon offset offering. The Tensas River Basin is part of a large block of critical habitat in the Lower Mississippi Valley.[27] It's worth noting that Caldeira, the climate scientist, would call this project a waste of time, considering its location north of the Tropic of Cancer.

Several large conservation groups have dispensed with the precise measurements altogether and simply ask for donations, assuring supporters that their money will help address global warming by protecting forests and other critical habitat.

But do offsets reduce the carbon dioxide that's warming the planet? Not really. It's basically another payoff system. While companies that purport to take care of our carbon sins use our money for ecologically positive investments, questions have been raised about the effectiveness of those endeavors. Many of the green investments touted by carbon offset companies have provided dubious environmental boons.

TerraPass experienced roller-coaster press coverage. First the company received accolades and landed the gig to green the Academy Awards. The added scrutiny, however, led to its outing by *Business Week* for the poor quality of its green investment portfolio.[28] Critics have questioned the environmental value of some of its projects and whether others wouldn't have taken place even without the infusion of TerraPass cash. The company has sought to address the concerns with an annual "stakeholder comment period" on new projects to improve transparency.

Even when carbon offsets are well planned and executed, factories continue to pollute the air. Your car still spews the same amount of climate-changing greenhouses gas into the air. Even a hybrid car has carbon issues, related to the nickel battery that makes it run and the transportation emissions racked up as the various raw materials and auto parts traveled around the world before being assembled and sold. While purists are holding out hope for the next generation of electric cars, they will still need to plug into the electricity grid, which is still powered primarily by dirty coal. The offset system doesn't necessarily discourage polluting. In fact, some suggest removing the guilt trip may lead to an overall increase in carbon emissions.

The carbon credit concept has been likened to the Roman Catholic Church's medieval practice of doling out indulgences to any sinner with deep enough pockets. In the poor countries lacking the wherewithal, it's been dismissed as a new twist on old imperialism, a way to transfer the brunt of the burden southward. People and countries without the money to pay for their carbon fix, they say, will face increasing pressure to actually endure the painful consequences of cutting industrial activity and personal emissions.

This point became clearer after measuring my own carbon footprint on the TNC site. The test inquires about home size, the annual miles you drive, and whether you recycle, use energy-efficient light bulbs, and try to conserve energy, among other things. I was relieved to find out my household's footprint was about 20 percent below the national average. Nevertheless, it was nearly four times the world average.

While carbon credit schemes may have some small role to play in coping with climate change, clearly we cannot buy our way out of global warming.

Epilogue

All of the Earth's living systems are in decline today including the human ones, which are exhibiting sobering warning signs. There are more than twenty million environmental refugees in the world, surpassing the number of people fleeing wars and political unrest, according to the United Nations. The UN estimates those people forced from their homes by environmental disasters will balloon to 150 million by 2050. If we go on this way, many scientists say we could drive our own species into extinction. And we won't go quietly. Already as many as 55,000 other species become extinct each year, a trend that is accelerating as global warming takes hold.

While the forecast is bleak, there are promising technologies available right now that could move us to a cleaner economy. According to one study by McKinsey & Co., not only is it possible to reduce greenhouse gas emissions and stave off environmental disaster, it can be done without creating irrevocable damage to our economy and way of life. McKinsey, the high-powered consulting firm where TNC's John Sawhill once worked as an energy industry expert, is one of a growing number of business organizations debunking the idea that we must choose between a healthy economy and a healthy environment. After a two-year study, McKinsey concluded that the cost would be "quite low on a societal basis" with much of the initial investment providing big savings in operating and energy costs over the long term. All this could be achieved using tested approaches and the most promising new technologies and would likely stimulate the economy and create new business opportunities. The report concluded that the options are "time perishable," however, meaning every year we wait, fewer options are open to us and at ever rising costs.

So far, energy companies, auto makers, and most other corporations have balked at making the expensive initial investments necessary before they (and society) can start reaping the environmental and bottom-line benefits. The world's leading companies are dragging their feet and the groups profiled in the previous chapters are helping them. The leaders of the largest environmental groups in the country have become all too comfortable jet-setting with their handpicked corporate board members, a lifestyle they owe to those same corporate moguls. So it is little wonder that instead of prodding their benefactors to do better, these leaders—always hungry for the next donation—heap praise on every corporate half measure and at every photo opportunity.

We need our environmental organizations more than ever today. But the biggest and best funded among them are failing us. By taking corporate dollars and giving corporate executives the keys to the boardrooms, these nonprofit groups have abandoned their missions at a critical moment in history. Their argument—essentially "the ends justify the means"—doesn't hold up to scrutiny. While it is true that cultivating corporate sponsors has allowed big environmental groups to expand their operations (and increase salaries), those same donations help polluting companies to greenwash on previously unimagined scales as we've seen with CI's relationships with Newmont Mining and Bunge; WWF's deal with APRIL, the Asian logging conglomerate; and CF's embrace of coal-fired power companies; among the many corporate-environmental dalliances previously discussed.

If only it were true that companies stung by the Rainforest Action Network, EIA, and other confrontational groups actually find "green awakenings" in the arms of more "polite," pro-business outfits such as CI, ED, TNC, CF, and WWF. It doesn't take a very hard look at the operations of these so-called "green corporations"—companies such as Alcoa, BP, Consol, and Wal-Mart—to see that improvements made to their environmental footprints are tiny compared to their overall negative impact on the planet. These relationships seldom lead to substantive changes on the order of what McKinsey & Co. has prescribed.

The groups that have become the minions of corporations need to examine themselves and get back on course. Why must conservation leaders make more than 99 percent of U.S. taxpayers? Once they get used to such lavish pay, doesn't it follow that fundraising—to keep those salaries coming—would trump their core mission? In some countries, nonprofit leaders are volunteers, legally barred from taking a salary from their organizations. That's one way of avoiding the kinds of unseemly behavior illustrated by some U.S. environmental leaders. But, there is also a strong argument for a "professional class" of nonprofit activists, who work fulltime for their cause. Perhaps there should be a cap on salaries. By limiting pay to $100,000 a year, top leaders would still make more than most Americans but without draining an organization's resources or creating a fundraising treadmill that could compromise its values and effectiveness. Another advantage: The movement would attract fewer careerists and more of what Bill Turnage refers to as "warriors," activists committed to protecting the environment not their future corporate job prospects.

Perhaps there should also be term limits on leading a nonprofit group. Too many leading environmental organizations are run for decades, sometimes for the entire life of the outfit, by the same small cadres of leaders. According to a wealth of scholarly literature about "founder's syndrome," leaders who stay too long and develop a sense of proprietorship over their organization can lead a group to ruin.

Limits should also be introduced governing the number of corporate executives allowed on nonprofit boards. While business leaders bring some valuable insights to an organization, many groups, where corporate board members dominate, have troubling track records. While an outright ban may be too draconian, limits seem in order. As Huey Johnson says, corporate board members "are like salt in a stew, useful in limited amounts."

There is also an obvious need for stricter federal guidelines and institutional policies on conflicts of interest and public disclosure of funding sources. When groups strike up marketing deals with companies, for instance, the amount of cash changing hands is hardly ever revealed. That should change. And conflict of interest rules need to be stronger to avoid the kinds of controversies seen in recent years. There is no shortage of recommendations out there: After TNC's public scandal, both the independent panel the organization itself convened and investigators working for the Senate Finance Committee came up with lengthy suggestions for reforms at TNC that are relevant for other groups. Scholars and nonprofit consultants have also chimed in with suggestions aimed at making groups more transparent and trustworthy.

To prod them to do the right thing, we could call, write, and e-mail the leaders of these groups and tell them they had better stop being such lapdogs and return to their watchdog role if they want to keep us as members. And there is plenty more we can do as individuals.

Only a serious change of mind-set will get us out of this global warming mess we're in. The last two hundred–plus pages of this book have been devoted to the failings of big conservation groups and big corporations, but what about our individual roles? Wal-Mart stands accused of a "no questions asked" policy. But couldn't we all be accused of the same thing? How much do we *really* know about the environmental footprints of the cars, houses, furniture, clothes, and groceries we purchase?

Better than sending a $20 annual membership fee to a conservation group is consistently asking retailers where their products came from, how the raw materials were acquired, and how far they traveled before arriving at the factory. How were they manufactured? How did those finished goods get to the stores where we bought them?

When you buy new furniture, ask the salesperson where the wood came from and whether it is certified sustainable. NRDC has a wood guide on its Web site that gives the lowdown on environmental and the human rights abuses associated with the different endangered lumber products. It also has thumbnail images of each species to help you steer clear of stolen timber. You can download it here: www.nrdc.org/land/forests/woodguide. pdf. With the wood guide in hand, you're in a strong position to make an ethical purchase and send the message to the retailer that customers care about where their products come from. When you go to the supermarket, get to know the manager. Ask about the company's sustainability policy. Inquire about the origin of the produce, and make it clear you want answers. If every supermarket, big-box retailer, and department store in the country receives just a few comments, letters, and e-mails a day from customers concerned about the environment, they will react to protect their reputations and profitability.

Get savvy about the different certifications and standards. Be aware, for instance, that when buying coffee not all brands labeled "Fair Trade" adhere to the highest biodiversity protections. While the Fair Trade products must meet some environmental sustainability standards, the label mainly assures that the growers were paid fair prices. The best biodiversity protections come from Fair Trade coffee that was "shade grown," which usually means it was grown under a rainforest canopy, where trees, birds, and other wildlife have been allowed to remain and coexist.

Deciphering today's environmental "dos and don'ts" can be very confusing. Buying organic vegetables might be good for your body but bad for the wilderness, plowed under to expand pesticide-free fields. Buying sustainably produced goods at Wal-Mart is good for the planet, while driving to Wal-Mart to get those goods is not so good. Throwing out one's entire wardrobe and home furnishings to buy new ones that meet environmentally friendly standards offers instant gratification but is bad for the already overburdened landfills (not to mention one's pocketbook). Biofuels replace gasoline, but they fuel habitat destruction and destabilize food prices, setting off an array of negative human and planetary impacts.

For me, the many contradictions remind me of my relationship with chocolate. Since I was a kid, I've always loved chocolate, so an abundance of chocolate is deeply ingrained in my mind as a good thing. But the more chocolate I eat, the less likely I'll fit into my favorite jeans—bad, very bad! Thus the chocolate paradox: while eating a lot of chocolate is not just good but the closest thing to nirvana by one measure, it's the very worst thing in the world by another, a-hem . . . let's just call it a tape measure. The same is true on the environmental front: Shopping is a national pastime, as is our proclivity for driving gas-guzzling cars, but something's got to give if we want to keep enjoying the planetary health that our economic well-being depends on.

The idea behind the corporate–conservationist partnerships is sort of like the notion that we can have our cake (chocolate in my case) and eat it too. They would have us believe that we can gobble up all the Earth's resources and belch out enormous quantities of greenhouse gases, and still have a healthy planet. Well, things don't work that way. Just like the chocolate paradox—in which chocolate is good and fitting into our jeans is good but the two have an inverse relationship—we can't continue our unbridled consumption without serious planetary consequences.

Corporations can and must play a role in addressing global warming and the other environmental crises looming before us. But they have to stop greenwashing and start following through on their rhetoric. If the companies want credit for being good corporate citizens and practicing environmental sustainability, let's show them what that means to us and hold them to their promises.

Recycling, conserving electricity, and driving less are also good places to start our personal carbon diets. Calling on government to make mandatory carbon emissions limits, whether it is through a cap-and-trade system or carbon taxes, is also essential. Companies have already shown they will go where governments and their customers lead, but let's stop believing they will do it voluntarily. Demanding to know where the products we purchase came from and how they were made is maybe the most important thing we can do to press corporations to clean up their operations and supply chains.

In a global economy, we are all contributing to ravishing the last remaining rainforests, devastating fish stocks, and leveling mountaintops to sustain our lifestyles. But globalization also gives us the voice, the tools, and the opportunity to reverse this downward spiral before things spin out of control. We don't have much time. The most important thing I learned while writing this book is that we all need to get educated and demand answers to fundamental questions governing our daily purchases.

Notes

Chapter One

1. Urban Institute, *Nonprofit Sector in Brief: Facts and Figures from the Nonprofit Almanac 2007,* 2007, 3.

2. Mark Dowie, *Losing Ground* (Cambridge, MA: The MIT Press, 1997), 2.

3. "In Oregon and U.S. Green Groups Are Mostly White," *Oregonian,* January 27, 2008.

4. Katherine Fulton and Andrew Blau, *Looking Out for the Future: An Orientation for Twenty-First Century Philanthropists* (Cambridge, MA: Monitor Group, 2005).

5. Center for Civil Society Studies, *Global Civil Society at a Glance: Major Findings of the Johns Hopkins Comparative Nonprofit Sector Project* (Baltimore, MD: Johns Hopkins Institute for Policy Studies, 2003).

Chapter Two

1. "Where the Money Is," *Time,* November 26, 2007, 59.

2. "Fat of the land: Movement's prosperity comes at a high price," *Sacramento Bee,* April 22, 2001.

3. Wirthlin Worldwide, *Corporate Partner Research Findings,* Memorandum, June 20, 2001.

4. Cone LLC, *The 2007 Cone Consumer Environmental Survey,* April 17, 2007; others include: EcoAlign, *EcoPinion Survey,* March 10, 2008.

5. "BP refinery pollutes US," *Chemistry and Industry,* 10, May 15, 2006, 4.

6. "Environmental Group Behind the TXU Deal Hires a Banker," *The New York Times,* March 8, 2007.

7. "TXU faces a Texas coal rush Energy," *Fortune* magazine, February 5 2007.

8. "The Devil's Advocate: Is Fred Krupp an Environmental Savior or a Corporate Stooge?" *New Republic,* September 24, 2007.

9. "Global Warming: Who Said What—and When," *Wall Street Journal,* March 24, 2008, R2.

10. "Anti-Nepotism Rules: The Legal Rights of Married Co-Workers," *Public Personnel Management,* March 22, 1989.

11. Carolyn Mathiasen and Heidi Welsh, *Social Policy Shareholder Resolutions in 2007,* RiskMetrics Group, February 2008.

12. "Statement 24, Form 990, Schedule A, Part III—Explanation for Line 2a," The Nature Conservancy FY 2004 tax return.

13. Graham Baines, John Duguman, and Peter Johnston, "Milne Bay Community-based Marine and Coastal and Marine Conservation Project: Terminal Evaluation of Phase I," United Nations Development Programme, July 2006, p. 14.

14. *Seligmann, Peter A. v. Seligmann, Susan,* Superior Court of the District of Columbia, Family Court branch, 2002 DRB 000256, March 12, 2003.

15. Senate Finance Committee, *Report on The Nature Conservancy,* June 7, 2005. First Session of the 109th Congress, www.senate.gov/~finance/sitepages/TNC%20Report.htm.

16. "Smithsonian Documents Detail Chief's Expenses, Invoices Include Work on Home of Secretary Small," *Washington Post,* March 19, 2007, A01.

17. GuideStar, *IRS Increases Enforcement Focus on Nonprofit Executive Compensation,* 2008.

18. Studies include Center for Corporate Citizenship, *The State of Corporate Citizenship 2007 Time to Get Real, Closing the Gap Between Rhetoric and Reality,* Boston College Carroll School of Management, 2007.

Chapter Three

1. Ulrike Bickel and Jan Maarten Dros, "The Impacts of Soybean Cultivation on Brazilian Ecosystems, Three Case Studies," commissioned by WWF Forest Conservation Initiative, October 2003, p. 11.

2. Jan Willem Van Gelder and Jan Maartin Dos, *From Rainforest to Chicken Breast,* Milieudefensie, Friends of the Earth Netherlands, and Cordaid, January 17, 2006, 9.

3. Sâmia Menezes, "Wellington propõe parceria público-privada à Bunge," Governo do Estado do Piauí, August 31, 2004, http://www.hdic.pi.gov.br/materia.php?id=8960.

4. Ibid.

5. Justica Global and Terra de Direitos, "On the Front Line: Human Rights Defenders in Brazil 2002–2005," December 2005.

6. Judson Barros, telephone interview, February 2008; Fundação Centro Brasileiro de Referência e Apoio Cultural (Cebrac), "Articulação Soja-Br Ouve Proposta Da Bunge Sobre Funaguas-Pi," press release, May 30, 2005, http://www.cebrac.org.br/v2/destaques/default.asp?c=35. Barros's version of the meeting largely jibes with the press release

issued by the Brazilian organization Cebrac. Cebrac hosted a meeting in May 2005 in Brasilia, Brazil's capital, attended by Barros and several representatives of Bunge, two executives of CI-Brazil, and a representative of CI's local partner Fundação Oréades and others, in which Barros was asked to abandon his fight against the company. The only major difference between Barros's and Cebrac's versions is that the press release says Barros promised to discuss the proposal with Funagua's supporters and lawyers and get back to Bunge with an answer. Barros says he immediately refused the proposal.

7. Baines, Duguman, and Johnston, "Milne Bay," Annex 5, 8.

8. *Seligmann, Peter A. v. Seligmann, Susan,* Superior Court of the District of Columbia, Family Court branch, 2002 DRB 000256, March 12, 2003.

9. "The Superfund," *San Francisco,* January 2004; "Donor Who Crossed High-Tech Frontiers Now Conserves Natural Ones," *Chronicle of Philanthropy,* November 4, 1999.

10. *Fortune,* "The Green Machine," July 31, 2006; "The Superfund," *San Francisco,* January 2004.

11. "How Companies Think About Climate Change," *McKinsey Quarterly,* February 2008.

12. Center for Corporate Citizenship, *The State of Corporate Citizenship 2007 Time to Get Real, Closing the Gap between Rhetoric and Reality,* Boston College Carroll School of Management, 2007.

13. "Rainforest Politics Strides onto the Boardwalk," *The New York Times,* June 24, 2007.

14. "Environmental, corporate accords create discord," The Associated Press, August 18, 1991.

15. Climate Counts, *The Climate Counts Company Scorecard,* December 14, 2007.

16. Christopher J. Bosso, *Environment, Inc.* (Lawrence: University Press of Kansas, 2005).

17. "Nonprofit Land Bank Amasses Billions, Charity Builds Assets on Corporate Partnerships," *Washington Post,* May 4, 2003.

18. Marcelo Marquesini and Gavin Edwards, "The Santarem Five & Illegal Logging—A case study," *Greenpeace Amazon,* October 2001.

19. Brazilian appeals court decision: Tribunal Regional Federal Da 1a. Região, Apelação Cível No. 2003.40.00.005451-0/PI Processo na Origem: 200340000054510, March 5, 2008.

20. Conservation International, *Centers for Biodiversity Conservation,* January 2008.

21. "George Soros vs. the planet, Soros, Goldman Sachs financing destruction of Brazilian forests," *Grist.org,* Aug 2, 2007.

Chapter Four

1. Ikea, "Ikea Actively Works Against Illegal Logging," press release, April 2, 2007.

2. WWF-Indonesia, "Gone in an Instant: How the Trade in Illegally Grown Coffee is Driving the Destruction of the Rhino, Tiger and Elephant Habitat in the Bukit Selatan National Park, Sumatra, Indonesia," January 2007.

3. "GM Invites Green Critics to Join Online Debate," *Financial Times*, February 11, 2008.

4. Several studies exist, including the *McKinsey Quarterly* and Boston College corporate mind-set reports cited earlier, also Avastone Consulting, "Leadership and the Corporate Sustainability Challenge," 2007.

5. Edelman, *Edelman Trust Barometer 2008*, January 2008.

6. Harris Interactive, *Harris Interactive Poll #91*, December 16, 2005.

7. "For Fiji Water, a Big List of Green Goals," *The New York Times*, November 7, 2007.

8. The Nature Conservancy, http://www.nature.org/joinanddonate/corporatepartnerships/tnccard/.

9. Mark Pryor, Attorney General, Arkansas, et al. "What's in a Nonprofit's Name? Public Trust, Profit, and the Potential for Public Deception," April 1999.

10. "US environmental group expels Florida chapter amid endorsement row," *The Guardian*, April 7, 2008.

11. "Clorox Courts Sierra Club, and a Product Is Endorsed," *The New York Times*, March 26, 2008.

12. Senate Finance Committee, *The Nature Conservancy*.

13. The Nature Conservancy, *Report of the External Science Review Committee*, May 2001, 98.

14. J. P. Rodriguez et al, "Globalization of Conservation: A View from the South," *Science* 317 (August 10, 2007).

15. Natural Resources Defense Council, http://www.nrdc.org; Sierra Club, http://www.sierraclub.org.

16. Timothy W. Luke, "The (Un)Wise (Ab)use of Nature: Environmentalism as Globalized Consumerism." *Alternatives: A Journal of World Policy*, 23 (1998), 175–212.

17. The Nature Conservancy, *Marketing as a Conservation Strategy*, 1999.

Chapter Five

1. Bill Birchard, *Nature's Keepers* (San Francisco: Jossey-Bass, 2005).

2. "HBS Lecturer, Environmentalist, Sawhill, Dies at 63," *Harvard Gazette*, June 1, 2000. Other sources include: "John Sawhill, Ex-N.Y.U. Chief Who Led Conservation Group, Dies at 63," *The New York Times*, May 20, 2000.

3. "McTNC? Behind the Scenes, McKinsey & Co. Recreates TNC in Their Own Image," *Range*, Summer 2003.

4. "Surviving Success: An Interview with The Nature Conservancy's John Sawhill," *Harvard Business Review*, September–October 1995, 109—118

5. Ibid., 113.

6. "Remembering an Establishment Revolutionary," *High Country News*, September 11, 2000.

7. "The Nature Conservancy," *Living on Earth* (National Public Radio show), February 21, 1997.

8. "John Sawhill, Ex-N.Y.U. Chief Who Led Conservation Group, Dies at 63," *The New York Times*, May 20, 2000.

9. Environmental Defense Fund, *Environmental Defense Statement on John Sawhill*, May 19, 2000.

10. Sources include "Establishment Revolutionary," *High Country News.*

11. "Surviving Success," *Harvard Business Review*, 116.

12. "How a Bid to Save a Species Came to Grief," *Washington Post*, May 5, 2003, A1. Part of a multi-day series of articles on The Nature Conservancy published May 4–6, 2003.

13. Senate Finance Committee, "The Nature Conservancy."

14. "Environment, Inc," *Sacramento Bee*, April 22–26, 2001.

15. Ted Nordhaus and Michael Shellenberger, "The Death of Environmentalism," 2004.

16. "Charity Fat Cats: The IRS Is Cracking Down on Excessive Pay and Perks at Nonprofits. Could the Scrutiny Go Too Far?" *Time*, November 6, 2006.

17. Ira M. Millstein et al., "The Report of the Governance Advisory Panel to the Executive Committee of the Board of Governors of the Nature Conservancy," March 19, 2004.

18. "Nature Conservancy Goes Back to Nature," *Grist*, June 14, 2003.

19. "Where the Cattle Herds Roam, Ideally in Harmony with Their Neighbors," *The New York Times*, July 11, 2006.

20. John Sawhill and David Williamson, "Measuring What Matters in Nonprofits," *McKinsey Quarterly* 2 (2001).

21. Steven Sanderson, "The Future of Conservation," *Foreign Affairs*, September/October 2002.

22. Jon Christensen, "Auditing Conservation in an Age of Accountability," *Conservation in Practice* 4 (Summer 2003).

23. Telephone interview, February 2008.

24. Benjamin S. Halpern et al., "Gaps and Mismatches Between Global Conservation Priorities and Spending," *Conservation Biology* 20 (1): 56–64.

25. Elizabeth O'Neill, *Conservation Audits: Auditing the Conservation Process Lessons Learned, 2003–2007,* Conservation Measures Partnership, July 2007.

Chapter Six

1. U.S. Department of Justice, *Fact Sheet: Exxon* Valdez *Oil Spill Reopener Provision,* June 1, 2006.

2. U.S. Department of Justice, Environment and Natural Resources Division, *FY 2008 Performance Budget Congressional Submission,* 10; February 20, 2007.

3. House Committee on Energy and Commerce, Subcommittee on Oversight and Investigations, "2006 Prudhoe Bay Shutdown: Will Recent Regulatory Changes and BP Management Reforms Prevent Future Failures?" http://energycommerce.house.gov/Subcommittees/ovin.shtml, Richard Fairfax, director of enforcement programs, OSHA, testimony, May 16, 2007.

4. House Committee on Energy and Commerce, Subcommittee on Oversight and Investigations, "2006 Prudhoe Bay Shutdown: Will Recent Regulatory Changes and BP Management Reforms Prevent Future Failures?" http://energycommerce.house.gov/Subcommittees/ovin.shtml, Carolyn W. Merritt, chairman and CEO of the U.S. Chemical Safety Board, testimony, May 16, 2007.

5. U.S. Department of Justice, *British Petroleum Exploration (Alaska) Agrees to Plead Guilty to a Criminal Violation of the Clean Water Act and Pay $21 Million in Criminal Penalties,* October 25, 2007.

6. BP, "BP Sustainability Report 2006," www.bp.com/downloadlisting.do ?categoryId=9010741&contentId=7022970, May 9, 2007.

7. House Subcommittee on Oversight and Investigations, Carolyn Merritt testimony, 6.

8. "Enron Also Courted Democrats," *Washington Post,* January 13, 2002, A1.

9. Robert Novak, "Enron's Green Side," January 17, 2002.

10. Earnest A. Lowe and Robert J. Harris, "British Petroleum's Decision on Climate Change," *Corporate Environmental Strategy,* Winter 1998.

11. Ibid.

12. "Ogilvy Campaign Backs BP's Interactive Stations," *Ad Week*, February 5, 2001.

13. Landor Associates, *ImagePower Green Brands Survey*, 2007.

14. "BP: Coloring Public Opinion?," *Ad Week*, January 14, 2008.

15. BP, *Fourth Quarter and Full Year Results 2007*, February 5, 2008.

16. "Observer: Green Backlash," *Financial Times*, July 6, 2007.

17. The Energy and Biodiversity Initiative, "The story of the EBI," http://www.theebi.org. http://www.theebi.org/abouttheebi.html.

18. "Protecting Habitats, Neglecting People?," *Living on Earth* (National Public Radio show), December 17, 2004.

19. The Energy and Biodiversity Initiative, *EBI Phase III Final Report*, June 2007.

20. U.S. Climate Action Partnership, http://www.us-cap.org.

21. "Hoax Misrepresents Corporate Consortium's Climate Change Goals," *Wired*, December 3, 2007.

22. The Yes Men, http://www.theyesmen.org.

23. Joanna Ossinger, "Vivoleum is People!," *Wall Street Journal* Environmental Capital blog, June 15, 2007, http://blogs.wsj.com/environmentalcapital/2007/06/15/vivoleum-is-people/?mod=WSJBlog.

24. The Goldman Environmental Prize, "Ken Saro-Wiwa," http://www.goldmanprize.org/node/160. This brief biography of Saro-Wiwa is one of many sources giving the background of Shell's legacy in Nigeria and its part in the conflict leading to the writer's execution.

25. "For Peru's Indians, Lawsuit Against Big Oil Reflects a New Era," *Washington Post*, January 31, 2008.

26. *Tomas Maynas Carijano, et al. vs. Occidental Petroleum et al.* Los Angeles Superior Court, May 14, 2007.

27. "Vestey's Vegan Grandson Sees off Shell," *Sunday Times*, January 27, 2008.

28. "Sakhalin Gas: Shell Loses, Whales Win," *Asian Times*, December 15, 2006.

29. "New Voices for a New Era," *Time*, April 13, 1981.

Chapter Seven

1. National Mining Association, *The Economic Contributions of the Mining Industry in 2005*, 2007.

2. EPA, *2006 Toxic Release Inventory*, February 2008.

3. Earthworks and Oxfam America, "Dirty Metals, Mining, the Community, and the Environment," 2004.

4. Ibid., 8.

5. Ibid., 9.

6. Ibid., 17.

7. EPA, Mine Waste Technology, "Progress & Goals," http://www.epa.gov/ORD/NRMRL/std/mtb/mwt/pg.htm.

8. Newmont Mining Corp., "Newmont Commences Development of Phoenix Project; Production Accelerated by One Year to 2006," press release, January 6, 2004.

9. "Mine, All Mine," *Grist*, March 10, 2004.

10. Ibid.

11. House Senate Committee on Natural Resources, Full Committee Oversight Hearing: Hardrock Mining: Issues Relating to Abandoned Mine Lands and Uranium Mining, http://energy.senate.gov/public/index.cfm?FuseAction=Hearings.Hearing&Hearing_ID=576bf0a1-bb72-435b-3d43-1ec215903dcf, *Hardrock Mining: Issues Relating to Abandoned Mine Lands and Uranium Mining*, Debra Struhsacker, Northwest Mining Association, testimony, March 12, 2008

12. Great Basin Mine Watch, *Newmont's Latest Failure*, February 2005, www.greatbasinminewatch.org/mambo/index.php?option=com_content&task=view&id=49&Itemid=108.

13. Senate Committee on Natural Resources, Full Committee Oversight Hearing: Hardrock Mining: Issues Relating to Abandoned Mine Lands and Uranium Mining, http://energy.senate.gov/public/index.cfm?FuseAction=Hearings.Hearing&Hearing_ID=576bf0a1-bb72-435b-3d43-1ec215903dcf *Hardrock Mining,Information on Abandoned Mines and Value and Coverage of Financial Assurances on BLM Land*, Robin Nazzaro, U.S. Government Accountability Office, testimony, March 12, 2008

14. Ibid.

15. National Mining Association, *Economic Contributions*.

16. EPA, "Progress & Goals."

17. Associated Press, "Barrick Defends Chile Mining Project," July 18, 2007.

18. Business & Human Rights Resource Centre, "Ok Tedi Mining," http://www.business-humanrights.org/Categories/Individualcompanies/O/OkTediMining. This is one of the center's feeds to news stories on companies embroiled in human rights cases.

19. "Shoshone Use Film, Courts to Fight Gold Mine on Sacred Land," *Environmental News Service*, December 6, 2007.

20. Bloomberg. "Rio Tinto Wins Review of Ruling on Papua New Guinea Claims," August 20, 2007.

21. Reuters. "Islanders Win Appeal in Claim Against Rio Tinto," August 8, 2007.

22. Rio Tinto, http://www.riotinto.com/media/news_6472.asp.

23. Earthworks and Oxfam America, "Dirty Metals."

24. "Retailers to Hold Mine to Higher Gold Standards," *Los Angeles Times*, February 12, 2008.

25. Joan O'Callaghan, ed. "Development Without Conflict: The Business Case for Community Consent," World Resources Institute, May 2007.

26. "Tangled Strands in Fight over Peru Gold Mine," *The New York Times*, October 25, 2005.

27. Conservation International, CELB, http://www.celb.org.

28. BBOP, "Biodiversity Offsets and the Business and Biodiversity Offset Program (BBOP)," 2008.

29. WWF-Australia, "The Heat is On: The Future of Energy in Australia," December 6, 2006.

30. "Coal Can't Fill World's Burning Appetite," *Washington Post*, March 20, 2008, A1.

31. "Goodwin Declines to Clarify Mountaintop Removal Ruling," *Charleston Gazette*, September 1, 2004.

32. National Public Radio, "American Electric Power Settles $4.6B Pollution Suit," October 9, 2007.

33. The Environmental Integrity Project, http://www.environmentalintegrity.org/pub385.cfm.

34. "The Toxic Ten," *Portfolio*, March 2008.

35. Reuters. "Erin Brockovich Joins Down Under Refinery Fight," August 7, 2007.

36. Rio Tinto, "Kelian Media Briefing," http://www.riotinto.com/media/news_4414.asp.

37. "British Miners Get Tough with China," *Telegraph*, March 3, 2008.

38. International Council on Mining and Metals, "No-Go Pledge Signals a New Era of Collaboration with the Conservation Movement," *ICMM Newsletter* (2) September 2003, 1.

39. Mathiasen and Welsh, *Social Policy*, 62 (see chap. 2 n. 8).

40. Jim Kuipers and Ann Maest, "Comparison of Predicted and Actual Water Quality at Hardrock Mines: The Reliability of Predictions in Environmental Impact Statements," Earthworks, Washington, D.C., December 7, 2006.

Chapter Eight

1. Environmental Investigation Agency, "Attention Wal-Mart Shoppers: How Wal-Mart's Sourcing Practices Encourage Illegal Logging and Threaten Endangered Species," December 2007.

2. *Fortune*, "The Green Machine," July 31, 2006.

3. Wal-Mart, *Sustainability Progress to Date,* November 15, 2007.

4. "Some Uncomfortable Findings for Wal-Mart," *Business Week,* October 26, 2005.

5. "Keep Your Eyes on the Size: The Impossibility of a Green Wal-Mart," *Grist,* March 28, 2007.

6. TerraChoice Environmental Marketing, *Six Sins of Greenwashing,* November 2007.

7. BBC News, "Shrimp Farms Harm Poor Nations," http://news.bbc.co.uk/2/hi/science/nature/3728019, May 19, 2004.

8. Reuters, "Child Laborers Toil in Thai Seafood Factories," http://uk.reuters.com/article/worldNews/idUKBKK26683020070425,April 24, 2007.

9. "Soft Soap?" *Financial Times,* September 9, 2007.

10. Telephone interview, February 2008.

11. "Shrimp Farmers Dispute Wal-Mart," *Nation,* August 23, 2007.

12. Associated Press, "Wal-Mart Nudges Foreign Suppliers," *Washington Post* October 21, 2005.

13. "Wal-Mart's China Inventory to Hit US$18B This Year," *China Daily,* November 29, 2004.

14. "Don't Discount Him: An Interview with Wal-Mart CEO H. Lee Scott," *Grist,* April 12, 2006.

15. Oxfam International, "The Rural Poverty Trap," June 2004.

16. Van Gelder and Dos, "From Rainforest to Chicken Breast."

17. Environmental Investigation Agency, "Attention Wal-Mart Shoppers."

18. American Forest & Paper Association, "'Illegal' Logging and Global Wood Markets: The Competitive Impacts on the U.S. Wood Products Industry," November 2004, 13.

19. Environmental Investigation Agency, "Attention Wal-Mart Shoppers."

20. Ibid., 19.

21. Jeffrey Goldberg, "Selling Wal-Mart," *The New Yorker,* April 2, 2007.

22. "What Price Reputation," *Business Week,* July 9 and July 16, 2007.

23. "At Wal-Mart, 'Green' Has Various Shades, Environmental Push Earns Mixed Results," *Washington Post,* November 16, 2007.

Chapter Nine

1. Wal-Mart, *Sustainability Progress to Date,* 55.

2. "Banking on Conservation 2007," Ecosystems Marketplace, 45.

3. U.S. Fish and Wildlife Service, Endangered Species Program, http://www.fws.gov/endangered/.

4. The Nature Conservancy, "External Science Review Committee" (see chap. 4 n. 11).

5. "Metro Area 'Fringes' Are Booming," *USA Today*, March 16, 2006.

6. "No Joke: Land-Use Policy Is Not a Laughing Matter," *Grist*, January 14, 2008.

7. U.S. Forest Service, *Current U.S. Forest Data and Maps*, http://fia.fs.fed.us/slides/current-data.pdf.

8. Centex, "Land Legacy Fund," http://www.centex.com/landlegacyfund.asp.

9. "Developer Cancels Offer of $22 Million to Town," *Washington Post*, August 5, 2006.

10. "Banking on green gesture?" *BBC News Online*, May 30, 2007.

11. World Bank, "Sustaining Forests," 2003, 7.

12. Environmental Investigation Agency, "No Questions Asked: The Impacts of US Market Demand for Illegal Timber—and the Potential for Change," 2007, 12.

13. Greenpeace Australia-Pacific Ltd., "Merbau's Last Stand," April 2007.

14. Environmental Investigation Agency, "No Questions Asked," 3.

15. "Corruption Stains Timber Trade," *Washington Post*, April 1, 2007, A1.

16. Environmental Investigation Agency, "Attention Wal-Mart Shoppers," 5.

17. Environmental Investigation Agency, "Forests for the World Campaign," www.eia-international.org/campaigns/forests/.

18. World Conservation Union, *Intsia bijuga2007 IUCN Red List of Threatened Species*, http://www.iucnredlist.org.

19. Nicholas Stern, "The Stern Review: The Economics of Climate Change," October 30, 2006, XXV.

20. Greenpeace, "Carving Up the Congo," April 11, 2007.

21. John W. Williams, Stephen T. Jackson, and John E. Kutzbach, "Projected Distributions of Novel and Disappearing Climates by 2100 AD," *Frontiers in Environment and Ecology* 104 (April 3, 2007).

22. "Weyerhaeuser, Environmentalists Argue Logging's Effect on Floods," *Seattle Times*, January 11, 2008.

23. "Two Timber Firms Pretending To Be 'Green,' Groups Allege, Environmentalists Want Companies' Lucrative Certification Revoked," *Washington Post*, December 24, 2006, A3.

24. "Is It Really Green? Advice for Navigating the Wild World of Products with Eco-Claims," *Grist*, January 28, 2008.

25. "FSC's 'Green' Label for Wood Products Gets Growing Pains," *Wall Street Journal*, October 30, 2007, B1.

26. "Corruption Stains Timber Trade."

27. "It's Way Too Easy Being Green," *Slate*, December 26, 2007.

28. "When a Home Wasn't as Much of a Castle," *Washington Post*, February 1, 2007, A1.

29. Telephone call to National Association of Home Builders' press office March 2008.

30. Centex, "Land Legacy Fund."

Chapter Ten

1. IUCN, "Protected Areas," media brief, 2003.

2. Daniel Brockington and James Igoe, "Eviction for Conservation: A Global Overview," *Conservation and Society* 4 (September 2006): 466.

3. Mark Dowie, "Conservation Refugees: When Protecting Nature Means Kicking People Out," *Orion*, November/December 2005.

4. Charles C. Geisler, "More on the Case for Compensation, Endangered Humans, How Global Land Conservation Efforts Are Creating a Growing Class of Invisible Refugees," *Foreign Policy*, May/June 2002.

5. Reuters. "UN Indigenous Protector Rodolfo Stavenhagen's Statements," March 20, 2007.

6. Michael Cernea and Kai Schmidt Soltau, "National Parks and Poverty Risks: Is Population Resettlement the Solution?" Paper presented at the World Park Congress (Durban, September 2003). An abbreviated version was published as "The end of forced resettlements for conservation: Conservation must not impoverish people," *Policy Matters*, 2003 12: 42-51.14.

7. "Zawa to Evict Settlers in Chief Mpashya," *Times of Zambia*, January 29, 2008.

8. "Eviction of Bushmen Is Ruled Illegal, Botswana Game Reserve Was Ancestral Home for Thousands," *Washington Post*, December 14, 2006, A20.

9. Brockington and Igoe, "Eviction for Conservation," 449.

10. Ibid., 425.

11. Reuters, "African Countries Brand Themselves with Eco-Labels," http://www.boston.com/news/world/africa/articles/2006/06/12/african_countries_brand_themselves_with_eco_labels/,June 13, 2006.

12. "WWF's Secret Bid for Summit Funding," *Post Courier* (Papua New Guinea), April 3, 2003.

13. Baines, Duguman, and Johnston, "Milne Bay," 11–13.

14. Conservation International et al. "Community-Based Coastal and Marine Conservation in Milne Bay, Papua New Guinea," project prospectus, 2001.

15. Baines, Duguman, and Johnston, "Milne Bay," Annex 5, 1.

16. Rodriguez et al., "Globalization of Conservation" (see chap. 4 n. 12).

17. Mac Chapin, "A Challenge to Conservationists," *World Watch*, November/December 2004.

18. "Protecting Habitats, Neglecting People?"

19. Hermes Justiniano, "Forging Effective Partnerships with Oil and Gas Companies for Protected Area Conservation, The Chiquitano Forest Conservation and Sustainable Development Plan," Fundación para la Conservación del Bosque Chiquitano, paper presented at the Vth World Parks Congress, Durban, South Africa, September 2003, pp. 2–3.

20. Chapin, "Challenge to Conservationists," 28.

21. "Paper Mates: Environmentalists, Loggers Near Deal on Asian Rainforest; The Talks in Indonesia Signal Rising Corporate Readiness to Engage Activist Groups; The Elephants of Tesso Nilo," *Wall Street Journal*, February 23, 2006, A1.

22. BBOP, "Biodiversity Offsets," 27–30

23. Agence France-Presse, "Vanishing Forests a Counterpoint to Indonesia's Climate Crusade," November 15, 2007.

24. David Pearce, "Paradoxes in Biodiversity Conservation," *World Economics* 6 (July–September 2005): 67.

Chapter Eleven

1. Intergovernmental Panel on Climate Change, "Climate Change 2007: Synthesis Report," November 2007.

2. "Climate Changing for Pollution Pacts," *Chicago Tribune*, March 23, 2008.

3. "Honeybees Vanishing Leaving Keepers in Peril," *The New York Times*, February 23, 2007.

4. World Bank, "Forest Carbon Partnership Facility," 2007, 1.

5. Stern, "The Stern Review," XXV.

6. World Bank, "Forest Carbon Partnership Facility," 1.

7. Ibid.

8. WorldBank, http://carbonfinance.org/Router.cfm?Page=News&ItemID=24669&NewsID=37173.

9. New Forest Pty Limited, "New Forest and Sabah State Government Announce Biodiversity Program in Borneo," press release, November 26, 2007.

10. Lauraine G. Chestnut, David M. Mills, "A fresh look at the benefits and costs of the US acid rain program," *Journal of Environmental Management 77* (2005), 252–266.

11. Ecosystems Marketplace, "Banking on Conservation."

12. BBOP, "Biodiversity Offsets," 21–26.

13. Ibid., 27–36.

14. Ibid., 27–30.

15. Ibid., 29.

16. Senate Finance Committee, "The Nature Conservancy," Part Two, 26.

17. K. Caldeira et al., "Climate Effects of Global Land Coverage Change," *Geophysical Research Letters*, September 6, 2005.

18. "Planting Trees to Save the Planet is Pointless, Ecologists Say," *Guardian*, December 15, 2006.

19. Ecosystems Marketplace, "Banking on Conservation," 28–32.

20. Senate Finance Committee, "The Nature Conservancy," Part Three, 62–65.

21. Ecosystems Marketplace, "Banking on Conservation."

22. HSBC, http://www.hsbcus.com. http://www.hsbc.com/1/PA_1_1_S5/content/assets/csr/080206_hsbc_and_carbon_neutrality_feb_2008.pdf.

23. Stockholm Environmental Institute, "Making Sense of the Carbon Offset Market," March 2008. Study paid for by WWF.

24. The Nature Conservancy, http://www.nature.org, http://www.nature.org/initiatives/climatechange/strategies/art22129.html.

25. "Another Inconvenient Truth," *Business Week*, March 26, 2007; "Why the Biofuels Movement Could Run Out of Gas," *Smithsonian*, November 2007; and other news reports.

26. TerraPass, http://www.terrapass.com.

27. The Nature Conservancy, http://www.nature.org/initiatives/climatechange/calculator/?src=search.

28. "Another Inconvenient Truth."

Index

Index

About the Author

Christine MacDonald, a journalist who has written for the *Boston Globe, The Dallas Morning News, Los Angeles Times,* and *Chicago Tribune,* was formerly manager of the Media Capacity Building Program of Conservation International's Global Communications Division. She lives in Washington D.C.